The New How to Keep House

AUTHOR OF

All About Modern Decorating

THE NEW
How to Keep House

by Mary Davis Gillies

Interior Design Consultant,
former Decorating and Building Editor,
McCall's magazine

Illustrations by Cobean

1817

HARPER & ROW, PUBLISHERS

New York, Evanston, and London

LIBRARY OF CONGRESS CATALOG CARD NUMBER: 68-15991

Contents

FOUR ABOUT THE LAUNDRY

FIVE ABOUT MANAGEMENT

SIX ABOUT THE FAMILY

Foreword

This book is about the mechanics of living. There are certain inescapable household tasks that must be done if we are to maintain a reasonably orderly life, whether we are married or single, male or female, young or old, live in a house or an apartment. It is all very well to talk about automatic devices, instant products, and easy-to-care-for clothes, but there is more to coping with them than pressing a button if these wonders are to be used successfully.

The methods of laundering, shopping, or cooking a meal of even ten years ago may no longer be the way to get the best results. My mother's housekeeping procedures and those I used when I first married are as completely outdated as the open-cockpit airplane in this jet age.

It would be naïve not to expect some of the scientific developments in this fast-moving world to rub off on everyday things. After all, with man circling the globe, putting television cameras on the moon, and generating life in a test tube, the wonder is that more magic has not invaded the household. The problem today is to keep one foot in the commonplace world of yesterday and the other foot in the rapidly developing world of tomorrow.

A new sense of freedom from conventions is having a disintegrating effect on old standards of household upkeep. Paper napkins, paper dresses, and paper furniture, whole meals on plates ready to serve in the freezer, plastic dishes, drip-dry shirts, trousers with a permanent press, and informal social life help the housewife escape from drudgery. But carried too far, freedom leads to chaos.

For generations the days of the week had their allotted tasks: Monday was for washing, Tuesday ironing, Wednesday mending, Thursday shopping, Friday cleaning, Saturday baking, and Sunday was for churchgoing. Today each housekeeper makes up her own schedule to fit the family's habits or her job outside the home. However, if a fixed weekly schedule of some kind isn't made, housekeeping can be a burden because every task requires an individual decision as to when it should be done.

Time must also be allotted to professional study of housekeeping. It is exciting and interesting, but also time consuming, to discover new products and equipment. This experimentation gives new life to homemaking. These new things must be tried and the results and cost measured against standard methods and products, for this is all a part of the modern pattern of living that the present generation is developing.

In this book apparently unchanging housekeeping procedures are given in detail because every housekeeper should be familiar with them. But, once they are learned, adaptations can be made to suit the individual household. These procedures may vary with the size of the house or apartment, the number of people in the household, their ages and work schedules and needs, both inside and outside the house. They will even be influenced by environment—urban, suburban, or rural—and by heredity and social background. Once these procedures are mastered and accepted, housekeeping can evolve into a series of projects that give a pleasant pattern and activity to the days.

MARY DAVIS GILLIES

1 *About the House*

1 Where to Live

Finding a place to live and making a home aren't the simple operations they used to be. Time was when your first house was almost inevitably in your own home town and you knew all the angles. Moreover, that first home, bought or rented, housed a bride and groom. Now the first home may be anywhere in the world and it may be for a family or for a single man or a woman.

Again, a home may be the second or thirteenth in a succession of moves to distant parts of the country or the world. It may be in a small community, in a suburb, or in a large city, in a new or old house or apartment. It may be a status-building structure or a discouraging nothing. Whatever the situation, it isn't a home until you make it one.

There is a knack to turning a house into a home; it requires a certain cheerful spirit as well as a knowledge and application of home-making procedures. Someone has said that mankind always has the

. . . orioles are good housekeepers

type of home it deserves. This statement can be applied to the individual. The home you achieve expresses exactly the interest, will, energy, knowledge, and cheer you put into it.

For an analogy consider the birds. The plaintive dove throws a few sticks together for a nest in any sort of tree or bush. It shifts location every season and has practically no home life. Orange-and-black Baltimore orioles, on the other hand, are cheerful birds and both male and female spend days building themselves handsome hammock-like nests in the highest branches of tall trees, safe and secure from marauders. They use the same nest for years, have a happy song and a pleasant family life.

A happy home for bird or man is seldom an accident. Its location, size, cost, and appearance must be planned and personal effort must go into its development and upkeep.

KNOW YOURSELF

Whether you realize it or not, your home deeply affects your attitude toward life. The more interest and energy you put into your home and the more charming it is, the more you will enjoy entertaining and all of the simple everyday joys. Whether it is a one-room apartment or a mansion, your home should and can express your personality, goals, and ambitions.

You may think you are just looking for a roof over your head, but with your first rented room, one-room apartment, or house you should begin setting standards, developing a personal point of view about your immediate environment. Each move offers an opportunity for a reappraisal and advancement. Life is too short to wait for your ship to come in; have pretty things now.

Requirements for a home fall quite naturally into age groups. Demands vary for single people, for married couples with children, and for those without children. Those with the clearest understanding of their current problems achieve the most delightful homes. Outlined below are the adult years divided into the periods which have differing housing requirements.

Your status and its particular demands plus what you can afford to allot to shelter are the strongest influences on your choice of a house or apartment. In the average budget one-fourth of the annual income, after taxes and social security payments, is allotted for rent. Pay more

Family Status	*Parents' Age*	*Years Married*	*Children's Age*
Single adult	18 up		
Married	18 to 23	1 to 5	1 to 4
Young children	24 to 30	6 to 12	5 to 11
Teenagers	31 to 40	13 to 20	12 to 17
Children married off	41 to 60	21 to 40	18 to 20
Alone at last	41 up	21 up	Grandchildren
Retirement	62 to 65	42 up	Great-grandchildren

than this and you may have to pinch pennies on food, clothing, and savings. Pay less and you should be able to build a reserve fund.

Single, men or women of any age. Time was when you took the helm of your own life only when you married. Now youth does not wait for life or luck. At eighteen, with college or that first job, young people may acquire their first *pied-à-terre*. As one twenty-year-old who had just rented her first apartment remarked, "You have to start when you're young if you're going to get anywhere."

But, though there are a growing number of single-member families, some landlords still hesitate to rent or lease to young single persons. They fear lack of responsibility in upkeep and payments as well as noise and incidents. In such cases financial as well as personal references may be required.

Notwithstanding this attitude, some delightful quarters are being put together by young men and women. One young man just out of college found himself stationed on an Indian reservation in New Mexico. His quarters consisted of a two-room cabin and one iron bedstead. Three months and $125 later Eddie was entertaining in a pleasant room with a book-shelf wall, Indian-made furniture, baskets, pottery, a mineral display, bleached antlers, handwoven rugs and hangings. He had achieved the transformation entirely with his own hands and the aid of the Indians whose children he teaches. His plans include the addition of an adobe fireplace built under the direction of an old Apache.

Sisters who gave up their jobs in advertising in Chicago designed and served as contractor for their own home in Florida and it is as personal as a house can be. It is square and all rooms face onto a screened central garden. The furnishings are family pieces of Victorian vintage. Painted violet with a shining white trim, the house is known to everyone in the community.

There are also an increasing number of older people living alone. Life will be richer for them if their homes are pleasant and well run.

Just married, or the first five years. This is the period of learning to be a homemaker, a wife, an adult. It marks the transition period between premarriage dating and true companionship: It is the time for personal examination and joint determination and these may be the most critical years of married life. In this period an intelligent, adult-minded couple map their future, set standards, aims, and ambitions for themselves. They conduct a private study of other couples, both younger and older than themselves, to determine the factors which contribute to a successful marriage. If marriage is worthwhile, it is worth this intensive research.

During these early years, there are advantages in having a small, simple establishment. It leaves more time free for one to learn about management, human relations, personal responsibility, as well as cooking, shopping, housekeeping. Moreover, furnishings are expensive and take time to accumulate. The argument is almost entirely in favor of an apartment which is small and easy to care for, where such extras as water, heat, and garden upkeep are included in the rent and do not add to your responsibilities. When such services are provided one has time to concentrate on the intricacies of cooking, shopping, cleaning, entertaining, and family development.

This is the time for modest rent. The address and the neighbors are usually less important during this period. Sound routines have not yet been established and there are usually no social requirements in connection with the husband's job. Until the children are ready for school their activities can be circumscribed.

The young K.'s experience with housing is worth noting. When they were married they thought they were fortunate to find a charming house in the suburbs. True, the rent was a little high. To furnish it properly would take considerable doing and for real convenience they needed an automobile. But the K.'s moved in with their odds and ends and the grand dreams of what they would do to their home. Then the baby came. From that time on, what with too-high rent, food, clothes, and doctor's bills for the baby, month by month they slipped behind. Life turned into an unspeakably dull grind and money was a constant worry. There wasn't a cent left over for a baby-sitter, and even an occasional guest with a big appetite did disastrous things to the budget.

Just when the K.'s situation seemed insurmountable they heard of an old-fashioned walk-up apartment in the city. Not only was the rent just two-thirds of what they were paying for the house, but they would save the cost of Mr. K.'s commutation ticket.

Draw a kindly curtain over the next six months in the K.'s life. It involved scrubbing, painting, and contriving on a scope they had not known they were capable of. Finally came the day for open house. Everything was sweet and clean and colorful, a condition which they had accomplished with their own hands.

Friends arrived a little aghast at the address and the building only to rave when they saw the apartment. Now they have guests two or three nights a week. An occasional baby-sitter can be financed. Succulent menus are everyday affairs and a young savings account is growing rapidly. But, even more important, the K.'s know that they can share living problems, that they can meet emergencies, and that they have the courage and inner fortitude to live on the wrong side of town in a slum if it means getting ahead.

Young children are the key to the next term which stretches from the sixth year of marriage to the twelfth. When the K.'s first child is six, ready for school, and needs the companionship of other children, the K.'s may have to move to a more desirable neighborhood. These first school years in an average family have been referred to as the crowded years and carry a family up to teen time.

This is a period when children are most active and need neighbor children to play with. It is a time to select a community where there is a good grade school within three-quarters of a mile and an accessible high school. There should be children of similar ages nearby, a feeling of neighborliness, and interest in community affairs. There should be a church and a library and ways and means of getting about. And the house should be large enough to zone for noisy activities as well as quiet ones.

This is the period when the communal life of a town or the suburbs may be preferable to a farm or country retreat. Children want and need each other to play with. It is part of their training. Make your home attractive to your children and their playmates by allotting them certain areas in the house, as well as outside, where they can play freely with toys, boxes, sand piles, and jungle gyms. At no time is it necessary or desirable to give children the run of the whole house or yard. There should always be quiet areas and adult areas as well as play areas. If the reason for these areas is understood, the children will respect them and you for laying down and enforcing reasonable laws.

Teenagers create the problems between the thirteenth and twentieth years of marriage. Suddenly sweet, happy children become critical and hypersensitive about everything relating to their parents and their home. If things don't suit them at home, their answer is to escape it. It is all quite normal and marks the beginning of growing up.

This is one of the periods when families often move, remodel, or redecorate. The former playroom will become an auxiliary living or game room so that both children and elders can entertain at the same time but separately, and provision will be made for dating daughters. A thought will be given to country-club membership, church societies, and summer camps where the children will meet their kind. Marriageable years are approaching, and the wise course is to expose children to suitable mates before it is too late.

Too often these social aspects are not linked with housekeeping. But actually, if there are children, the community and the neighborhood may be more important than the design of the house or the condition of the roof.

Married off. Marriage is one of the goals of parents for children. But first come college, summer jobs, and then perhaps travel. Suddenly the family that has completely absorbed your attention for so many years begins to scatter. The children are deep in important plans of their own. They get married, have jobs in different parts of the country, or want their own apartment.

These years call for deep study and a fresh point of view. If creatively faced, they may lead to the richest years of your life.

Alone at last. By the time parents are in their late forties most of the children are probably on their own or should be. In some cases the contraction of a family calls for greater adjustments than the years of expansion. At first there is a feeling of emptiness, a desire to keep things as they are for family reunions. But after a little consideration the responsibility and care of a big house may outweigh the occasional visits of children and grandchildren and you may want to move to a smaller house or an apartment.

For a successful businessman this may be a period of peak earning. It is also often the time when both husband and wife are most active in community life. But by the middle fifties retirement looms ahead and the time has arrived to plan for the years from sixty-five on, even if you don't retire.

The years after sixty-five. This is a period that usually involves important changes. For most people, whether retired or not, the best solution is to simplify the pattern of living. If you haven't already done it, now is the time to dispose of a too-large house and move into an easy-to-care-for apartment or house with every labor-saving device available.

Some people may remodel a summer cottage into a year-round home. Others will build the compact house they have dreamed about for years. During the early years of retirement a country house or even a mobile home may hold interest, but during the later period an apartment that entails few responsibilities is often the wisest choice. If living and house care are simplified and organized, it is amazing how long an elderly couple can cope with the problem successfully and happily.

The entire country can be scouted for the right location, Florida, Arizona, California, even Hawaii or Mexico. Air transportation has brought the world so close together that family emergencies are no longer a reason for huddling together in one location.

It is clear then that it will help you to decide where to live if you will consider both the present and the future. You must see yourselves as an expanding, contracting, or stable unit and plan for what may happen. If you can do this, influenced by surrounding elements, and responsive to environment, you are well launched.

2 How to Rent

It is usually more economical to rent a house or apartment than it is to own one. But there is not nearly as much satisfaction in renting. Also, if the rent equals the carrying charges on a home at the end of ten years, a renter has nothing but rent stubs, whereas an owner has a growing equity in a house or apartment. As a renter you have maximum flexibility. Within the scope of your lease you can move any time you want. The owner, of course, after building an equity in a small unit, can sell it, buy a larger one, and eventually, as his income and equity increase, can parlay his investment into the home of his dreams.

It is easier for a renter to control living costs because there are fewer extras. If the furnace breaks down or the roof leaks, it's the landlord's expense and responsibility. The landlord also keeps your house accounts. He pays the taxes, insurance, and school and road assessments on the property. He also provides fresh paint and repairs and it is his money that is tied up.

Because there are fewer extras, an apartment in the city may be less expensive than a house in the suburbs. But of course a rural home may be the cheapest of all because of the low rent and simpler life with less expensive demands.

In a city apartment the rent, or carrying charges if you own it, include all major operating expenses. If the apartment is in the suburbs or country, commutation costs to and from town to a regular job must be added to monthly expenses, as well as the upkeep of an automobile which may be necessary. There may also be garage fees and other extras.

In a house, in addition to the monthly payment on the house in the form of rent or mortgage, the following items should be included under housing costs:

care of garden
water
light and heat
window washing
cooking fuel
handy-man services
garbage disposal
higher insurance

In the country, in addition to normal living problems, consider the means by which fuel for cooking and heating, water, and garbage disposal are handled. Can you cope with them? Think about transportation summer and winter. Reflect on problems snow may impose. How much will it cost to have a snow plow clear the driveway? Is there a doctor available? Are neighbors and the shopping center within a reasonable distance? Is there telephone service? Are you self-sufficient enough to manage without being lonesome? Are you competent in the face of an emergency? Do you know what to do with squirrels in the attic and skunks under the porch? Can you cope with rats and mice? Are you afraid of snakes?

In a city it is possible to find the widest range of rentals, but usually for the same amount of money there are fewer rooms and less service than on the fringes of a city or in the suburbs. However, less goes into transportation and there are fewer enforced extras, though there are more temptations to spend money. Additional pleasures include picture galleries and museums to visit, the theater, concerts, and auction galleries. During the first few years of marriage excursions into such activities will broaden your interests and may become a life-long avocation.

In the suburbs life seems simpler, but it is more complicated. The advantage and the drawback lie in the same thing—the greater opportunities for community and social life.

For children there is no question about it, small towns and suburbs are ideal. In the city some people may think private schools a necessity, but usually the public school offers the best all-around education.

The danger of the suburbs lies in trying to keep up with your neighbors, living beyond your means, and squandering time on meaningless social activities. It is much more difficult to be a nonconformist in a small town or suburb than it is in the heart of a city or in the country. The years for nonconformity are those before there are children and after they have left home when you are alone at last.

Wherever you decide to rent—city, suburbs, or country, house or apartment—finding just the right place to live is an exciting business and brings its own reward. Some people seem to have all the luck. They find the perfect apartment while you search. They find a brand-new house and all you can find is an old barn of a place. They find the perfect, remodeled hundred-year-old salt-box house with a fireplace in both the living room and the dining room while all you can find is a modern horror. Why is it?

The answer is easy. The others are successful because they used the right technique, which is 90 percent concentration and good hard work.

. . . it's difficult to be a nonconformist in a small town

Before setting out to find a rental, plot the attack and allow no loopholes. Plan at the beginning to be successful and get there first. These are the avenues open to you. Work on them all simultaneously.

1. Register your requirements with renting agents operating in communities in which you are interested.
2. Study for-rent and for-sale ads in the newspapers. In one town where the clamor for houses was intense one couple went down to the newspaper office at one o'clock each morning for a week to get a paper hot off the press in order to be the first to see the for-rent listings.
3. Put an advertisement in the newspaper—and don't overlook small-town weeklies. Make your case appealing.

4. Walk up and down streets looking for both signs and vacant houses.
5. Tell every friend and acquaintance, including the butcher, the baker, and the dry cleaner that you are house or apartment hunting. This is the most effective method if you have a wide circle of friends.
6. Read the society columns for announcements of families leaving town on extended trips. Such tips often lead to excellent sublets or furnished rentals.

WHAT TO LOOK FOR

Shop for rentals with an open mind but observant eyes. Your thoroughness in inspecting a house or apartment for rent will vary with your need. If you are desperate for a place to live, who will blame you if you close your eyes and use your imagination? Often makeshift quarters turn out beautifully if you have the energy to cope with them and don't feel sorry for yourself.

Consider these points whether it is a house or an apartment.

1. Plumbing. Is it modern or ancient? Is there evidence of rust in the pipes? Try the water for pressure and flush the toilet to check the valve. Is there a shower?
2. Hot water. Is there a constant supply or is the supply intermittent? Is it included in the rent or do you pay for the fuel? Is the system automatic, electric, or gas, or is the water heated by a pot-bellied coal stove?
3. Heating system. Is heat included in the rent or is it extra as in a detached house? Is the furnace automatic or must it be stoked? If you pay for fuel, is the house insulated? Are there storm windows? Is the system reasonably efficient? Check the pipes or flues, registers or radiators, and valves. Ask what the normal fuel bill is. If it is electric heat, consult the local utility and discuss rates.
4. Condition of the basement. Is it clean, dry, and free of odors?
5. Age of building. The answer will give you a point of view on what you may expect of working parts of house or apartment.
6. Laundry facilities. What is provided? Are there tubs in the basement, kitchen, or back porch? Is there a machine? What type? Is there a charge for using the laundry?

. . . privacy may be impossible

7. Electric outlets. Check and see how many are available. Are there ceiling fixtures? What type?
8. Wall spaces. Is there a place for the sofa, beds, chest of drawers, piano, and buffet if you have one?
9. Storage facilities and closets. Where are they?
10. Closets. Are there garment poles, shelves, hooks?
11. Daytime and nighttime light. Apartments with little daylight—and houses, for that matter—should rent more cheaply than bright ones. Thus apartments opening onto a court rent for less than outside apartments of the same size on the same floor. If the location is in the middle of town, consider electric signs which might be annoying.
12. Noises. Check on transmission of sound through inside walls as well as noise from outside, buses, heavy traffic. A nearby school may make a place untenable if you have sensitive ears. In poorly built apartments privacy may be impossible. In one large housing operation, the pipes running through the bathrooms serve as a sound lane and carry amazing scraps of conversations. In another apartment, if you sit attentively in a particular spot, every word of a neighbor's telephone conversation can be heard!
13. Shades and blinds. Are they clean? Do they work?
14. Conditions of floors. Can they be kept clean? Will your floor coverings fit?
15. Kitchen equipment. What is included?
16. Decorating. What painting, papering, refurbishing, if any, can be expected? Is there any regular schedule for future decorating? If standard colors aren't used there may be a double charge, first for applying a different color and on leaving for restoring it to the original color.

If the rented unit is an apartment, here are special subjects to review:

1. Is there a resident superintendent?
2. How are packages and mail handled?
3. What system is used for garbage collections?
4. What type of tenants occupy the building and how long do they usually stay?
5. Are there any special rules covering dogs, cats, babies, and subleasing?

6. Who is responsible for cleaning the windows? What laundry facilities are available?
7. How often are halls and corridors cleaned? Are there any odors?
8. Who owns the building? How long has it been under the same management and what is the financial standing of the owner?
9. Is the electric current submetered? Are the gas, water, and electricity included in the rent or do you have your own meter and pay separately? Is the apartment air-conditioned?
10. How good are the door locks? If there is a choice of apartments, as there often is in a large development, pick the plum. There are certain apartments which for the same price are better than others. The ideal apartment has large living-room windows facing south, has cross ventilation, is high enough for one to see over the tops of buildings across the street, has the elevator far enough away to minimize the noise, and has big closets.
11. What are the car-parking facilities?

ESTIMATING RENT

Not many people are clever enough to figure out whether or not a rental deal is absolutely fair. It seems to be a take-it-or-leave-it business with the owner having the whip hand.

However, a calculating soul with a slight knowledge of the going interest rate on loans, mortgages, amortization proceedings, insurance, taxes, and the cost of upkeep can arrive at the correct rental on a property if the original cost is known.

In most sections of the country a fair monthly rent is one-twelfth of the carrying costs on a house. Another way of checking rent is to allow 6 percent of the assessed valuation. If a house has an assessed valuation of $15,000 the owner is within his rights to charge $900 annual rent or $75 a month. Usually one month's rent in advance is required.

Renting a house or apartment furnished is an uncharted sea without a compass to guide the navigator. If it is a sublease, in other words if you are renting from a renter, not an owner, be sure it is a legitimate deal and that you will not be put out.

Both parties involved in a furnished rental should check credit ratings if the furnishings have any real value. There should also be duplicate inventories. It is permissible for the owner to retain one closet in which his personal possessions are locked. Often it is sealed with a strip of gummed tape put over the crack. This is a protection against moths as well as vandalism. In the average furnished rental, silver, china, and bed coverings are not included. Finally, if a survey of the house has convinced the would-be tenant that certain pictures and accessories are an impediment and wholly useless, it is desirable to have the owner remove them. If he seems unwilling, collect all such articles, pack them, and put them aside in an easily remembered location before moving in.

What is the total rent? The mere quotation of the rent due the landlord or owner does not represent the complete cost of shelter. A new home or apartment may make far deeper inroads into your pocketbook than the rent quoted. In other words, before you sign a lease or estimate the expense of moving, add up the extra expense which may be involved in the new location. Review these points:

1. How much will moving cost?
2. Is there a garden to care for? Have you tools and can you do the work yourself?
3. How much will daily transportation cost for working members of the family? How much will occasional trips to town for the family cost?
4. Is there a garage or will you have to rent space?
5. Is the water free or do you have to pay water rates, which may be as much as a hundred dollars a year?
6. Are gas and electricity included in the rent? They are in many large housing projects. Are gas and electricity submetered? This is bad as you may have to pay more than city rates. Do you deal directly with the city public utility? If so, find out what the rates are and the average bill you may expect.
7. What are the telephone rates?
8. Have you enough furniture? If you have to buy more this should be counted against rent.
9. Will the children have to go to private schools?
10. Is there a charge for garbage removal? What is it?

Until the cost of operating the new property is calculated and the total added to the rent the monthly cost of shelter is not accurate. Not until this cost picture is examined in the privacy of your own home with your account book and checkbook at your elbow should you consider signing a lease.

THE LEASE

In renting a house or apartment look before you leap. Regardless of how affable the renting agent is, by all means examine the property and get in writing all adjustments, no matter how trivial, before signing the lease. Also read every word of the lease before affixing your signature.

Leases make disturbing reading. The tenant is always made to appear as the villian in the case and the landlord is the angel pure. The lease is drawn exclusively in favor of the landlord, who comes out of it having promised only what you can get out of him through typed inserts. It is the tenant who promises everything and is liable for everything.

Briefly, the tenant in the standard lease agrees to make no alterations, decorations, or improvements without the landlord's permission. Moreover, all improvements become the property of the landlord. The tenant must not drive nails or deface the building. He must take good care of the property. He must comply with all laws, orders, and regulations. But the landlord is liable for any injury or damage to persons or property resulting from falling plaster, steam, gas, electricity, water, rain or snow. He is not liable for latent defects in the building or the theft or damage of property in storage in the building. Mechanical refrigeration, if provided, is for the accommodation of the tenant and the landlord is not responsible for any failure of refrigeration or leakages or damage. The landlord is permitted access to the premises at all times. If at any time any windows become closed or darkened by new buildings, the landlord is not responsible, nor is he liable for the presence of bugs, vermin, or insects!

The tenant's greatest encouragement may come from a passage buried near the end of the standard lease. The clause varies, but in all leases there will be a similar item. The subtitle is "Quiet Enjoyment." It reads, "Landlord covenants and agrees with tenant that upon tenant paying said rent, performing all the covenants and conditions aforesaid, on tenant's part to be observed and performed, tenant shall and may peaceably and quietly have, hold, and enjoy the premises hereby devised. . . ."

Judging from this passage it is easy to see that to enter into a contract with a landlord has aspects even more involved than getting married. But a good Yankee trader can get concessions written into the lease before it is signed. The nature and extent of the promises will depend on economic conditions. During a period of depression when rentals are a drug on the market a deal is easy to make. "Redecorate? Certainly." "Enclose the terrace? I believe we can arrange it." "An oil burner? Why not?"

When there aren't enough houses or apartments to go around, a take-it-or-leave-it attitude prevails. Even in such cases redecorating walls and finishing floors is not unusual and may even be a matter of course.

Another point regarding the lease should be considered. Leases are almost impossible to break. The landlord can terminate a lease for cause, but almost no cause exists which will release a tenant. Therefore, if there is a possibility that you may have to move to another town before your lease is up, try to have a termination clause written into the lease.

If you have a lease and plan on moving, read your lease again. The lease may have an automatic renewal clause. Unless you have given three months' notice, the landlord may hold that the lease binds you for another year. By all means file your copy of the lease carefully where it can be easily located for ready reference.

Finally, if you are moving into a new house or apartment or one that is being remodeled, introduce a clause into the lease stipulating when it is to be ready for occupancy. Even then don't drive up optimistically in the moving van without checking to see if the house is ready or you may have to pay the moving company for moving you twice and find a place for you and your family to sleep, not for a day but for weeks.

DONT'S FOR THE DO-IT-YOURSELF TENANT

"Ask before you alter" is a rule worth remembering. Tenants who install a hood over the kitchen range, put down a new tile floor, paint a ceiling red or the walls black may find themselves in conflict with the lease, the landlord, and the law. So unless you want to live dangerously basic changes and improvements should be discussed with the landlord before they are executed.

In marginal, rundown units shrewd landlords have been known to concede several months' rent for improvements made by tenants. In other cases materials are supplied. But these are rare examples. In most cases if a tenant wants to make major changes, such as erecting a wall, removing one, or just eliminating a door, he should have the agreement in writing.

Basically anything that is bolted, cemented, or soldered to the walls or floors cannot be removed. Book shelves, mirrors mounted (not hung on walls), floor and wall tiles, and special locks must be left behind. There is often hairsplitting over chandeliers. If they are installed so that the wires are wrapped around the existing wires in the ceiling the tenant may remove the fixture when he leaves. However, if the wires of the new chandelier are soldered together, the fixture becomes a gift to the owner of the building.

Wallpaper is frowned on by all landlords, many of whom either demand a fee for its removal or deduct the sum from the rent-security. So be forewarned: renters should proceed on improvements with caution.

3 How to Buy or Build a House

Owning a house has become the American way of life: a privilege, sometimes a necessity, a status symbol, and, under favored circumstances, one of the great joys of life. Security, of course, lies in one's own self, not in the possession of things. However, there is a sense of security, a satisfaction, which comes from owning a piece of land and a house that cannot be had in any other way. When you plant a tree, when you repair the porch or paint the house, there is a feeling of kinship with the world around you.

Even though everyone seems to prefer ownership today, nevertheless there are hazards. Prices are high, quality is questionable, local taxes are soaring, and until you have bought or built and sold two or three houses you are pretty much of an amateur. It takes days of research to know what is available, years of study to be able to judge value, experience to recognize a faulty floor plan, and a trained eye to appraise design. If house buyers were more demanding about design, conveniences, traffic patterns, and the use of easy-upkeep materials they could revolutionize the house-building market overnight.

A HOUSE IS A WAY OF LIFE

Before you focus on the four walls of a house, it is important to know yourself and your aims and ambitions. More than you may realize a house affects the way you live, how you entertain, whom your children play with, the hours you spend on care and repair as well as the hours spent getting to and from your job.

To aid self-understanding, answer these questions: Are you a formal or informal family? Do you want a house that can take it or is your aim a certain amount of elegance?

Do you have lots of company? Do people just drop in or are they invited to arranged affairs? Do the children bring their friends home for meals? How often do you have dinner parties and how large are the groups?

Do you play bridge, chess, or other games regularly? What type of sports equipment will be needed? Are there or will there be pets which are a part of the family?

What hobbies must be provided for—pianos, painting, collections, etc.? How large a house is needed for today as well as tomorrow? This decision may be influenced by the possibility of changes in your job as well as by your family's expanding or contracting.

Answer these questions realistically. It is American to be ambitious, to want to improve your family lot, but improvement can be accomplished more easily if you have clearly outlined goals. Certainly ownership is wise if (a) you can reasonably expect to live in the house for five years or more. (b) If you can expect a sufficiently stable income to meet the costs involved. (c) If home ownership means enough to you to justify assuming the added responsibilities which it involves.

Fortunately, family wants will vary greatly. What constitutes good housing for one family will not be acceptable to another. The important thing is to classify yourself. The Housing Research Center of Cornell University, in the book *Houses for People,* divides families buying houses into four groups.

Economy-oriented families are most concerned with financial aspects—cost price, maintenance, and resale value of houses. These families are usually male-dominated, conservative, conventional, informal, and the children are well disciplined. They will gravitate toward plain, simple houses more notable for size and durability than for appearance. Masonry is favored as long as the house is compact, rectangular, simple, and economical to construct with nothing radical about the exterior or interior. A certain amount of inconvenience in plan is overlooked if economies result. Built-ins are eschewed.

When the family moves in, the furnishings will be as basic and practical as the house. As far as mechanization goes, this family may be ten years behind the average, not because they can't afford the latest, but because they feel that it is more practical to let others experiment with newfangled gadgets.

The "family" house is for the young couple who have common interests and are jointly ambitious for their children. They have close

family relationships and want space for family activities and projects. Health and safety are important and they realize that because the average woman has no household help mechanical aids and maximum convenience are "mother savers." In family houses rooms have a way of flowing into each other and many rooms have multi-uses. Much attention is given to washable surfaces, sun, ventilation, good lighting, and safety gadgets.

The furnishings that move into this house will be modern without being extreme. Upholstering and accessories will say clearly, "Children live here." The television, refrigerator, and washer may be the best and biggest available. Neither exterior nor interior of the house will have any particular style, and while the children are young little effort may be given to gardening. Most improvements and changes are made for the children's sake.

The "personal" house is for families who have moved up the ladder of self-improvement and discovery. The husband and wife are usually college graduates and individualistic, with a strong desire for independence and self-expression. They have developed a feeling for finer things. They want to grow themselves as well as expose their children to a cultivated background, but they are not completely child-oriented. Their house must supply more than comfort. Both inside and out it must have a feeling of refinement. The fireplace, the bookcases, the built-in record player, the simple lighting fixtures, all say, "Nice people live here." Families in this group are apt to have more possessions than the first two groups, so more storage space is supplied. Built-ins are used and the yard is landscaped. The house may be either traditional or good modern design.

The "prestige" house is for the status seekers who want to keep ahead of the Jonses. The house will not be so much a personal expression of the owners as an expression of the architect and decorator who designed and furnished it. If the designers were good, the house may be a showplace, a contribution to the aesthetics of the day; but, if the professionals were less exacting, the house may be nothing but garish exhibitionism with a high price tag.

The "prestige" house is usually more formal. It will have a separate dining room and a kitchen designed for a cook and a maid; even so, to be in the swing of things, the kitchen will be fitted with the last word in gadgetry. There will be a complete intercom system. The house will be air-conditioned and have a swimming pool and garden.

There will be batteries of push buttons to work doors, wall panels, and lights.

MAJOR INVESTMENT

After personal wants are resolved the next question is how much you can afford to pay for a house. The answer will not be determined by your bank account as much as by your income and prospects. A house is looked upon as a long-term investment and money may be borrowed to finance it. Nevertheless cash is still a consideration, and the larger the down payment, the less interest you pay and the less the house will cost in the end.

The old rule of thumb is that you can afford to pay two and one-half times your annual income for a home. Carrying charges or monthly payments on the loan, real-estate taxes, and fire-insurance payments should not take more than 25 percent of your annual income. Following the formula above, the chart below shows how much you can wisely spend for a house which is bought out of income.

Annual Income	*Cost of House*
$5,000	$12,500
6,000	15,000
7,000	17,500
8,000	20,000
9,000	22,500
10,000	25,000
12,000	30,000
15,000	37,500
20,000	50,000

Like all formulas this one does not always work. A great deal depends on your ability to manage, the size of your outstanding debts, your reserves, and freedom from emergencies. You should live as well as you can afford to, but it is unwise to try to live on a scale above your income. Thousands of young couples buy houses beyond their ability to pay. They live in houses without furniture and are under such financial strain that recriminations and unhappiness are almost inevitable.

Another error frequently made by young couples is to buy a house with no down payment. It sounds like a good plan, just like paying rent except that you own the house in the end. But is it so smart?

Meet three home buyers, George, Jim, and Bill. Each buys a house for $12,500. Each pays $66 monthly to pay off the mortgage loan, but each makes a different down payment. The table tells the story:

	Down Payment	*Years to Pay Off*	*Interest Paid*	*Total Cost of $12,500 House*
George	None	25	$7,300	$19,800
Jim	$2,500	19	4,787	17,287
Bill	4,200	15	2,986	15,486

The facts suggest that to get the most for your money when buying a house pay down as much as you can and pay off the mortgage as fast as you can. There are three types of mortgages: veterans loans, Federal Housing Administration (F.H.A.), and conventional loans. Inquire about all three. Information on mortgage loans is available through your own bank, savings and loan associations, savings banks, and mortgage houses. In any case a good mortgage will include a clause which permits you to pay off the loan ahead of the scheduled date. While balancing the pros and cons of interest it is well to note that all interest payments and real-estate taxes are deductible from your federal income tax.

CLOSING COSTS

Even though you are buying a house with no down payment, cash will be needed to cover closing costs. Since buying a house, even a simple one, involves considerable money and is wound up with legal entanglements, you need expert advise from a lawyer to look out for your interests and guide you through the negotiations. There are variations in regulations in every state and community, and even though you have had experience it is advisable to have the advice of a local man. This advice applies to the purchase of both new and old houses.

Before you take title there will be fees to pay called closing costs, which range from $150 to $1,000.

The charges cover the following:

Lawyer's fees for preparing documents and other professional services. The fee may run to as much as one percent of the purchase price, though usually it is much less.

Property survey. The price of establishing exact property boundaries.

Title insurance involves checking the validity of the title to be transferred. A title search is carried back to the original owner of the property. If the property has passed through many hands the search may be complicated.

Service and related charges. If borrowed money is involved in a mortgage, there will be a lender's fee, which is usually a percentage of the sum borrowed. It will include a credit check and copies of your payment schedule.

Other costs include recording fees, notary fees, payment of hazard insurance premiums, any unpaid property taxes, and cash for any portion of the down payment not yet covered.

To avoid embarrassment or surprise ask in advance of the settlement date for an estimate of the charges which will be made.

Notwithstanding all of these ands, ifs, and buts, approximately 65 percent of the population own the houses they live in, and with apartment ownership on the increase the combined ownership figures for houses and apartments would be still higher.

WHAT ABOUT THE HOUSE

In general in shopping for a house there are three choices: a new house in a development, an old house, or a custom-built house tailored to your needs.

According to appraisers representing loan associations the most frequent deficiencies they find in houses new and old are these:

Bad or inconvenient location
Too small for size of family
Poor floor plan
Too expensive
Meaningless or ugly design
Excessive maintenance costs
Zoning conflicts

Tucked away in these seven points are the factors which will affect the comfort and happiness of the family, the hours given to care and maintenance, and the resale value. Never fall in love with a house until you have calmly and objectively reviewed these seven points.

Location. A dream house poorly located is seldom a good buy. To judge it, consider the distance and expense of getting to work; proximity to shops, schools, churches, and recreation; the reputation of schools; and the age bracket and interests of neighbors. Then look at the immediate neighborhood. Are there curving streets or dead ends to minimize traffic? Have trees, brooks, and other natural features been preserved? Is the neighborhood developing or deteriorating? Are there factories near which are noisy, create traffic hazards, or give out noxious fumes?

Size. It is a mistake sometimes to buy a house that is too small. Often the choice is between an expensive, small new house and a cheaper but big old house. Even with several counts against it the big old house with more space may offer better living, especially if there is a handy man or woman in the family who can paint and do a little carpentry. A house with insufficient storage, with only one bathroom, with no foyer, or not enough bedrooms can be a costly error.

Poor floor plan. You may be entranced with the kitchen, delighted with the bathrooms, and pleased with the family room, but if the house has a bad traffic pattern, walk out and forget it. Such a house may be hard to clean. It will waste time and steps. Floor coverings will show early wear and the children will mess up the whole house. Check these features:

1. Is there an entrance hall from which you can reach any room without going through another? An extra plus goes to the house which also has an entrance hall or mud room near the back door.
2. Is the route from the car park or garage to the kitchen direct for bundle carriers? If you can go under cover, add another point.
3. Is there a quiet area for reading or study?
4. Is there a suitable place for children's play indoors?
5. Is there adequate storage for clothes, linens, cleaning equipment, games, and garden and maintenance tools?

Too expensive. The price of a house should be consistent with that of the other houses in the community. From a resale point of view it is better to own an inexpensive house in a good neighborhood than an expensive house in a poor neighborhood. Extensive remodeling may not always be a good investment.

Ugly design. In some respects this is the most difficult to guard against, since fashion is a factor. Favored styles change about every ten years; since the thirties, popular styles have moved through Cape Cod, to modern, to ranch house, to split level and two-story colonial.

Rather than think in terms of the popular style, study the design of the house. Is the design freakish? Is the front of the house dressed up with scallops or iron grillwork? Have more than two building materials been used? Has an imposing two-story entrance been grafted onto a simple split-level house? Tricks grow tiresome and date a house. Avoid them.

Excessive maintenance costs. As soon as construction starts depreciation begins. Investigate how well equipment and materials used will resist weather, fire, decay, corrosion, insects, scuffs, bangs, heat, and lack of heat. Constant upkeep will minimize depreciation but siding and roofing guaranteed to require no painting or care, equipment with warranties, gasket-free faucets, tile floors, tightly fitting doors and windows reduce the cost and effort.

Zoning. Large and small communities are often in a state of flux; they are being zoned for the first time or zoning is being changed. Communities are specifying the minimum size for lots in different areas and also what the land can be used for. If you plan to rent a room, have an office in your home, raise chickens, keep a horse, or do anything unusual on your property, clear it with the zoning board before buying the property or you may find yourself at odds with the community.

THE CARE OF A NEW HOUSE

There are pluses and minuses about any new house. If you have chosen wisely a new house should be maintenance free for several years. It should be easy to clean and care for, since it will have new fixtures in the bathroom, the latest appliances in the kitchen. It may be wired for hi-fi, have an intercommunication system and air-conditioning. At first you may think you need an engineer to operate all of the buttons and gadgets, but in time such problems will smooth out.

On the other hand the community may be a new one, the land barren except for one or two skimpy trees. If the builder is careless, and many are, you may find electric heaters without control units, gutters and drain spouts which are not connected, convenience outlets without plates over them, a badly drained basement, closets without shelves or poles, doors that will not close, bathroom doors without locks, and windows without screens.

Since perfection in house construction is seldom achieved, investigate the house and the builder thoroughly before buying and never give a down payment unless every feature of the house is in perfect working condition.

Talk to people who live in the same development. Are their furnaces adequate and basements dry? Does the builder respond to trouble calls? Does the builder give a year or more warranty? Is his financial rating good? Also look into local tax rates and utility rates. Many new communities are burdened with the cost of constructing new schools and the growing demands of police and fire departments.

THE CASE FOR THE OLDER HOUSE

Your money will usually buy more space if the house is old than if it is new. There is also a better prospect of a good buy if you are getting a house which was built for owner occupancy than if it was built to rent. In an old house the grounds may be developed and offer a real plus on the purchase price. Seldom is the value of the landscaping added to the price of a house. The remodeling and redecorating of the house itself should be added to the purchase price. Incidentally, the upkeep and care of an old house may be more than on a new house. If you find a house you are really excited about, put bloodhounds on the trail of every detail of its history.

1. When was it built? Go over all existing records, blueprints, spefications, deeds.
2. Who was the builder? If he is available, talk to him.
3. What was the original cost?
4. Who built the house and why, to live in, or to rent?
5. Was it designed by an architect?
6. Was it part of a development or independent?
7. What is the record on loans and mortgages? The local recorder's office can furnish the details.

This information is merely background for a close inspection of the house construction. See with your own eyes the following thirteen features. If the price of the house involves much money, call on experts to check the wiring, plumbing, heating, and general condition.

The basement. Look for evidence of dampness, cracks in the wall, a watermark on the wall, or standing water. With a knife, stab posts and joists. If rotten, they will cut like putty. Are there braces between joists, patches, or repairs? Is there any evidence of sagging? Are there means of ventilation? Are there termite tunnels on the walls?

Heating plant. What kind? How old? Is it automatic? What capacity is the fuel tank or coal bin? Are all pipes insulated with asbestos to prevent heat loss? Ask to see fuel bills for one year. Ask the opinion of an expert.

Exterior walls. What material? Condition of paint? State of flashings around doors and windows? Examine foundation line around the house where it meets the masonry, the sills. Look at porches, terraces, steps.

Roof. What kind? What condition? Does it need repair or painting? Is ridge straight and even? Is there evidence of sagging of house or porches? Are flashings around chimneys in good condition? Go to the attic for an inside inspection.

Doors. What kind? Are they heavy, with good locks, hardware, and hinges? Look at interior doors for weight and hardware. Warping, wide spaces at top and bottom, or sticking of doors are all bad signs.

Windows. What kind? Do they open easily? When partly open, can you shake them? They should be tight, with little give. Are there storm sashes and screens? Is putty in good shape? Can all windows be locked? Are they glued down with paint?

Walls. What is the construction? Are there cracks in plaster? Is there evidence of dampness? Are inside walls painted or papered? If papered, how many layers are there to remove to get a good base? Has wallboard been used? How was it installed? Will it support pictures and mirrors?

Ceilings. Look for same features as with walls.

Floors. What material? What is the finish? Do they need refinishing? If wood, are there any cracks? Jump on the floors. Do they shake? Are there squeaks? Are they uneven underfoot? Is there space between the floor and baseboard?

Woodwork and trim. Is it good? Is it well fitted? Does it require refinishing? Is there too much?

Plumbing. How many bathrooms? What kind of fixtures in kitchen, baths, and laundry? Will any have to be replaced? What size hot-water tank? Is pressure good? Does water drain fast without a gurgle or sediment? Run water in the kitchen and at the same time try the pressure in the bathroom. Is there evidence of rust? Are pipes iron or copper? Call in an expert on plumbing.

Electrical system. Is there a double convenience outlet every twelve feet? How many circuits? Is there a heavy-duty line in case you plan to use an electric range? Are the fixtures out of date? Will you have to remove unsightly wall brackets and center fixtures? If you plan to install many major electric appliances, consult an expert.

Design. Is the design of the exterior and interior simple and direct? Will remodeling be required?

Now draw a floor plan to scale and actually work out the furniture arrangement. Only when you get down to fine details can you be sure that there is enough space on each end of the sofa for lamp tables, that there is room for the buffet, and that the pair of chests will slide into place in the master bedroom.

What does the fireplace look like? Five times out of ten a person with a sensitive eye could not live with the fireplaces contractors cook up. Of course for a consideration fireplaces can be remodeled.

CUSTOM-BUILT HOUSE

Planning and building are exciting and should supply years of pleasure in study and anticipation. As the building industry is now operated, you are jumping into an uncharted sea of possibilities, rife with architects, contractors, subcontractors, mortgages, unions, landscape architects, and decorators. For a few months this crew will be working for you and, more than that, you will be footing the bill.

For an analogy consider the headaches you would have if you took over the local garage for about four months and had the crew build you an automobile by hand. When you consider that houses are built in this casual fashion, is it any wonder that they aren't as good a buy or as finished and standardized as your favorite car?

If a house is to be purchased ready built, a study course is desirable. If you are building, take a postgraduate course. At least two years of serious study should precede the attempt. Though you may consider yourself an expert, it is ridiculous to think that you can draw up the floor plan. Even experts in the business, trained architects and contractors, confess that they built half a dozen houses before they achieved one that they were proud of. In the same spirit a friend of mine advises young couples to build their first house as soon as they can swing it financially. By building and selling several houses as the family expands and ages, they will eventually evolve the perfect house. This plan could be a profitable adventure for anyone with a feeling for real estate but extravagant for anyone else.

I receive hundreds of house plans for criticism sent in by misguided souls trying to be their own architects. I have yet to see one that is good in design. A house is usually the most expensive purchase you will ever make. In order to get the best your money will buy, consult an expert and pay a fee. Such procedure will result in better living and it will also protect your investment.

The two important characters in your house drama will be the architect and the contractor. The architect will plan the house and supervise its construction. He will guide you through business routines and help with your decisions. Don't take just any architect. Pick out one and then visit houses he has designed. Study his work. If you don't like it, try another.

THE CASE FOR APARTMENT OWNERSHIP

In the late sixties, three in four families still lived in detached houses, but transportation problems, disappearing land, and the exploding population are forcing a change. It is predicted that by the year 2000, which is almost tomorrow, half the population will live in multiple housing: town houses, duplexes, garden or cluster units, or high-rise apartments.

Rentals with leases are the usual choice but increasingly apartments are offered for sale. Such apartments are either cooperatives or condominiums. They may be modest or luxurious.

In a cooperative tenants buy stock in a corporation and have a lease agreement covering their own apartment. A board of control is elected to run the corporation. Monthly payments are made covering maintenance costs, real-estate taxes, and mortgage. The carrying charges are based on the size of the apartment. In some cases alterations in your own unit must be approved by the board.

When the tenant wishes to dispose of the apartment, the board is notified. They set the price and select and approve the purchaser.

In a condominium a tenant holds individual title to the apartment unit he occupies and common ownership of all public areas. He arranges and holds his own mortgage. With the other owners he belongs to an association and makes monthly payments for services and maintenance of commonly held property. The tenant can sell his property at will and establish his own price.

When you are looking for an apartment to buy, do a thorough job of research and check off the same points that you would for a house. Today the variety of apartments and the special services offered by cooperatives and condominiums is fantastic. Buildings even in metropolitan areas offer swimming pools, health clubs, beauty parlors, catering services, and landscaped grounds.

There are city-center, suburban, new-town, and even rural apartments located on lakes. They have equestrian trails or golf courses, marinas, bowling alleys, and ice-skating rinks. Some apartments are restricted to the under-forty group, others to the over-fifty category.

A well-designed apartment has a good traffic pattern, offers privacy, and has ample storage. Check on the view, the exposure, sound-proofing, and ventilation. Balance the pros and cons of being high up or on a lower floor; height improves the view, the lower levels offer economy. Check on garage and laundry facilities and ask about rules covering children, pets, and redecorating. Also ask about mail and package deliveries, waste disposal, and other services.

HOW TO SELL A HOUSE OR APARTMENT

If you are shopping for a house or apartment, the chances are that you have a place to sell. Unless there is an unusual demand for houses in your area, turn the problem over to a real-estate broker. They are experts and can advise you on price. They will find a buyer, locate a loan company for the mortgage, and in other ways facilitate the sale.

When you go to a doctor or lawyer you give all the facts, good and bad, about the case. Similarly you should give your broker all the information about your house. Tell him about inadequate insulation, a leaky roof, pending street assessments, recorded easements, and other features which might come up while the sale is being made which would put both you and the broker in an awkward position.

With most brokers you can specify that you want the house shown only by appointment. Once your house has been listed, however, it is not ethical for you to make a private sale. All potential customers, including friends, should be referred to your broker. The law requires that the seller pay the sales commission no matter who sells the house during the period it is listed with the broker. Before signing any documents related to the sale of the house your broker should be present and approve them before you sign.

When your house is up for sale:

Don't do any major remodeling.

Don't keep apologizing for the appearance of the house or grounds.

Don't trail around after the broker and his customer listening to what they say.

Don't have the radio or television blaring when the house is being shown.

Don't go around turning off lights and cleaning ash trays until after the broker and potential buyer have left.

Don't try to sell a potential buyer draperies, carpets, or other furnishings until the deal on the house is made.

Do clean the grounds, paint the exterior, keep the grass mowed, and create an orderly look.

Do clean rubbish out of garage, basements, and attics. Repair walks and steps and remove clutter.

Do wash windows and make rooms look light and bright.

Do clean closets and cupboards as women have a mania for looking into all of the unexpected corners.

Do keep the house smelling sweet and clean; unaired houses can be very unpleasant.

Do see that all lamps and ceiling fixtures have bulbs in them which will give the rooms brilliance when they are turned on. Put extension cords and bulbs in basement and attic if no lights are there.

4 How to Plan the Furnishings

Assuming that you have located a house or apartment and set the day for moving, begin immediately to plan your furnishings. Don't waste time aimlessly trying to visualize how the rooms will look. Ask the real-estate agent or superintendent for a floor plan. For new units such plans are available, but on old houses or apartments you will have to make your own room charts.

Armed with a yardstick or extension rule, and if possible a helpful husband, work out a scale drawing of the major rooms. First draw a free-hand plan of the room, indicating all doors, windows, fireplaces, radiators, and juts in the walls. Next take overall measurements of these features. Then measure the wall spaces on each side of windows and other architectural features so that they can be accurately located. Check ceiling heights and window dimensions carefully as a guide in making draperies. Note how much wall space there is between the top of the window and the ceiling and also check the distance between the floor and windowsill.

Such a chart will make it possible for you to make all furnishing plans in advance of moving so that you can get settled more quickly. When you are shopping for a new house, the chart in your pocketbook will help you in making correct purchases.

The first decorating decision may be the color for the walls. Take time to think the problem through. Don't settle on cream or apple green just because the painter suggests them and it is the easiest way out of a dilemma. In almost any paint catalogue there are beautiful colors to choose from, such as sunshine yellow, delphinium blue, sand, white, or rich spruce green.

But to really do a good decorating job a complete plan should be made before the painting is done. The color must be checked with the floor covering, draperies, upholstery, and accessories. Take an afternoon off to study the light in every angle and corner of the new quarters. Brood about it. Visualize the way you will live, where you will sit and read, where meals will be served. Walk along the traffic lanes between doors in each room; plan to keep them free of furniture. This picture of how a room will be used precedes a furniture plan.

There is no magic formula for learning how to live in or how to decorate a house. As with shorthand, engineering, or chemistry it is necessary to learn the fundamentals before much success can be achieved. True, if you had the good fortune to grow up in a gracious, well-managed home, you are leagues ahead when it comes time to furnish your own home. But even so you should stop, look, and listen before duplicating your ancestral mansion, for decorating fashions change with the times.

Today, whether you are furnishing a room, an old house, or a new house, whether you are working on a $25 or a $5,000 budget, it is important to know yourself. As you study the room, also look at yourself. It is amazing how many people go through life and never discover what makes them tick. Some discover it accidentally. Only a few get down and figure it out for themselves. This is a must if you want something more than just a pretty room.

Ask yourself these questions:

Do I like fluffy or tailored clothes?

Am I a leader or a follower?

What are my aims and ambitions for myself and my family?

What atmosphere do I want to develop: conservative, bohemian, cultivated, gay, simple, luxurious, studious, musical, artistic?

Have I the courage to do things the way I want them or do I want to impress the Joneses?

What does my future hold—children, a step up in the social scale, a step down, a move?

These questions may resemble the tea-leaf fortune school of thought, but the answers affect the house and the furnishings you acquire.

KNOW WHAT MAKES A FAMILY COMFORTABLE

Decorating or furnishing a house is not a matter of appearance as much as it is a problem in comfort and convenience. If a decorator thinks only in terms of tables and chairs and this darling chintz and that sweet lamp, the resulting room may be disastrous.

Comfort in a room comes before a color scheme or any other foible of decorating. A home should be a place where adults may relax, read, entertain, listen to music, sew, paint, tinker, do carpentry and a thousand and one other things. A home should be a place that encourages children to do things by supplying the place and the equipment for doing them.

A living room where you can only sit, or sit and listen to the radio, is only half a living room; a bedroom where you can only sleep, or sleep and dress, is only half a bedroom; and the house is only half a home.

Before buying even so much as a table or chair one should list all of the activities and interests of the household and, regardless of what they are, weave into the decorating plan the facilities and storage space they require.

KNOW MERCHANDISE

Next find out what is available and something about current trends. Because hats and coats and shoes are purchased frequently, almost subconsciously women keep up with colors and styles in clothes, but rugs, chairs, lamps are widely spaced purchases. Perhaps only two living-room rugs are bought in a lifetime, so before each purchase a review of the market for price, quality, color, and style is important.

First, study magazines. Analyze each room you see for color schemes, for furniture arrangement, for pictures and accessories, and for its convenience and use aspects. Get acquainted with the merchandise shown in magazine advertisements. Clip the ads if you see rugs, wallpaper, or furniture you like and take them with you when you go shopping.

Second, study newspaper advertisements. Become as thoroughly acquainted with price brackets in home furnishings as you are with the current prices of coats, dresses, and shoes.

Third, forearmed as you are with ideas on style, color, and price, spend several afternoons just shopping from store to store seeing what your town has to offer. Become an expert in what is available.

Only after you know yourself, know what will make your family comfortable, and know merchandise are you ready to take a pencil and paper and plan your room.

HOW TO PLAN A ROOM

After this short course in decorating and merchandising, take the floor plan of your new apartment or house and arrange the furniture, using not only the furniture you have, but also the furniture you would like to add.

Putting your plan on paper is the only way to think through a decorating job and make it jell. It is the only way to hold the idea of a room which may have to be developed over a period of years. I have been decorating houses for many years and even with my experience I still think plotting the floor plan on paper is important. It is even more vital for the person with little experience.

After the floor plan has been plotted, the next step is to develop the color scheme for the walls, woodwork, and rugs, the furniture, draperies, lamps, and accessories. Not only have your color scheme in your mind but assemble little color clippings of fabrics, wallpaper, and color bits from magazines to represent accessories. Play with these color charts until you are thoroughly pleased with your combination.

When you have the furniture arrangement and the color scheme worked out, you are ready to get down to brass tacks. The next step is to review the furniture, rugs, and accessories you have to start with. Fit what you have into your plan and schedule the purchase of the changes and new additions you want to make. This schedule, of course, will depend upon the amount you can budget for the new furnishings.

If you could wave your hand and decorate your room with one majestic sweep it would be wonderful. But most of us have to proceed bit by bit and piece by piece and often it is more fun to do it gradually. By adding just a piece at a time you get a chance to enjoy each new possession more. However, such slow decorating makes a master plan even more important if you are to avoid the hodgepodge of the average room.

In decorating, naturally necessities come first, but for effect, redoing the background will cause a more dramatic change in your room than any other single thing. The four walls are the largest area and the floor is the next. Seating units and beds should be listed as necessities. Follow these with new chests or storage pieces and lamps, because they have such an important influence on a room. Curtains and draperies are classed as major additions and should be followed by the perfect tables and desk. Pictures and accessories should be as carefully chosen as your gloves and earrings. They are last on the list, but they are important and are seriously slighted in the average room.

WORK SCHEDULE

In almost no time I have outlined the fundamentals of a decorating project. Each point has been briefly made. To go into the subject thoroughly would require a book.

Even though you are renting, some carpentry work on the background may be desirable. Such work may involve bookcases, closets, removal or addition of partitions, restyling the fireplace, or renovating the kitchen. All this work should be done before the painting.

Since the furniture presumably has not been moved in, the only make-ready for the painter is to have samples of your wallpaper and actual color samples of paint on hand. Either give the painter a clear, room-by-room chart with color samples or write directions on each wall and stick the color sample on with tape. Always keep half the color sample for your own guide and for your file folder on the job.

Following the painting, floors may be scraped and finished. Always request walnut-brown stain, shellacked and waxed, not the light-yellow finish so often used. If vinyl tile or carpets are on your schedule, they should be laid, if possible, before the moving day.

If extensive repairs are being made, follow this schedule:

1. Plumber. Working on plumbing, the hot water, or furnace systems may involve tearing out sections of the wall in order to get at pipes. Such work should be done first.
2. Mason. The plumber may have ripped out tile floors or walls in bathrooms, which a mason will restore. At the same time the mason will repair fireplaces and chimneys.
3. Electrician. New electric convenience outlets may be needed. Often wall brackets must be removed and central fixtures capped. All this should be done before the carpenter comes. However, if bookcases are to cover a wall the electrician should be told so

that he can bring convenience outlets through and mount them on the back of the bookcase after the carpenter has finished.

4. Carpenter. Puts in bookcases and windows, blocks out unnecessary doors, and remodels fireplace.
5. Plasterers are needed only when large holes are made. Small cracks and holes can be handled by the painter.
6. Painter for woodwork and walls.
7. Paperhangers.
8. Floor refinishing, carpet laying.
9. Draperies.
10. Furniture.

All work—plumbing, carpentry, painting, and floor finishing—should start in the bedrooms or upstairs and the work should be carried through the house to the back door. This plan will reduce the tracking of dirt through the house, and final cleaning can be done room by room as the workmen leave. If there is any way to accomplish it, try to have all repairs and changes made before you move in. It will simplify life in the new location.

5 How to Pack and Move

Moving has become a part of the housekeeper's ritual. By the time the average couple has been married fifteen years, they have moved from one to ten times. The prospect of frequent moves is not an altogether happy one, but, since many of the moves represent a step up in income and many are financed by the boss, mobility is fast becoming a way of life and is something to be mastered physically and psychologically.

If frequent moves are written into your future, face them and plan accordingly especially when you buy furniture.

Avoid:

Grand pianos and other overscale furniture.
Eight-foot sofas; substitute a pair of love seats.
Triple dressers; get unit pieces that line up against the wall.
Breakfront bookcases with glass doors; substitute wall shelves.
Glass- and marble-topped tables; wood holds up better.
Carpeting; invest in handsome area rugs that will fit anywhere.
Breakable accessories; specialize in handsome antique pewter, copper, brass, and woodenware.

Moves fall roughly into four classifications and each entails a slightly different problem.

Moves across state lines. Such moves are regulated by the Interstate Commerce Commission, whose responsibility it is to fix the rate per pound and liabilities.

Moves within a state. Moves from one city to another within the same state come under state laws. Some states have regulatory requirements, others do not.

Local moves. Changes of residence within a city or its suburbs are usually not controlled by law. Here your own research into the reliability of the mover is especially important.

Overseas moves. Door-to-door delivery of household goods can now be arranged between the United States, Canada, Europe, the Middle East, South America, and Alaska. This service has been set up by the Aero Mayflower Transit Company, the American Express Company, and Pan American World Airways.

Perhaps you have moved before and know the ropes. If you haven't, do some research before plunging. About 20 percent of American householders move annually, so naturally moving has become big business. There are highly competent movers and those who give lesser service, while some local movers, subject to fewer controls, may be downright frauds. Your investigation should be keyed to getting a dependable mover, in business for years, with a good reputation, for, as you will discover, laws all seem to protect the mover and you are dependent on his integrity.

Begin by a study of the movers in the classified section of the telephone directory. Ask friends and relatives about their experiences. Call up several companies and ask about their service. Check their references and make inquiries of the Better Business Bureau.

As soon as you are satisfied that you have the right mover, make arrangements for him to look over the load. Before the estimate is made, make a complete survey, including the basement, attic, and garage. Determine exactly what is to be moved and what things are to be sold or disposed of. Estimates are important but are not necessarily accurate, especially on interstate moves, which are based on the actual weight of the shipment, distance, and additional services performed.

In the interview discuss the timing and the number of men who will handle the work. Inquire into the firm's financial rating and liability coverage. Regardless of any prior estimates received, you will be required to pay transportation charges filed by your mover with the Interstate Commerce Commission. Charges may be more or less than the estimate. Since the estimate is not binding, it is important to use a mover who will not overcharge.

Valuable furnishings, fine paintings, oriental rugs, irreplaceable antiques should all be covered with an all-risk insurance policy. Usually no overall liability insurance is given unless the movers also do all of the packing.

If the move begins or ends in a large apartment with an elevator, ask the superintendent for rules covering moving. Often the elevator may be used only at certain times of the day, and if there are other tenants moving in or out a definite schedule will be made. If your movers do not arrive on time, they will miss their turn on the elevator, which will necessitate a wait that may increase the cost of the job.

There are movers who will take over the whole project—packing, moving, and unpacking—but such operations are more legendary than real for most of us because of the fee.

However, ask for advice from your mover on packing. He may supply barrels for china, estimate the number needed, and suggest ways and means of handling books.

Don't start tearing up the house until the date for moving is not more than two weeks off. There is no reason to live in an upset house longer than necessary. From the beginning use a notebook and pencil as a double check on your memory. Each morning over toast and coffee make lists of things to be done. At the same time feel a fine sense of accomplishment by marking off tasks completed.

PEOPLE TO NOTIFY

Send plain post cards, which are available at the post office, announcing your move. Include your name, your old address, your new address with zip code, and the date of your arrival. Make the date on which you leave your present residence precise and clear. Include on your list:

1. United States post office in your town. A week's notice is sufficient. Your mailman can supply a form for you to fill out.
2. Magazines to which you subscribe. Four to six weeks' notification is desirable.
3. Local newspapers. A week's notice in advance is enough.
4. All charge accounts. A month's notice is considerate.
5. Insurance company. Transfer fire, theft, and employees' insurance to the new address so that you will be covered from the time your furnishings are moved.
6. Book clubs should have four to six weeks' notice. Include your account number.
7. Commercial laundries will appreciate a week's notice and don't forget articles you have in storage.
8. Dry cleaners. If you use a neighborhood cleaner, don't leave anything behind. If you are moving to a new location in the same

town, have cleaned blankets, carpets, and clothes delivered to the new address. The carpets should be laid before the van arrives.

9. Gas, electric, and water companies. Don't wait until the last day. Have connections made several days ahead of time. Check to see if utility deposits made when you moved to your present address are due you.
10. Telephone company. Allow a month as you may have to await your turn for a connection. Retain your old number if possible.
11. Fuel or oil company—and get the value of remaining oil.
12. Water softener, garbage, and pay TV service.
13. Public library if you or your children have cards.
14. A next-door neighbor.

Collect records from school, church, and tax collector. Give new address to charge-card companies, i.e., American Express, etc. If you are moving to another city, the Health Insurance Institute suggests that you gather as many family health records as possible, including eyeglass prescriptions and dental records. Have your physician forward records to your new doctor.

Retired persons should notify their Social Security office and pension sources.

Don't forget to notify your bank and your stock-market broker. Check your safety deposit box.

JUNK DRIVE

Before actually organizing the packing, conduct a private and ruthless junk drive. This idea comes from a woman who, though married only four years, has moved ten times. Most people are accumulators. Even a week's stay in one place accounts for a pile of papers or boxes to be discarded. After a month there is a rising tide of debris and after a year the problem of excess may be acute.

Weed out all unnecessary bottles, jars, boxes, clothes hangers, furniture, rugs, knickknacks, toys, and magazines that are no longer needed, and dispose of them. Also discard deteriorating cans of paint, all flammable fluids, and year-old medicine bottles. The thoroughness of the cleanout may depend on the distance you are moving and the character and size of the new home. Long-distance moving is expensive and so is storage; on the other hand replacements are expensive too so reckless discards are not recommended.

If you are moving to a retirement home, plan carefully. Take the things you love with you but be firm about discards. Sell what you can, but you won't find it easy to do. Disposing of furniture requires time, stamina, and know-how. There is little demand for even good commercial furniture; however, antiques, even young antiques of early twentieth-century vintage, have resale possibilities.

An item in the newspaper or mention on the local radio could result in some sales. Dealers and auctioneers prefer lots to single pieces unless the furniture being disposed of is choice. Furnishings which cannot be sold for cash sometimes can be given to the Salvation Army and thrift shops, which at least will cart the stuff away. You can then ask for a receipt and take a deduction on your income tax.

If by chance you have a vast accumulation of newspapers and magazines they may be bundled and sold. Better still, call the Boy Scouts and if they are interested they will collect them. If you can't get anyone to take away what's left over at a price, locate the city dump and dispose of the junk yourself.

Plan in advance satisfactory disposal of potted plants or move them yourself. Movers are not permitted to accept for shipment plants or flowers of any kind. Pets, birds, goldfish, dogs, and cats will also be your responsibility.

PACKING INSTRUCTIONS

Don't feel overwhelmed with packing. A systematic approach and a certain amount of patience are all that are necessary. Actually, organization is more important than anything else. The better you pack, the easier it will be to unpack, and on local moves you will be saving money. Rates for local moves as a rule are based on time for loading and unloading and a mileage rate for the distance between your old and new residences. It takes a minimum of six hours to load a six-room house of furniture. The busy moving season runs from May 15 to October 15, according to a national report. The peak months for moving are June, July, and August. If you can schedule your move in a slack period, you may get a discount and certainly better personal service.

PACKING

If you have decided to do some of the packing yourself, be professional. Use correct materials; do it the right way. Don't pack so that the movers will have to redo the work, and remember movers are not responsible for owner-packed articles.

Supplies needed:

Boxes, barrels, cartons
Old newspapers, and quantities of white tissue paper
Heavy wrapping paper and heavy cord
"Fragile" stickers
Felt-tipped package marker and tags

There are variables which affect the cost of moving. These include the heavy objects such as oversized sofas, grand pianos, and freezers; how close the van can get to the house for loading and unloading; narrow, winding halls and steep, narrow stairways. Delicate, old, or easily breakable furniture and even the weather may affect the cost of moving. If it rains or snows, special precautions are needed:

Don't pack lamps or shades. Just remove the shades, screw finials back on base. Packers prefer their own boxes.
Don't overload boxes or cartons. Allow twenty-five to thirty books to a box; aim for a fifty-pound maximum.
Don't remove large pictures and mirrors from walls; leave them for movers to handle.
Don't put liquids where they can spill and damage other things.
Don't ship flammable liquids.
Don't fill drawers and cupboards on long hauls with heavy sheets or other heavy objects; they may shift and damage the furniture. Sweaters, lingerie, and other soft objects may be packed in drawers.
Don't roll up inner-spring mattresses. Movers bring special cartons to protect them.

SPECIAL ADVICE

China and glass may be your greatest concern. Use barrels if possible. First pad the bottom with excelsior or shredded newspaper. Wrap each item separately and fit it in snugly. Put heavy bowls and platters at the bottom, cups and smaller items on top. Stand the plates on their side, nest cups, watch handles. Fine ware should be packed in compartmented boxes supplied by the mover. Leave space for padding on top. The aim is to have packing so tight that objects cannot click together.

Records like plates should be packed upright and exactly fit their container. Tape down the changer and tone arm of record players.

Pots and pans should be wrapped and packed carefully to prevent dents and breakage, with the heaviest objects at the bottom. Have a box specially labeled for things needed immediately. Include paper cups, tea, coffee, soap, scouring powder, towels, cleaning cloths, and hammer and nails. Have kitchen shelf paper mailed or delivered to the new house ahead of time to speed up putting kitchen in order.

Accessories should be packed according to rooms and each carton labeled. Reduce as far as possible the number of separate small items to be handled.

Plan to take with you fragile articles, antiques, or items of special value such as jewelry, watches, stocks, bonds, documents, certificates, deeds, stamp collections, and precious stones. Under rules and regulations covering interstate shipments, movers are not responsible for these things.

Rugs and carpets if cleaned should be delivered and laid in the new house before moving day. If they are to go with the van, let the movers handle them. Rugs and pads are rolled separately to reduce the weight. Rugs are rolled lengthwise, except orientals and other hand-woven rugs with no sizing on the back. Felt pads may be folded; rubber pads are rolled.

Freezers. For short hauls not to exceed 150 miles let the freezer operate until the movers arrive. If delivery is complete within twenty-four hours there will be no spoilage. If the trip is longer, begin reducing your freezer load at once so that it is empty when moving day comes.

Television antenna. These and window fans, air-conditioning units, curtain rods, traverse rods, as well as other fixtures should be down and ready to go on M-day. Also disconnect and dismantle hi-fi speakers and intercom units.

Custom-built wall shelving. This should be taken down, as well as all wall-mounted tools such as can openers, pencil sharpeners, tissue dispensers, etc.

Power mower. Drain the fuel. No flammables of any kind can be shipped by van. Dismantle and pack up the home workshop and garden tools.

Major appliances. Have the gas range, refrigerator, and other electrical objects disconnected. Movers are not responsible for mechanical failure of major appliances unless they have been disconnected by an authorized person.

AT OLD HOME—AFTER MOVERS ARRIVE

Tell movers exactly what goes and what stays. Arrange to have items needed first loaded last. If you have a floor plan of the new premises, give it to the movers along with your new phone number. Sign and get a copy of the bill of lading and of the inventory. Get estimate of time when goods will be delivered. If you do not have exclusive use of the van (unless otherwise specified on long hauls two or three shipments may be consolidated), no delivery time will be given.

After the movers leave check all rooms. Make sure nothing wanted was left behind. Leave the house or apartment in good order. Dispose of waste and sweep each room. If you do not have time for this, arrange to have it done. When the van is loaded and the movers are getting ready to leave, pull the master switch on the electric current, read the meter, record date, lock the house, and leave the keys in a place previously arranged.

AT THE NEW LOCATION BEFORE THE MOVERS ARRIVE

Have telephone, gas, water, and electricity turned on. Arrange with local trades people to have appliances installed. Arrange to have new auto licenses. Have the windows cleaned and the whole house spotless. Contact movers' local agent for reports on the progress of the van.

When the movers arrive at the new house be on hand with a duplicate floor plan. Be a traffic director. Notwithstanding your labels, station yourself at the front door and as each man comes in tell him where to deposit his load: front room upstairs, back room downstairs, kitchen, and so on. Such directions will facilitate the unloading and assure you of better sorting. You should be half settled when the men leave.

All charges must be paid in cash, by money order, or certified check at the time shipment is delivered. In the event of loss or damage, have the driver make an initialed note on the receipt or freight bill he gives you.

All claims for loss or damage must be filed in writing with the mover. Otherwise the I.C.C. cannot help you get settlement.

WHEN THE VAN LEAVES

Go ahead and collapse when the van leaves. A cold drink or a hot cup of tea or coffee will perk you and your helpers up and you will be ready to dig in again.

First get the beds put together and made up before you do another thing. This is in case you reach the end of your endurance suddenly. When this is done, put the living room to rights. It will help the family feel settled and will be good for morale if anyone calls.

Don't be fancy about dinner. Serve it picnic style and remember wonderful things come out of cans—spaghetti and tomato sauce, corned-beef hash, baked beans, and brown bread. Also consider paper plates and cups. Better still, park the children and pets with Grandmother or a willing friend. If such arrangements are impractical and you have reached the point where you must have peace and the children are too old to be put to bed at six o'clock, send them off to a movie. Then you can contemplate your problem and plan tomorrow's strategy. Or, better still, bundle up the whole family and spend the night in a nearby motel. Unpacking will look easier in the morning.

HOW TO CLOSE A SUMMER HOUSE

There is an art and a science to closing a summer house whether in the country, in the mountains, or at the shore. Do a good job in the fall and the house will welcome you in the spring. The precautions taken should be designed to ward off human and animal marauders and the ravages of weather; rust is the big enemy.

1. Install winter shutters over the windows. Remove the screen doors. Check the roof for leaks. If snows will be heavy, consider roof reinforcements.
2. Paint the wood stove, stove pipe, and other iron equipment with unsalted grease. Leave the wood box for stove and fireplace full of wood and kindling ready for a quick crackling fire. Thoroughly drain all plumbing, disconnect the pump, put kerosene in the traps of water closet and sink. Leave the screws, washer, and wrench beside the sink for quick use in the spring. Put all matches in glass jars or tin cans.

3. Store all tools indoors. Clean tools, coat metal parts with unsalted fat, and paint the handles. Store garden furniture under cover if possible. Leave nothing attractive outside for light-fingered passersby. Padlock shed. Close damper in fireplace; consider covering chimney top to keep squirrels out.
4. Go through the house with a basket or box and remove anything that could freeze: ink bottles, liquid lotion and medicine bottles, all canned goods, and bottled drinks. Sugar and salt solidify and should not be left behind. Flour, dry cereals, tea, coffee, cocoa, rice, and spaghetti may be stored in tin containers and left in the house. This is in the spirit of the West. Squatters' cabins cannot be locked. They are closed with a latch string and basic food supplies are left for use by anyone lost in the mountains.
5. Put all pillows in plastic bags and hang them from a clothesline. Remove blankets from beds and fold them. Stand seat cushions in chairs; leave no snuggly throws on sofas to invite mice. Take all last-minute washing home and make a list of things you want to bring back with you in the spring. Put polyethylene under and over the mattresses to discourage mice, keep out moisture, and protect from a leaky roof.
6. Scrub all garbage pails, sun, and leave under cover. Mice will nest in soap flakes and eat soap, so collect it from bathrooms and sink and store in a plastic, tin, or glass container.
7. Just before you leave and after all household pets have been put out of the house sprinkle mouse pellets liberally through the house. Put naphtha cakes in drawers and closets. Never leave pets behind. Either take them with you, make arrangements for their care, or turn them over to the A.S.P.C.A. or village pound.
8. Leave your city address and phone number with your nearest neighbor and the local police.

6 How to Get Acquainted

Moving into a new house or apartment is like starting all over again. It is the time to appraise yourself, your household, and the community, to make new resolutions, and to establish new family habits and customs. In fresh surroundings with new neighbors and shopkeepers it is easier to try new ways, to demonstrate growth in taste and neighborliness.

If you and your family have lived in one community for three or four generations, everyone knows you. You are established and almost no effort is required for you to be a part of the community. Because you are an old family, you are included in club, church, and community affairs, the children are invited to parties, and life flows smoothly.

In a new community the situation is entirely different. You and your family are unknown and you will receive merits or demerits on your own conduct and spirit. What your parents or grandparents were will mean very little. The fact that you are strangers in the community can lead to a sense of instability in the family, especially in the children, unless effort is made to put down roots or develop an identity in the new location. Adolescents especially seem to take the attitude, "Well, nobody knows me. I can do anything." This is a trouble-making point of view.

It is important to put out feelers in all directions when you move to a new location in order to become, as soon as possible, an active part of the neighborhood and the community.

ADVANCE PREPARATION

As soon as the move you are making is decided upon, talk it over in full with the children. Even three- or four-year-olds should be a part of the family council. Tell them why the shift is being made, let them feel a sense of adventure in connection with it—a going-forth to new places like an explorer of old.

Before moving day take the children on a visit to the new neighborhood. If you are moving to a distant city and a visit is not practical, get a map, pin it upon the family bulletin board, mark with a heavy line the route to the new location. Make a point of talking about the new house, city, state—the history, the scenic advantages. Perhaps there is travel literature available from the state or from the chamber of commerce of the town you are moving to.

Your own attitude will count more than anything else and the children's attitude will reflect yours. If you are happy about the move, if you have stilled all doubts and disturbances, the settling-in process will be happier for everyone. Approach the new neighborhood with positive good will. Don't compare it with the one you have left. Find the good things about the new town, the new neighborhood, the new house. Don't be standoffish; take an optimistic attitude. Everyone is drawn to a happy, outgoing personality.

THE NEIGHBORS

Experts in community life say that there is freedom from snobbery only in the lowest levels of society and the topmost brackets. Most of us fall in between these two extremes, which means that in this new neighborhood it is necessary to move carefully, but in a neighborly fashion. Antagonism can be avoided by being neighborly at heart. Petty snobbery melts before a pleasant smile and a cheerful "Good morning."

When you first greet the neighbors it may help if you realize that you are not a total stranger. The neighbors already have their opinions about you. It is amazing the deductions which can be made from your lares and penates as they are passed into the house from the moving van. In the few minutes belongings stand naked and unprotected on the street, the more astute neighbors have discovered your strengths and weaknesses, your taste in decoration, your favorite color, your age, your standard of living, and perhaps even your income! Children, yours and the neighbors, will facilitate the transmission of information so that even first contacts are not made without a small fund of personal data on both sides.

If yours is the average neighborhood, the neighbors will let you settle in peace. Neighborhoods are far more miscellaneous than they were at one time. New families of all races, nationalities, religions, incomes, and standards may live within a few blocks of each other and even in the same apartment house.

If by chance you have a foreign accent, remember that the human animal instinctively resists contacts with the unknown. Only a small group reaches out for new experiences. If you don't celebrate the same holidays, and if you eat borsch, shashlik, or vichyssoise, instead of meat, potatoes, and apple pie, at first you may be regarded with suspicion, but if you are generous, helpful, and considerate and don't draw within yourself, you may be surprised at the generosity and friendliness you will uncover.

Callers. In the early years in this country it was customary to call on new neighbors as soon as they were settled. It was a completely routine affair. This was before neighborhoods were as mixed as they are now. Today if you are a newcomer, and the doorbell rings, it probably won't be a neighbor. It may be a Fuller-brush man or a Fullerette, a vacuum-cleaner salesman, an agent for a magazine, an unusually active insurance solicitor, or a representative from a nearby church.

About this group of callers you may use your own judgment, but if by chance a neighbor appears invite her in and chat with her. If you can manage it easily and without being out of the room more than a few minutes, serve a cup of tea or coffee. Don't let any disarrangement of the living room disturb you. What can be expected in the first week?

When the new household is in order it will be time enough to appease the curiosity of friends. There is no ceremony. Perhaps your club will meet with you, or by ones or twos or threes friends may be invited for luncheon, tea, dinner, or the evening.

If you are a bride setting up housekeeping in your husband's home town and none of his friends call, after a reasonable length of time, if your husband wishes, you may invite his more intimate friends to your house. This will start the ball rolling toward social success.

CHILDREN AND THE COMMUNITY

If you have children, present-day lack of neighborliness will be automatically broken down. Children, yours and the neighbors', are without inhibitions. As naturally as puppies, they will get acquainted with any youngster who fares forth in the street in their block.

To facilitate getting acquainted, which is very important for children, it may be wise to provide some interesting outside activity, something irresistible like a tricycle, bicycle, pogo stick, or, for older children, a basketball and basket or a football or baseball. Any one of these activities should prove an admirable icebreaker.

School adjustment for young children will come much faster if they are taken to school the first day. Your presence will help dissipate a feeling of strangeness. One clever primary teacher, who realizes how forlorn and out of place a youngster feels in a new class, tries to locate a book the child is familiar with to read aloud to the class. She appoints a "big brother" or "sister" to show the newcomer around and see that he takes part in games at recess. With such consideration, in a few days the child is no longer a stranger.

While at the school meet not only the principal but also the child's teacher. Point out your child's good points as well as the weak ones and frankly ask for help. Inquire about school clubs, the Parent-Teacher Association, and other community activities which may be directed by the school. Also find out who directs the Boy Scouts, Girl Scouts, and the Camp Fire Girls. These are fine organizations and every child should have such directed group experience.

Becoming personally involved in a new community is one of the best ways of making friends. Whether it's Rockport, Maine, or Ferndale, Washington, if you show a spirit of willingness, interest, and responsibility you will be welcome. One woman, new to a community, volunteered to give lessons in astronomy to Scout groups. A man who gives talks on rock collecting and shows his own exhibits in less than a year has made a unique place for himself. An Eastern couple new to the West are frequent volunteers for weekend ski parties sponsored by the high school. Their two teen-age daughters are the beneficiaries. There is also always a place for women who wish to do civic or charitable work, in hospitals, charity thrift shops, Red Cross, or Scout work.

Adult education classes offer another means of meeting others with like interests. Classes are offered in interior design, art, music, languages, ceramics, and woodworking. Little theatre activities are also rewarding.

Whether in the States or abroad follow the custom of the country, "do as the Romans do." Get acquainted with the foods of the area and local schedules for doing things. Be understanding and considerate. Smile.

CHURCHES AND THE COMMUNITY

Probably members from several churches will call on you. Return the courtesy by attending services and go more than halfway in getting acquainted. Look up the person who called on you and tell her how much you enjoyed the service.

Enter children in Sunday school and personally escort young children on the first several occasions just as you did at day school. Participate in church activities and in a short time you will find yourself with friends.

Churches in this country are traditionally the nucleus of neighborliness and community life. In frontier towns the church was often built before the school. The church is still ready to serve, but it is the people who attend a church who determine the extent of that service. If you belong to a church by all means have your membership transferred to your new location.

SHOPS AND STORES

Two or three generations ago housekeepers went to original sources for household supplies. They baked their own bread, canned their vegetables, butchered their meat, hemmed their own sheets, and made their own clothes. Women understood quality because they knew what went into things. But times have changed. Now the mark of a clever woman often comes down to the way she markets, the out-of-the-way shops she discovers, and her rapport with the butcher, the baker, and the candlestick maker.

Make your own tour of discovery. Be systematic about it. Do it as thoroughly as you would a market study you were being paid to make. Armed with a pad and pencil, visit the shopping centers. Check within a radius of several miles to locate the most convenient one that will serve your needs, but don't overlook specialties offered by others. Treat shopkeepers like human beings and take time enough to get acquainted with them.

Our shopping manners in this country are really bad and should be changed. In France, for instance, the only way you can get service is to be reasonably polite. On entering a store shoppers customarily greet the shopkeeper with a "Bonjour, madame," and on leaving with "Au revoir, madame." In France you follow your greeting to the shopkeeper with an elaborate explanation of what you want and who you are shopping for and you are almost sure to get results. "Have you a pretty scarf? I want it for my aunt who lives in St. Louis. She has green eyes and I would so like to find something to match them." With such an introduction to the problem the average French shopkeeper will take the place apart for you. Indeed she will continue the search long after you are satisfied.

. . . butchers offer a particular problem

Believe it or not, this human approach brings results on Main Street. My husband's prowess as a shopper offers an example. He is an exuberant soul who goes shopping for entertainment and to entertain. Without question he receives superior service whether he shops in person or on the telephone. After a little raillery, all of our suppliers outdo themselves for him. The special service we get is proof that affability and the special approach pay off in business contacts.

Even the local supermarket personnel will be more gracious if you treat them like people instead of cogs in a wheel. Make a point of getting acquainted with the butcher, have a heart-to-heart talk, and call early in the morning before the store is crowded. Under these conditions it's amazing how much special service you can get even from the supermarket where most meat comes prewrapped.

Important too are dry-cleaning and laundry services. Explore them fully as the offerings in different localities vary widely.

When your market study is completed, you will know the location of the one or two closest shopping centers and several routes for going and coming. You will have located the nearest supermarkets and your address book will contain store names, managers' names, addresses, and telephone numbers of some or all of the following stores and services:

auto repairs
baby-sitter
Blue Cross headquarters
church
clothes cleaner
delicatessen
dentist
doctor
drugstore
fire department
florist
fuel dealer
garbage-disposal service
gasoline station
hairdresser
hardware store
housemaid
milkman
newsdealer
oculist
poison-control center
police department
post office
public library
public utilities
restaurants or tearooms
school
shoe-repair service
snow-plow service
social security service (for recipients)
taxicab service
television repairman
town manager or mayor

Armed with your own private directory of supplies and services, you will begin to feel like an established member of the community. Any feeling of inexperience or strangeness will be dispelled and you can focus your attention on your own household management.

2 *About Cleaning*

7 How to Run a House

Running a house is a most exciting and interesting job, for you are not only making a home—creating a background for you and your family—but you are also enriching your own life, adding to your own pleasure and convenience, as well as demonstrating your power over things. Moreover, the better you run the house, the more you will enjoy it, and the faster you work the more time you have for avocations.

Even though running a house has a far deeper significance than having a job in an office, the two can be approached in the same way. In an office only those who look upon their work as a career will have enthusiasm and put heart into the job. The same factors operate with the homemaker. Only homemakers who are sincere and are willing to apply both mind and hands can hope to cope with the intricacies of keeping house. It is without question one of the most complicated and many-sided operations one person is ever expected to handle. The homemaker is both boss and helper, manager and flunky. She sits on the board of directors and is the purchasing agent. She is head of personnel, social secretary, and in charge of public relations, and at the same time she is chambermaid and cook, laundress and handyman. Finally, as wife she is a companion, confidante, social partner, and love mate, and usually a mother.

All this adds up to a challenging job, and the fact that you were once a good secretary, a good teacher, beauty queen, or a Phi Beta Kappa is trivial compared with it. Two of the most pathetic and unhappy homemakers I know are Phi Beta Kappas. They have not grasped the importance of homemaking; they have not applied their minds to the problem. As a result two more badly operated homes cannot be imagined.

After a visit, the mother-in-law of one of these girls exploded to me. "I've just spent two of the most difficult weeks of my life with Sally, Bob, and the baby. Believe me," she sputtered, "I've been sitting

Mother
Furnace Man
Cook
Chambermaid
Laundress
Soul Mate

on both my hands and holding my tongue to keep from doing or saying the wrong thing. Sally works all the time washing, ironing, sewing, and cooking. She starts at seven o'clock in the morning and some days she is still working at ten o'clock at night."

When I murmured that, yes, it was a job looking after a house and baby, Mother Jan burst out again. "My eye, don't tell me that. I had five and I didn't have diaper service, strained baby foods, ready-made clothes, or all the gadgets Sally has to make the job easy. Still, I never worked any such hours. The difference is," and she faced me with a stern look, "I knew my job and I had respect for it. Poor Sally hasn't seen the light. She was a Phi Beta Kappa and taught school before she married and she doesn't know the first thing about babies or running a house. She is scared of the baby, as uncertain as a hog on ice in her beautiful kitchen, and on top of that she feels put upon, and I don't know what to do about it."

Obviously the only solution for Sally is to learn how to handle the job she has now. With her mind she can if she will recognize the value of it. Then she will be able to dispatch her job smoothly and have a margin of time to write the short stories she was too tired to attempt when she was teaching.

Some of the best housekeepers I know are men. They do the job efficiently, get if over with, and don't talk about it. As a rule their houses are in order before they leave for work and their homes convey a feeling of competence and order lacking in many households.

Homemaking is a skill and a profession. If you want to do it well, you acquire standards and learn how to measure up to them. Frustration with housekeeping is not caused by the work as much as by the attitude. The fact is that the average woman gets tired of being alone; she gets bored with conversations with babies. She needs to master the techniques of keeping house so that she can get it done and out of the way. Then she will have time for refreshing contacts and hobbies.

JOB ANALYSIS

In order to understand the job or the jobs to be done, homemaking must be divided into its various parts. Planning is nine-tenths of any job. An architect may work a year and a half on plans for a house it takes three months to build. A decorator may work six months designing a room which can be assembled in two days. A job is usually as good as the planning that goes into it. In other words, with homemaking as with any other job big or little, one must first draft the program, then select the tools, and finally develop the logistics.

Homemaking involves dealing with people and their needs. The people who have to be dealt with are the family and that involves:

child health and education
social life and recreation
community activities
companionship

The needs that have to be handled are:

cleaning, care, and upkeep of house
food, cooking, nutrition
clothing, its selection and care
finances and purchasing

It takes understanding and skillful management to weave together the many problems and tasks of homemaking into a comfortable, smooth-running routine which takes into account daily, weekly, and seasonal variations.

Until housekeeping becomes automatic, written schedules are good discipline. Later, when you become an old hand, work schedules, meal timing, menus, and family relationships are handled subconsciously and written schedules may lapse. Even then you cannot relax your vigilance. Never let a habit ride you. Investigation of new developments should continue. Change methods when a better one presents itself. Take advantage of the parade of new tools and new products. That's the way to stay young.

WORK SCHEDULES

No one schedule could possibly serve all households. Variations are imposed by the size of the house, whether it is urban, suburban, or rural, the number and age of members of the household, the materials, textures, and colors of surfaces, the section of the country, air pollution, personal standards of cleanliness, who does the work, and the quality of the tools. If there are only two people, it is easy to make programs agree, but, if there are five or six in the family, some fine and fancy coordination is necessary, for the more people there are in the family group and the greater the age span, the more detailed the scheduling should be. By this I do not mean that a house should be run on a timetable like a train, or even an office. Nothing could be more deadly. But a household run completely without schedule leads to chaos.

The chart below divides the major jobs into four groups. Daily schedules revolve around food preparation, serving and cleaning up after meals. Weekly tasks are fitted into the daily schedule whenever it is convenient. As the seasons roll round, in addition to these daily and weekly tasks there are the seasonal ones. Summer or winter clothes must be cleaned and put away and new ones acquired, holiday activities must be arranged, and the house itself refurbished.

In brief outline a work chart may look like this:

DAILY TASKS

preparation, serving and cleaning up after meals
straightening up and routine housecleaning
care of children, if any
period of relaxation
personal grooming

WEEKLY TASKS

thorough housecleaning
washing and ironing
menu planning and marketing
baking and special food preparation

SPECIAL TASKS

entertaining and trips outside the house
mending, sewing, clothes care
accounts, correspondence, records

SEASONAL TASKS

special cleaning
annual conversion of house to winter
annual conversion of house to summer
annual conversion of clothes to winter
annual conversion of clothes to summer
holiday preparations
canning
gardening

A good manager spreads special tasks and seasonal tasks over the year. I think of Mrs. X., who without help runs a dude ranch. She cleans daily and prepares and serves three meals for ten to twelve people. In addition, she also takes the dudes horseback riding for an average of two hours each morning.

She gets up at six-thirty and serves breakfast from seven-thirty to nine o'clock. During this period she also prepares lunch and often makes soup or dessert for the evening meal. Between nine and ten o'clock she washes dishes and cleans the cabins. From ten to twelve she rides with dudes. At twelve-thirty luncheon is served. Until two-thirty dishes and extras occupy her. Then she has a period of relaxation followed by more horseback riding or extra tasks until dinner.

During the six days I observed Mrs. X.'s amazing management, in addition to the excellent meals and the daily horseback riding, she managed to:

crochet a hat
make butter
make candy
bake a cake
call on a friend
hand feed and care for
  a half-dozen delicate baby turkeys
supervise the farmer
start knitting a sock
arrange flowers
work in the garden
write letters
handle milk from two cows
take a Sunday-afternoon drive

Mrs. X. is able to accomplish these tasks easily because of her fine mechanical aids. She insists that they are far superior to one or two people she had in the pre-electrical days. As helpers she rates first her constant supply of hot water, then her dishwasher and frozen-food locker, followed by the refrigerator and vacuum cleaner. The electric coffee maker and big dining-room hot trays save steps to and from the kitchen. Coffee is available almost twenty-four hours a day for those who want between-meal snacks.

Another remarkable manager, a young woman of twenty-seven, has four children—three boys, seven, five, and three, and a girl aged one. With her large family a careful daily program has proven to be the only solution. Her weekly schedule goes like this:

Monday: Vacuum shades, rugs, upholstery, moldings, doors, windowsills—literally everything in the house.

Tuesday: Polish everything—silver, glass, mirrors, pots and pans, brass, and andirons.

Wednesday: Change the beds, collect and count laundry to be sent out Thursday.

Thursday: Thoroughly clean the kitchen, bathroom, and porch.

Friday: Buy weekly groceries, clean all vegetables before putting in refrigerator. Do weekend baking.

There is an automatic washer and a dryer and every morning the children's clothes and table linen are washed. This schedule leaves every afternoon and Saturday and Sunday reasonably free for family projects and fun.

Mrs. S. has four jobs. Another schedule, far more involved, has been developed by a young woman of thirty-one who has her doctor's degree as well as three girls—five and a half, three, and one—and a boy of four. She is active in the community, is conducting a study group on international relations, has been in charge of a church group collecting clothing for its rummage sale, belongs to a preschool study group, is a member of the executive board of the National League of Women Voters, and has just accepted the chairmanship of the annual church carnival for children.

This program sounds like more than a full-time job, but Mrs. S. handles it easily with only a part-time maid who comes in while Mrs. S. is away from home. The secret of her management seems to be her complete confidence and understanding of nutritional problems and the operation of the household. She knows the job, wastes no time doing it, and is having a magnificent time.

True, her house never has a scrubbed look. Glass curtains have been eliminated along with the clutter of unnecessary accessories. The three girls share one room, the boy has one to himself, and a third bedroom has been designated a playroom. The children are trained to keep their toys and confusion confined to that room.

In this household there is only one trip a week to the supermarket for groceries and that is on the one day a week that Mrs. S. has the use of the car. The neighborhood runs a car pool for taking children to and from school. Monday is the day delegated to Mrs. S., so on that day her husband uses the bus and Mrs. S. taxis the neighborhood children to and from nursery school and dancing class. She does the week's shopping, takes shoes out to be mended, and drops clothes at the cleaner. She begins the day with a list of the errands to be done and collects all of the items which are to be delivered to assorted places. As each job is taken care of it is checked off.

Mrs. S. handles all household jobs on this streamlined mass-production basis. Dishes are done once a day, cleaning once a week in a terrific swoop. The laundry may accumulate several weeks, then be done in an operation that goes on from dawn to midnight with Mr. S. pitching in to help.

Mrs. S.'s is not a normal schedule, since she does the work of four women, but it serves her and that is the important thing. She has the fond hope that after the children are all in school she can take a part-time job. But, since she wants two, maybe four more children, that time seems a long way off; meanwhile she is running her household with vim and is enjoying every minute of it.

Since even a brief survey shows that family activities are as varied as the homemakers' noses, no exact recommendations can be made. But there are a few overall rules which appear in all programs of well-run houses:

Shopping is done once a week. The food is put into the refrigerator and freezer in a half-prepared state whenever possible. A big food-storage pantry is essential.

No time is wasted getting a job done and the day's work begins with alarm-clock precision at six-thirty or seven o'clock.

At breakfast a note pad at the elbow accumulates a list of activities for the day. The special jobs for the day are noted, such as sending a suit to the cleaner, spraying the closets for moths, or sewing or pressing name tapes on the children's camp clothes.

Actual work is supported by a fine array of labor-saving aids, such as vacuum cleaner, an electric sweeper, automatic washer and dryer, a dishwasher, and refrigerator-freezer.

There is complete understanding and respect for the job of housekeeping, but there is also the enriching experience of hobbies and outside activities.

The successful housekeepers are always the happiest and the ones most vocal about their hobbies. One woman is fond of music, has collected good records. As she shines silver, sews, or does the quiet jobs she does it to music. She arranges at least one thirty-minute musical program each day.

Another woman is fond of birds and has turned her whole family into an active Audubon Society. She has a collection of feeding stations catering to different types of birds outside the dining-room window. Close at hand are a pair of binoculars and a bird field guide.

Some women feel refreshed by having one day a month completely free of household tasks. It may mean luncheon in town with friends, personal shopping, a concert, visit to a picture gallery or museum, the freedom to paint a picture or just loaf.

As an alternative to a trip away from home which would involve a baby-sitter, one woman has worked out an elaborate Friday-afternoon program. She brushes, washes, and sets her hair. Perhaps she has a special rinse or a home permanent. Then nails are manicured and she gives herself a facial. Sometimes she treats herself to the works and has a facial mask and a bubble bath, followed by a pedicure, especially in the summer when bare legs are in evidence.

In one neighborhood the young mothers take turns baby-sitting in order to get their afternoons off. The group report that their morale has improved remarkably since this relief program was started.

I can hear thousands of women who read this chapter saying, "All of your ideas are fine but I'm always tired; at the end of a day I'm just too exhausted to think." I've heard girls with jobs in offices say the same thing, in the same way, with tense lines furrowing their foreheads and with harsh voices. I'll confess that during several periods of my life I've had this feeling of hopelessness, and felt as tired when I got up as when I went to bed, unable to smile, just dead-beat.

Within the last few years a variety of studies have been made on fatigue. Without exception the tests show that in more than three-fourths of the cases there was nothing physically wrong and that the work being done was not severe enough to exhaust the subject. The sensations were the result of boredom or personal disturbance rather than lack of energy.

Mental discipline is what's needed when things look a little black and out-of-joint. Wipe out fear of any big task; develop a feeling of confidence in yourself and in other people. Don't let that female bugaboo, self-pity, get you. Make a frontal attack on boredom, because only you are to blame if that is your problem. Practicing a sunny outlook is half the battle and in doing it you are saving yourself.

The trick, then, to running a house is based not so much on magic as on planning. The task is eased by organization and knowledge of the right methods. It is speeded up by schedules, good generalship, family cooperation, and the right tools. It is saved from monotony by thoughtful strategy, by broad interests and enthusiasms, and by development of a conscious practice of mental discipline.

8 How to Tool Up

Let's put our cards on the table right in the beginning and admit that it isn't easy to keep a house bright and shining. It is a never-ending job. The saving grace of this constant effort lies in the fine sense of accomplishment which comes when a house is all sweet and clean as a result of personal effort.

The trouble about housecleaning is that it is never completely finished and it involves such varied activities. There are just plain never-ending dust and dirt to cope with. There is also the care of endless surfaces—which soil, stain, mar, tarnish, mildew, burn, lose their luster or wear out.

But if you think your spring cleaning is a chore imagine what it would be if your living room were 215 feet long, had a 100-foot ceiling, and was tracked over once a week by 10,000 people. This is the problem of the superintendent at the Riverside Church in New York. He has 75 full-time workers and 200 part-time workers. They tackle every inch of the building, even to chandeliers and the bell tower, with an impressive array of equipment. "After all," he says, "all the ladies wear their white gloves on Sundays."

Only the stained-glass windows are never washed. Dust picks up the light and, believe it or not, gives the windows added sparkle. This could be a handy story to remember and bring out when you can see only dimly through your own windows.

EQUIPMENT AND MATERIALS

The first step in housecleaning is respect for the job to be done and a certain philosophy, even detachment, about it. The second step is to assemble the right tools and cleaning agents. The third and inescapable move is to get to work.

It is possible to do a surprisingly good job of cleaning with nothing but a corn broom, a dustpan, soap, water, innumerable cloths, and muscle power. The fact that the task can be done with simple equipment makes a dirty house inexcusable, yet to resort to such primitive methods is to play the martyr's role and that's a temptation that should be avoided at all costs.

The saying "A workman is only as good as his tools" can be paraphrased to read "A housecleaner is only as good and as fast as the tools used." For even though soap, water, and a broom bring good results, there are literally hundreds of tools and cleaning agents available to make the job easier.

It's smart to try out new cleaners and tools. In fact, it isn't a bad plan to visit the best household-supply store in town every six months just to browse, reading labels on cans and asking about this and that just as you do at a library or bookstore. If possible, take your husband along with you on these trips. A man seems to have a feeling for gadgets and cleaners and he may spot something you would overlook. The chances are you will leave the store with something under your arm to speed a task.

Scientists may seem to be spending all of their time in the pursuit of science-fantasy projects based on far-out research, but some few are studying household chores and are coming up with incredible job shrinkers. An English engineer, for instance, has developed a robot that may in time revolutionize housekeeping by doing all of the odious jobs from scrubbing floors to ironing clothes. It is a real cast-iron Minnie with a computer brain. Since we are still in a man-machine interphase and have no robot in the closet, we might as well tool up with the best available manually operated equipment to make the job easier.

Here is a list of the essential cleaning tools and supplies plus desirable additions, if the budget allows them.

ESSENTIAL TOOLS

broom
dustpan, short or long handle
dust cloths, lintless rags
scrub cloths
scrub pail, 10-quart capacity
mops, dry and wet
toilet-bowl brush
whisk broom

DESIRABLE ADDITIONS

vacuum cleaner and attachments
electric carpet sweeper
electric floor scrubber
treated polishing cloths
cellulose sponges
lintless cheesecloth

electric floor polisher
rug shampooer
brushes—wall, radiator, Venetian blind
window squeegee
paper towels
basket for cleaning supplies
denim apron with big pockets
rubber gloves
stepladder, preferably aluminum
step stool

ESSENTIAL SUPPLIES

ammonia
chlorine bleach
drain cleaner
soap
detergent, dry and liquid
metal polish
moth repellent
silver polish
scouring powder and paste

DESIRABLE SUPPLIES

floor wax, paste and liquid
furniture polish
window and glass cleaner
paint cleaner
furniture glue and plastic wood
oil, rust-preventing
oven cleaner
rug cleaner
upholstery cleaner
saddle soap (for leather)
sandpaper, fine
French chalk
water softener

Vacuum cleaners are listed in the desirable, not essential, classification. The world got along without these cleaning windbags until the beginning of the twentieth century, so they cannot be called essential. However, today any woman without at least one has a right to feel

underprivileged. A good vacuum cleaner will take the place of a broom, dust cloth, a floor mop, and upholstery cleaner.

Before selecting a vacuum cleaner know your needs. In many households, two or more may be desirable, each different. Learn to use the attachments. Today's assortment includes the following:

Upright cleaner, with motor-driven beating brushes. This is a heavy-duty machine for use primarily for floors carpeted with deep-pile, hard-to-clean weaves and in homes where children track in grit and pets shed hairs.

Tank cleaner. This is a lighter-weight cleaner with strong suction. In addition to cleaning carpets and rugs it can be used on draperies, upholstery, moldings, and windowsills. It will not unravel scatter rugs, will whisk dust from the surface and cracks of bare floors, and will clean close to baseboards and under low furniture.

Electric broom. Ease of use and economy are the twin virtues of power-driven electric sweepers. They can be used on carpets or bare floors, are ideal for the quick daily pickups and for small households.

Hand vacuum. Used for above-the-floor cleaning, they are small, low priced, and light to handle. Excellent for use on draperies, upholstery, for dusting books and bookshelves.

Built-in central-system vacuum cleaner. This is a heavy-duty system with a central motor. The hose is plugged into inlets, like convenience outlets in baseboards, which carry dust to a dust receiver installed in basement or garage. This is a luxury installation.

Shop vacuum cleaner. Powerful portable vacuum for rough cleaning, designed for use in home workshops, garages, basements, and on terraces and driveways. The cleaner is capable of picking up wood chips, sawdust, nails, and grass cuttings. It can even be used to clean the ashes out of the fireplace and on outdoor carpeting.

When there are children and pets and the rugs or carpets really get dirty, the upright cleaner is more efficient and does a faster job. The revolving brush will dislodge the clinging material from the surface and at the same time vibrate loose the embedded grit, making it easy for the suction to carry it all into the bag. They are not recommended for fine orientals and antique rugs.

If you have large areas of bare floors and rugs which can be rolled back, or if you have dusting problems, acres of draperies or Venetian blinds, the tank type has advantages. The tank cleaner which cleans with suction only will not ravel scatter rugs or damage antique rugs. It will whisk dust from the surface and cracks of bare floors, clean close to baseboards, and under low furniture.

If you have a small house or apartment or want an extra cleaner for use in the bedroom wing, the problem may not warrant either a tank or an upright cleaner, but an electric broom, small, lightweight, and efficient.

CARE AND CLEANING OF TOOLS

The best tools do only half a job if they are not used correctly, are not kept in good condition, and are not readily available. Begin by reading the book of instructions which comes with the tool until you thoroughly understand it. Ask for a demonstration if any point isn't clear. If a periodic oiling is necessary, note when and where and keep oil on hand.

Keep tools clean. A dusty vacuum cleaner, dust cloth, or mop can resoil what you are trying to clean. Care of a vacuum cleaner is simple. Nine out of ten service calls aren't necessary. If the motor on your upright cleaner works, but it doesn't pick things up, check the three B's—the bag, the belt, and the brush.

The bag. The suction of any type of cleaner is dependent on the bag. Only as much air will come through the nozzle as will pass through the bag. If the bag or tank is full, a cleaner will not pick up properly and the motor will overheat. Never let the bag or tank get overloaded. Change the filter occasionally.

The belt. If the bag is in good condition and the action still isn't good, in an upright cleaner check the belt which drives the brush. It may be too loose, it may have lost its resilience from age, or it may have slipped off the pulley. To check, turn the machine upside down and see that the belt is in place. Then turn the switch and with the palm of a gloved hand press lightly on the brush. If it stalls under light pressure, the belt is loose and needs replacement. Belts need changing every six to twelve months, depending on use.

The brush. The bristles on the brush wear down after long usage. If they look worn, replace the brush. Clean brush roll frequently; keep it free of matted thread, lint, and hair. Snip matted material with scissors to free it.

The hose. When your tank cleaner does not pick up, and the bag is empty, check the suction at the cleaner opening. If this is in order, connect hose and check suction at end of hose. If there is no suction or it is weak, the hose may be clogged. Pass a broom handle or a yardstick through the hose to remove the obstruction. A badly worn hose lining may also reduce suction and should be replaced.

The motor. If the motor doesn't start at once, first test the plug. See that it is properly connected. Next check for a blown fuse. Connect a lamp to the same outlet. If outlet is active and the motor still won't start, a service man is needed. Get a report on the switch and the cord before agreeing to a major overhaul. These are the usual sources of trouble. If the motor sparks while in operation, shut it off at once, for a major repair may be needed.

In general, keep all screws, nuts, and bolts on your cleaner tight. Before storing cleaner wind the cord loosely. Tension may cause wires to break inside the cord. When using, make sure all connections are tight to avoid loss of suction.

STORAGE

The importance of keeping cleaning equipment in an orderly way is dramatized by the story of an elderly bachelor back in 1755 who couldn't decide which of three girls to marry. With the help of his sister he gave them the "broom test." His sister invited them to tea on three separate days. Each day before the guest's arrival, the gentleman placed a broom across the entrance door. One girl stepped over it, one moved it, but the third picked up the broom and carried it to the broom closet in the kitchen. This so pleased orderly Henry that he married her.

It may be harder to find a place to store your equipment than to collect it. The puny two-by-four mop closet found in the average house just isn't big enough. Turn thumbs down on a shambles under a stairway. If cleaners and equipment are not stored in an orderly and easily available fashion, every cleaning bout will start with a frantic search and a short temper.

As simple a thing as placing articles used daily on shelves no higher than the shoulder has been found to reduce exertion. It takes nineteen times as much energy to get something three inches from the floor as it does something at elbow level. A difference of even 15 percent too high or too low doubles the strain. Line cleaning closets and doors with shelves, wall clips, and hooks for orderly disposal of supplies and equipment.

Store brooms, mops, and vacuum cleaners so that they can be easily reached. Assemble in a basket frequently needed supplies, such as dust cloths, furniture polish, metal polishing cloths, whisk broom, oil can, glass cleaner, self-polishing and paste wax, a spot remover, art-gum eraser, magic mending tape, plus a roll of paper toweling.

Equipment and supplies should be stored as close to the point of use as possible. In a two-story, split-level, or long ranch house, with widely separated living and bedroom wings, assemble two cleaning closets. Also keep a broom in the basement and one in the garage. Quick clean-up jobs will be done that would be skipped entirely if the equipment was not at hand.

Clean all equipment before it is put away. Empty vacuum-cleaner bags and clean brushes. To prevent fire, never store wax- or oil-soaked cloths in the cleaning cupboard.

Equipment to end it all. Today one of the best ways to keep a house clean is not to let it get dirty! It is one of the surprises and delights of air-conditioning to discover that the washed, cooled, humidity-conditioned air reduces housework. There is less free dust in the air, no smoke or soot, and hands free of perspiration leave fewer marks on furniture and upholstery. There is less dust on curtains and draperies.

Radiant heating systems and electric heating also contribute to cleaner houses. Radiators and air currents are eliminated so that dust-laden air doesn't travel through the whole house. The heating systems of tomorrow will offer total air control; they will heat, cool, humidify air automatically. They will remove odors from cooking and smoking, and pollen, dust, dirt, and other airborne particles, to make air fresher and cleaner. Such systems are available now but few of us have them.

9 How to Clean Rooms

If your aim is to keep your house in an absolutely antiseptic condition so that you can eat off the floor, the plan outlined here won't help. An old saying says you have to eat a peck of dirt before you die, so what is the use in slaving away too zealously? At an early date it is important to establish a reasonable balance in all things, including cleaning standards.

The answer is to study the chores involved until you understand them. Once understood, each job can be dealt with daily, weekly, and seasonally in an efficient manner which will put the whole business in the category of automatic activity. Once having attained this state you really can dismiss the whole thing from your mind. It won't mire you down or become an obsession. There are a lot more interesting things than housecleaning to become neurotic about, so don't worry about the dirt. Just get rid of it.

Even though a clean house holds satisfaction, mere cleanliness is never the goal of housekeeping. The goal is family pleasure, pride, and convenience. If using a room gets it rumpled up and out of order, why that's that. It can be straightened out again when the hour for cleaning arrives. It does not require any tush-tushing or constant restraints on the family. As Theodore Roosevelt said: "Order without liberty and liberty without order are equally destructive."

The cleaning plan outlined here isn't as exacting as my mother's, but I have always thought it was desirable to set an attainable goal. This plan can be carried through and still leave a margin of time to do any number of other things. That isn't to say that my mother didn't accomplish wonders in the way of outside activities in addition to the care of a family of seven. But something seems to have gone out of female flesh today. We have succumbed, I'm afraid, to a softer way of living.

Professional cleaners report that homes are about 20 percent dirtier today than they were twenty years ago. Dust enters through and

around windows and outside doors. Papers, magazines, holiday decorations, and visitors, pets, pipes, and cigarettes follow as sources of house soil. Another menace is the backfiring of oil-burning furnaces. This can leave a deposit of soot on every surface in the house and it may cost hundreds of dollars to recondition the interior, an expense often anticipated and covered by insurance.

Almost any anti-dust and -dirt measures are helpful. Tightly fitted doors and windows, paved paths leading to the house, surfaced roads, an entrance hall at the front of the house and a mud room near the back door, where soiled clothes and shoes can be removed, foot scrapers and floor mats at each entrance door, and a cooperative family all help reduce the amount of dirt brought into the house. A good exhaust system in the kitchen will carry away airborne fats and oils. Satin-finished hardware for knobs and switch plates require less polishing than bright metals. Stain or varnish finishes on handrails and stair risers are easier to care for than paint, and high-gloss enamels will resist soil and clean better than flat finishes.

Upholstery may be processed to repel stain, and carpets and flooring selected which camouflage soil, such as tweed textured carpets and darker patterned vinyls. Plain whites and pastels used on floors and counters in kitchens will show more soil than those with pattern and a tone. Other cleaning liabilities include louvered doors, ornate lighting fixtures, vaulted ceiling, high clerestory windows, lavish draperies and valances, and a vast clutter of bric-a-brac that must be dusted.

Valuable, too, in giving a house a semblance of order is a family room that siphons from the living room children's play and other activities which create disorder. This does not mean that the living room need be off limits for all but guests. It's a living room, isn't it? If each person cleans up in a rudimentary fashion, reasonable order can be maintained.

Probably the most rewarding task of the day is creating order in the family room and living room just before going to bed. The five minutes needed will help give the next day a more cheerful start. Nothing is as discouraging in the morning as the sight of an untidy room. If your husband is a neat soul, with a little concealed direction he will lend a hand. The once-over should include:

straightening chairs
plumping pillows

. . . have an activity room

returning books, games, and toys to shelves or drawers
emptying ash trays
returning apple cores and empty glasses to the kitchen
brushing up the fireplace

The daily pickup should be scheduled the minute the family is disposed of and the kitchen is in order. The old cliché applies here—he who hesitates is lost. If you decide to have a glance at the paper, to write a note to Jane, or to call someone on the phone first, there's a chance that the best of intentions will go astray. But if the daily cleaning is approached with a gleam in the eye and firm intent, even a large room can be put in order in less than fifteen minutes. "Ifs" in this time limit concern the family's habits, the personal possessions that must be straightened up. Other "ifs" affecting the time factor are a baby, telephone calls, callers, and miscellaneous demands and interruptions.

When the nightly pickup is observed, the daily routine cleaning is often omitted in busy households where everyone is off to school or to a job right after breakfast. This, of course, only delays more thorough cleaning. For the daily brushup, equip yourself with the supply basket, apron, hand or electric sweeper, and dust mop, and follow this routine:

1. Open windows. Fresh air is a wonderful antidote for stale smells, ashes, smoke, and dust. It will freshen the room more than anything. Even in winter open a door or window five minutes every morning.
2. Remove debris. Empty wastebaskets, ash trays, faded flowers, and other trash into a paper bag. Check over newspapers and magazines; pile those to be discarded to one side and organize the remainder. Brush up hearth if fireplace has been used.
3. Dust. Make desk, tables, and mantel top orderly and dust surfaces. Dust windowsills. Keep a roll of paper dusters or a chamois in the drawer of a table in the living room; other members of the family may be tempted to administer a quick bushup through the day.
4. Sweep. Clean the rug or carpet with a hand or electric sweeper. If necessary, run a dry mop over the floor.
5. Create order. Put all furniture and chairs in place. Plump pillows and cushions on chairs and sofa. Close the windows and adjust blinds or shades.

Weekly cleaning. Time was when this was a Saturday chore. Now with so many offices closed on Saturday, the men around, and the children home from school, it seems too bad to have the house in a turmoil. More and more the weekly cleaning is done on a weekday. In some households it is done Monday and Tuesday, in others Thursday and Friday, and in many it is done when the mood strikes.

Equip yourself with apron, basket, dust mops, and vacuum cleaner. The routine is more complete than the daily brushup. It begins with the theory that dust and dirt fall down. Work begins at the ceiling and progresses down walls and windows to furniture tops, baseboards, and finally the floor.

Concentrate on what you are doing as you clean and it will go faster. All movements should be steady and controlled. Flourishing a mop or dust cloth may help you think you are being efficient, but it is a wholly false impression. Learn to work with both hands. Pick up a lamp in one hand and dust it with the other. Pile magazines using both hands. It is comparatively easy to cultivate ambidexterity and it certainly speeds a task. I have been impressed recently by this in going through a champagne winery. Men go through the cellars giving each bottle a sixth of the circumference turn. By making both hands do an equal share they turn five thousand bottles an hour. All one can hear in the cellar is the almost mechanical click of the turning bottles.

Also face the fact that to get a room in order it must be put into disorder. Many pieces of furniture must be moved to clean under and dust them. So heave ho or be shocked at the condition underneath a piece of furniture when you do move it.

The order of cleaning:

1. Clean ashes out of fireplace with doors and windows closed.
2. Remove all faded flowers and leaves. Groom plants.
3. Open a window but avoid strong cross drafts. Dust windowsills inside and out. A vacuum cleaner does this nicely.
4. Dust ceilings and moldings, walls, doors, and screens, book shelves, books, and radiators. In old houses inspect corners and under cornices for spider webs. To dust use (1) the wand of the vacuum cleaner, (2) a hand vacuum, (3) a long-handled brush, or (4) a broom with a clean cloth tied around it, or a bag made for the purpose with a draw-string top which ties around the broom handle.

5. Brush all fabrics—draperies, curtains, pillows, upholstery, and lamp shades. Use a whisk broom or vacuum cleaner. If there are any grease spots on rug or upholstery, remove with cleaning fluid. Likely locations are under dining table, on upholstered dining-room chairs, in front of sofa or fireplace if food has been served there.
6. Wipe off or polish all vases, ash trays, ornaments, lamp bulbs, and reflectors. Even a trace of dust on a light bulb or the reflecting surfaces of a lamp reduces the light in the room. Use a damp cloth or a processed cloth or processed tissue paper for polishing and cleaning metals.
7. Dust and polish all furniture and baseboards. Wipe finger marks off doors and doorknobs.
8. Now, if you are using a vacuum cleaner, do the carpet or wood floor. But if you are using a carpet sweeper do the rug next, then last dust the floor, using a dry mop.
9. Vacuum the rug thoroughly. Turn back the corners and sides of the rug and clean the back. Finish by rolling back the rug pad and clean under it. Once a week allow twenty minutes to vacuum thoroughly a nine-by-twelve area.
10. Return the room to order. Replace all chairs, tables, and accessories.
11. Clean equipment and put away. Remove the vacuum-cleaner bag if it is full, clean out brushes, shake mops, shake and/or wash dust cloths and sponges, depending on their nature. Put stoppers on bottles or cans of cleaning agents.
12. Put out fresh flowers and leaves.

Seasonal living-room cleaning. If the living-dining room has received its daily and weekly quota of care, no back-breaking seasonal operations are needed. However, when draperies are changed from winter to summer and vice versa, when rugs are lifted or laid, when slip covers and lamp shades are changed, whenever pictures and accessories are tucked away or moved about, it seems logical to make a few additional slick-and-shine strokes.

In an increasing number of households the seasonal or occasional cleaning may be turned over to professional cleaners, who put the whole house in order. Three types of professional home cleaning and maintenance are available and the field is growing. The three packages offered are quarterly heavy-duty cleaning, monthly service, and bi-weekly light cleaning. Prices for this service are higher than for a maid but there is the assurance that the work will be done in an expert and efficient manner.

Most professional cleaners, instead of cleaning one room at a time, carry one operation throughout the house until the whole house is clean. They clean all glass, windows, doors, mirrors, glass-topped tables, light bulbs, etc. Then they vacuum all ceilings, walls, woodwork, and shelves requiring a vacuum wand. Washing follows if it is necessary. Next, they remove all spots and stains throughout the house. Then they shampoo carpets, rugs, and upholstery. This method saves time in assembling tools. When each job is done, the tools required can be put away. If a house is to go through total cleaning in minimum time, this method is excellent, but few women work this way. By doing only a room at a time the job doesn't seem as overwhelming, the whole house isn't in turmoil, and the cleaning can be spread out over weeks, even months.

Occasional or seasonal cleaning, when done a room at a time, is done in this order:

1. Take down and remove everything that is not to stay in the room —curtains, draperies, rugs, lamp shades, slip covers, accessories, and pictures. Dust off and wrap lamp shades to be stored. Wrap and pack pictures and accessories in labeled boxes or plastic bags. List items to be sent to cleaners. All wool things should be cleaned before storing. If they are stored at home, protect them against moths.
2. Sort and discard magazines and miscellaneous accumulation.
3. Next, thoroughly clean walls and ceilings. Wash them if necessary. Also wash woodwork. Remove pictures and wipe off front and back.
4. Remove all books from shelves. Wash shelves and dust books with cloth or vacuum cleaner. Return books to shelves.
5. Scour tile hearth and fireplace.
6. Polish all metal—the andirons, radiators, light fixtures, doorknobs, fireplace tools.
7. Wash windows, mirrors, and all the glass parts of lighting fixtures. Wash venetian blinds, windowsills, and mantel.
8. Dry clean, vacuum, or brush upholstery.

9. Wash all leather on table tops, wastebaskets, desks, and chairs.
10. Wipe wood furniture with a damp cloth and apply furniture polish.
11. Give carpet and rugs a deep cleaning or shampoo. If floor is exposed, wax with an electric polisher. Now the room smells clean and is clean. Hang fresh curtains and draperies. Put on fresh slip covers and rearrange accessories.
12. Add fresh flowers or plants.

Note. Develop an adaptation of the living-room routine for cleaning the dining room, family room, entrance hall, and study.

HOW TO CLEAN BEDROOMS

Is there a girl who hasn't cleaned her own room since she was ten years old? If she has been relieved of this chore, she has missed something of a normal responsibility in the routine of a normal home. It is a job that goes on for a lifetime, a homey, simple task, but the degree and quality of the job reveal much.

Don't get careless about throwing back bedclothes to air the bed. Do this as you get up in the morning. See that every member of the family takes care of his own bed, starting with the two-year-old. This is a habit to acquire like brushing your teeth.

Daily bedroom cleaning

1. Open windows.
2. Put away all clothes, shoes, and odds and ends.
3. Empty all ash trays, faded flowers, and wastebasket contents into paper bag for discard.
4. Make the bed.
5. Vacuum the rugs if necessary.
6. Dust table tops, chests, and windowsills.
7. Dry-mop exposed floors.
8. Put furniture and accessories back in place.

Weekly bedroom cleaning

1. Pick up room as in daily cleaning.
2. Remove all covers from bed. Vacuum clean or brush mattress and bed frame. Every other week turn mattress end over end.

3. Good mattresses should be protected by a mattress cover. Over the mattress cover use a quilted mattress protector which fits exactly the top of the bed. Pads should be washed frequently, especially through the hot months when they are exposed to perspiration.
4. Change the pillow cases and sheets. Incidently, the top and bottom hems of a sheet are not the same width. The wide hem goes at the head of the bed. About eight inches of the top sheet is folded back over the blanket.
5. Proceed to dust, clean, and vacuum the rest of the room. By all means use the vacuum for cleaning under the bed. If there is no vacuum, remove "dust kittens" with broom and dustpan. On wood floor follow with the dust mop.
6. Wipe down walls with vacuum or soft brush; check corners carefully to remove spider webs. To remove a spider in a web cleanly, take the head off the vacuum-cleaner wand, then hold it up to the web. The suction will pull in web and spider and leave no smudge on the wall.
7. When cleaning the room keep the closet door closed, but while the vacuum is connected, open the door and clean the closet floor and shelves.
8. Put on fresh dresser scarves where needed. Wipe off perfume bottles; they seem to attract dust like a magnet. Arrange furniture and accessories.

Seasonal bedroom cleaning. As in the living room the seasonal cleaning comes spring and fall when bedspreads, draperies, and rugs may be changed. The general routine should follow that outlined for the living room. However, a few modifications are evident and the first problem is how to cope with the closets.

1. Empty closet. Wash walls and shelves with a dampened cloth wrung out in water with a trace of disinfectant in it. For amount of disinfectant read label on the bottle. Consider using the pine-perfumed type because it leaves a pleasant odor. Next, spray closet with moth preventive, using hand equipment or vacuum cleaner.
2. Separate clothing into three piles: clothes to be stored, clothes to be used, and clothes to be discarded. Brush and mend all garments to be returned to the closet. Brush, air, or send to cleaner other things. Spray all clothes to be packed away. If your storage space is limited, it pays to send out for storage heavy winter coats and

other bulky items. Decide what to do with clothes to be discarded. Balance between the needs of some member of the family, a neighbor or friends, the Salvation Army, church, or other charity.
3. Wash, store, and moth proof blankets. Bring out ones for the next season.
4. Sun or launder feather pillows. When washing do not remove from ticking as loose feathers are uncontrollable.
5. Sun hair mattresses. Air innersprings and cotton pad. Dust and wash bed frame and springs.
6. Follow outline of living-room seasonal routine.
7. Empty all bureau drawers. Wipe out with damp cloth. Air until dry. Put in fresh paper lining. Put back only garments that are being worn.
8. Put up fresh curtains. Lay clean rugs on freshly polished floor. Arrange furniture and reassemble accessories.

HOW TO CLEAN THE BATHROOM

Each person using a bathroom must assume responsibility for it each time he uses it. This should be taught at an early age. Each user must flush toilet, wash the bathtub, pull the shower curtain out to dry, leave the soap where it will dry, and hang his own washcloth and towels neatly. If this routine is adhered to daily, the cleaning task is simple. (In hardwater areas, if you do not have a central water softener, bathtub rings can be reduced to a minimum if a dash of Calgon water softener is used in the bath water. It also makes the water feel silky.) Keep cleaners, cloths, sponges, disinfectants and drain cleaners in or near the bathroom.

Daily bathroom routine

1. Open the windows when you start to clean the bedrooms.
2. When you return after finishing the bedrooms, arrange towels neatly; replace soiled ones.
3. Wash basin, bathtub, mirrors, faucets, and toilet seat, using household cleanser and a cellulose sponge. With a brush or paper towel wipe the underside of the rim of the toilet. Drop the paper towel in the bowl and repeat until no more soil comes off on the paper. Flush the toilet.
4. Wipe up splashed water or floor spots. Close window.

Weekly bathroom routine

1. Using a disinfectant and brush, clean toilet bowl. Wash the top, bottom, and hinges of the seat, clean tank, metal fittings, and base. Put a few drops of disinfectant in bowl; a pine-scented type is pleasant. If none is available, use ammonia.
2. Polish all metal faucets and parts. Dry to prevent water spots.
3. Scrub wash bowl, tub, and shower. Wipe off strainers with a paper towel. If there are bits of paper or bobby pins in the drain, remove. Flush with hot water.
4. Wipe off windows, mirror, and light fixtures.
5. Wash down tile or marble walls with soap and water. Use a soft brush on painted and wallpapered walls. Dust frames and backs of pictures.
6. Scrub floors; wipe off bathroom scales.
7. Replace towels.
8. Empty and replace wastebasket.
9. Clean and replace rug or carpet.

Seasonal bathroom routine

1. Wash and replace shower curtain.
2. Wash and replace window curtains and wash window and screen.
3. Empty medicine closet, wash and replace items being used. Discard drugs more than a year old. Instead of keeping empty bottles with prescription numbers that might be wanted again someday, write the numbers and other neccessary information on a piece of paper fastened to the back of the medicine chest door.
4. Empty towel closet or chest, wash, reline, and replace towels.
5. Empty clothes hamper, wash inside and out, wipe off with dry cloth, leave open until aired out.

10 How to Clean Overhead

In addition to the daily, weekly, and annual cleaning here are special jobs which should be attended to when they are necessary. If these tasks are spread out over the year, they involve no headache or backache and major seasonal bouts may be unnecessary.

To keep walls, furniture, floors, glass, and tile in perfect shape, they must be individually understood and periodically cared for, washed, waxed, and coaxed into pristine condition.

In routine cleaning, walls, ceiling, and woodwork get first attention. This is also true when a thorough cleaning is to be administered. If those areas have been dusted weekly or even monthly, a once-a-year cleaning in depth will suffice. Schedule this cleaning when help is available. A stepladder will be necessary to clean high places and a rescue squad should be available. Never climb a ladder when you are alone in the house.

WALLS, CEILING, AND WOODWORK

Push all furniture to the center of the room and cover with a sheet or plastic cover. Dust walls and ceiling with the dusting brush of the vacuum cleaner, a long-handled broom covered with a cloth bag, or a long-handled soft hair brush. Work from the ceiling down. Go over all woodwork, cornices, ledges, and shelves, behind pictures and mirrors, around windows and doors.

To wash walls. Most wall coverings, paint, wallpaper, and coated fabrics, are washable but in different degrees. Properly applied, all modern paints are washable but they must be allowed to set or "ripen" at least thirty days before they are subjected to washing. Gloss paints and enamels withstand scrubbing better than semi-gloss and flat finishes. Enamels with an alkyd-resin base are the toughest and are recommended for kitchen and bathrooms.

Wallpapers fall into three categories: water-resistant, plastic-treated, and water-sensitive. Only the latter cannot be washed. On these use a doughlike cleaner available at hardware stores. There are many nonpaper wall coverings; the vinyl-coated family are as tough as the vinyl-processed papers. If there is any question about washability, test wash an inconspicuous area behind a piece of furniture.

In general walls should be washed from the bottom up, from baseboard to ceiling. This prevents hard-to-remove streaks which develop when water trickles down over the unwashed area. Wipe one section at a time with thick detergent suds, using a sponge or soft cloth. As the work proceeds let the cleaned areas overlap to prevent streaks. Change to clean suds, and rinse well. To avoid using excess water, use thick suds. To make, add detergent to a pail of water and swish with your hand.

To remove a spot put some detergent on a wet cellulose sponge and squeeze it. After applying suds, pat spot with a clean damp sponge. For a larger area mix detergent and water in a bowl with an egg beater. The resulting thick suds can be used on almost any surface without harm.

When washing walls and ceiling wear a bracelet made by wrapping a sponge or wash cloth around your wrist, pin it or hold it in place with an elastic band. This prevents suds from running down your arm.

Woodwork and paneled walls. If frequently dusted these will seldom need washing. However, the high temperature and lack of humidity in our houses dry out wood.

If varnished, wood walls and woodwork should be wiped down once a year. Use a quart of warm water mixed with one tablespoon turpentine and three tablespoons boiled linseed oil. (The label will read "Boiled Linseed Oil.")

If painted, wash with mild suds, then wax.

Open-grain woods like oak or chestnut respond to an oil finish. Occasional treatment with equal parts of raw linseed oil and turpentine thoroughly mixed will add luster to the wood. Apply and rub dry.

If wood is shellacked, don't use water; clean and feed with liquid wax.

After they have been cleaned, windowsills, cupboard doors, all surfaces exposed to soil should be waxed. This preserves the finish and makes cleaning easier. Apply liquid wax with a cloth and rub to a dry polish with a clean cloth.

Ceramic tile walls. The glaze on ceramic tile makes it waterproof. Soil can be easily removed with detergent suds and fresh water. Scrubbing is seldom necessary.

In an old house there may be stains or black mildew between the tiles. Iron stains, if not too heavy, may be removed with scouring powder containing a bleach. To remove heavy stains dissolve one-part sodium citrate crystals in six parts of water. Add to this an equal amount of glycerin and mix. Make a thick paste with whiting (French chalk) and this solution. Apply one-eighth inch thick. Let dry, brush off. Repeat if necessary. Any laundry bleach also may be used. All should be well rinsed with clear water.

If a black shadow remains in the joints when they are thoroughly dry, outline each tile with white washable paint and a small brush. If tile is an objectionable color, it can be successfully painted with an enamel having an alkyd-resin base.

WINDOWS

Smog, air pollution, soot, and dust leave deposits on the outside of windows, and plain house dust, smoke, grime from unwashed air of a heating system, and grease in fumes from the kitchen leave their mark on the inside. How often windows should be washed will vary with the individual problem, but once a year is a minimum, and to be crystal clear several once-overs are desirable at least on the inside.

There are many commercial window cleaners in the form of sprays, creams, and powders which are easily applied and just as easily wiped off. If there are many windows, it is more economical and just as satisfactory to use four tablespoons of household ammonia, vinegar, or denatured alcohol to one quart of warm water. After applying, wipe dry with a rubber squeegee, cellulose sponge, or lint-free cloth. Paper towels give a fine high finishing polish. Better still, used crushed newspapers, which give an even higher polish with a soil-resistant quality.

Miscellaneous points:

Cloudy days are good for window washing, for cleaners dry more slowly and fewer strokes are needed to remove them.

In freezing weather wash windows with a blend of one-half cup denatured alcohol and two quarts of warm water. Apply with a sponge or lintless cloth, wipe off with a chamois, cloth, or squeegee. No frost will form.

Remove any paint from windowpanes as quickly as possible. Turpentine may be used when the paint is fresh. After it has dried a razor blade is most efficient. Hardware stores have handles for blades. Ammonia helps remove putty smears.

For a new house select windows and/or storm sashes that can be snapped out of their frame for washing.

Wash sliding glass doors and window walls with a hose and a long-handled squeegee mop.

A team of washers, one working inside and the other outside a window simultaneously, reduce spots and streaks because each can see the other's failures.

If a window sticks, apply floor wax, candle wax, soap, vaseline, or a silicone spray to the runners. Next, with a padded hammer, tap the wood sharply at several points. If it still doesn't move, from the outside insert a wedge or chisel under the window and pry it up. Incidentally, be sure that the window is unlocked and that there are no nails holding it.

Screens should be vacuum-cleaned or scrubbed inside and out with a stiff brush. Occasionally turn the hose on them. Use a hand vacuum to clean the tracks on roll-up screens; then wax the tracks. Paint wood-framed screens every two years. Paint screens with a rag or roller, working with the screen flat so the paint won't run while drying.

SHADES AND BLINDS

Blinds should be operated daily to keep them in good condition. Dust with soft cloth, brush, or vacuum cleaner frequently, especially at the top of the roller and along the hem. Finger marks along the hem may be removed with a damp cloth or dough-type wallpaper cleaner, available at a hardware store.

If shades are shabby, be sure they are washable before washing. There are a great variety of shades today. Do not wash "Holland" type, or other novelty shades. However, many of the shades are vinyl-coated and are guaranteed washable. These may be removed from the brackets, stretched out on a table, and both sides washed with a detergent and water. Hang them unrolled in shady windows to dry. When dry, remove, roll up evenly, tighten springs at the end, and rehang.

VENETIAN BLINDS

Regular dusting is important. The best tools are a vacuum cleaner, with either the round brush or the V-shaped tool, a pronged, wool-covered brush, or soft home-made gloves of four thicknesses of cheesecloth. The tapes, which may soil more quickly than the slats, can be cleaned with a brush and detergent suds followed with a clean-water rinse. Dry-cleaning fluid is an alternate method, but be sure the room is well ventilated and let tapes dry completely before pulling shade up. For a more thorough cleaning, blinds may be taken down and washed in the bathtub or on the lawn. If you are ambitious, slats can be removed, repainted, and reassembled in new tape. This is a major project and not recommended for the timid.

REGISTERS AND RADIATORS

Heat creates air currents and inevitably the source of heat will acquire a dust deposit. Surfaces of heating units should be dusted in your routine cleaning. Occasionally, using a brush or the tube end of a vacuum, clean the coils, valve, pipes, and the wall back of radiators. If a brush is used for cleaning, lay damp papers under radiator before cleaning. To clean thoroughly, wash coils and the floor underneath.

Registers or hot-air systems collect dust and redistribute it. To clean, lift the grid, clean the back and the opening with the vacuum-cleaner brush. Heatalator grids in a fireplace and in electric radiators cannot be removed, but they should be vacuumed periodically.

FIREPLACES

While cleaning walls and woodwork give the fireplace some special attention. Wash smoke stains from slate or tile with a strong detergent, rinse well. Also use detergent on marble, then polish with a felt buffer. If marble is badly stained and yellowed, apply black shoe polish. After buffing, the marble appears to be a mellow gray.

Scour stone with a stiff brush and scouring powder; rinse well.
Scour brick with a stiff brush and strong washing powder; rinse well.
Scour black iron with steel wool and kerosene to prevent rusting.

Scour brass andirons and other accessories with a copper-and-brass cleanser.

MIRRORS AND PICTURES

While the stepladder is around, wash mirrors and the glass on pictures. Use a window cleaner. It can be controlled better if applied with a cloth, not sprayed on. Never spray a liquid at or near a joint in the mirror for it might run between the frame and the mirror.

Often denatured alcohol is used to clean mirrors. Apply it with a cheesecloth pad, but avoid contact with the mirror frame; it may remove or soften the finish.

Never hang a valuable mirror where the sun will hit it. The heat may affect the backing.

While at it, dust picture frames and wipe off the wall back of them. Wax wood frames.

Gilt picture frames must be handled gently. Moisten a sponge with a solution of equal parts of ammonia and denatured alcohol and pat the frame lightly. Then pat dry and apply a little lemon oil on a cheesecloth pad to revive the luster. Avoid any contact with the picture itself.

The Metropolitan Museum of Art in New York City gives the following instructions on the care of oil paintings, but takes no responsibility for any home treatment. These are the instructions:

Superficial dust and dirt can be removed from an oil painting in sound condition by light brushing with absorbent cotton or a soft brush. Either of these can be used dry or moistened with a gasoline-type dry cleaning fluid. These are inflammable; proper precautions must be taken. The canvas must be firmly and uniformly supported from the reverse while any pressure is put upon the face of the painting. Paintings should not be treated, on front or back, with soap, water, bread crumbs, erasers, raw potato, sliced onion, or oil of any kind. Some of these may improve the appearance of a painting temporarily, but all can be harmful in inexperienced hands.

A painting whose surface has become dull can frequently be brightened by the use of a good quality prepared wax-emulsion cream furniture polish. If the manufacturer's directions for use on fine furniture are carefully followed, no harm should result, and the thin film of wax left on the surface is a safe and moderately durable protection.

No other treatment should be tried by inexperienced persons. Paintings deteriorate very slowly and seldom need emergency first aid. If there is any doubt about the condition of a painting, it should be left alone until it can be examined by a professional restorer. Neglect is less dangerous than inexpert home treatment.

LIGHTING FIXTURES AND LAMPS

Dust lighting fixtures and lamp bases with a hand vacuum cleaner.

Fixtures can be further cleaned with a damp cloth. Use ammonia in the water for sparkle on crystal chandeliers.

Never submerge lamp bases in water; just wipe with a damp cloth and wax. Don't neglect the bulbs; dust reduces their efficiency.

Dust shades regularly with hand vacuum without letting it touch shade, as this might smudge soft dust.

Fabric shades can be washed if handled carefully and the fabric has not been weakened from the heat. Make suds. Dip the shade up and down in it; repeat with clear water. Then swing through the air like a French lettuce basket to rid shade of excess moisture and dry in a breeze.

11 How to Clean Waist High

Furniture, whether wood, metal, or upholstered, and accessories come in the waist-high category, and in caring for them an ounce of prevention is worth you know what.

WOOD FURNITURE

Wood is alive; it breathes, expands, and contracts, and responds like a child to loving care. It looks shabby and wan if it is neglected, but gets glum or blushes if it's fussed over too much. Simple, regular care is all that it needs.

Use a soft vacuum-cleaner brush to dust table bases and heavily carved pieces. Frequent dusting by hand, using a soft cloth with nothing on it, will improve the finish of table tops and chests. Always wipe with the grain of the wood; never rub in circles. A chamois is ideal for dusting wood.

The patina or sheen on well-cared-for antique furniture is the result of just such constant, gentle rubbing. However, twice a year feed wood furniture with oil or wax. The best times are just before the furnace is started in the fall and just after it is turned off in the spring.

The type of polish used should vary with the finish of the piece. Whatever you use, use it sparingly as polish or wax gums up the surface and collects dust.

French hand-rubbed. This finish, found only on quality furniture, is built up by repeated coats of wax applied by hand. Use a cloth and rub with the grain.

Oiled finish. The oil finish is used on custom-made furniture and most Scandinavian imports. Buy boiled linseed oil. Apply it slightly warm and leave it on overnight. Next day finish by rubbing off every trace of surface oil. If old finish is soiled, mix a little turpentine with the oil, rub in till dry, using a soft cloth.

Lacquer or a synthetic resin varnish. Inexpensive or medium-grade furniture is often finished in this way to close the pores of the wood. A surface cleaning with paste or liquid wax and polishing are all that are required.

Plastic-surfaced furniture. This needs only dusting to clean and polishing with paste or liquid wax. If lint from table pads or mats sticks to the surface, rub blemish with vaseline, salad oil, or lard. Wash with suds, rinse, dry, and polish.

Old furniture. When the furniture is old and the finish is unknown, it can be rubbed with lemon oil, or use this formula developed by a museum:

> In a quart jar mix 1⅓ pints of olive oil, ⅔ pints of alcohol and 1 teaspoon of vinegar. Wet cloth with solution, wring, polish furniture and follow at once with a dry chamois or soft cloth.

Old furniture, or furniture which has been stored, may be dirty. Make a thick jelly of mild soap and soft water; whisk to a lather. Wring a cloth out in this and wipe off soil. Rinse with a cloth or sponge wrung out in clear water. When dry, polish with paste wax. Use wax on antiques and all worn, damaged, or porous woods. It gives more protection and a rich satiny polish. Never let water stand on furniture. Wipe on, wipe off detergents may be used on painted furniture.

White rings are caused by heat, steam, or moisture. Prevent by using table pads, hot pads, and coasters. Remove white rings by one of these five methods:

> Rub with a paste of linseed oil and powdered pumice.
> Rub with turpentine (flammable).
> Rub with a mixture of half oil and half turpentine.
> Rub with camphorated oil.
> Rub with salad oil.

Never use an unknown polish on furniture. Use only polishes made by well-known manufacturers. Many polishes peddled from door to door have been found to contain kerosene and other finish-destroying agents.

Care of wood furniture. Take care of scratches, attending to such repairs when they are discovered. Wood is not delicate, as antiques, hundreds of years old, in any museum bear witness. In fact, it is silly to suffer over every little scratch and mark on furniture. On higher-priced furniture so-called "distressed finishes" are common. The unmarred furniture is beaten with chains, it is burned here and there, tiny wormlike holes are bored, the finish is shaded from dark around the edges to lighter in the middle. Bright, shiny brasses are chemically treated with iodine to darken them. All this is done to simulate old furniture, to give the new pieces a used look. Why, then, get upset over a scratch or a burn? It's all a part of aging gracefully. If first-aid treatment is needed use one of these methods:

Scratches. David Barrett, well-known New York interior designer, like a doctor, always carries a kit with him for emergency furniture repairs. In the kit are eyebrow pencils, matches, a white candle, fine steel wool, and brown shoe polish. If one of his clients is disturbed about a scratch on a dark piece of furniture, he produces an eyebrow pencil the right shade, draws it along the line, then smears it dry. The brown shoe polish is used on blond furniture, but if the piece is painted he produces the candle, lights it, and drips wax over the area. In burning, the wax is mixed with the carbon black, the better to antique the finish and soften the scratch. While the wax is still soft he smears and works it into the wood. The fine steel wool is used on any blemish or edge that needs to be smoothed down.

For deeper scratches, wash with benzine or carbon tetrachloride to clean the area. Sand lightly with very fine finishing paper to smooth down rough edges. Wipe the area clean and apply a thin coat of varnish. When thoroughly dry, sand and varnish again; repeat the thin coats, perhaps three or four times, until the scratch is filled in. Rub the area with fine powdered pumice stone until varnished area merges with the rest; then polish entire surface.

Gouges. Clean hole and area as outlined above for deep scratches. Then, using a shellac stick of the right color, fill the hole. The shellac should be melted with a soldering iron over a gas or electric range or any flame which will not leave a sooty residue. A simple method is to heat a spatula or paring knife (not your best one) until it will cut the shellac. Get a small portion on the knife, heat until softened, drop hot shellac into the hole. Repeat until hole is filled.

When the shellac has set, slice away surplus with chisel or sharp edge. Sand lightly. Apply a final coat of varnish, let dry, and polish.

Burns. Cigarette burns are common and are of all degrees from shallow to deep. For light burns make a creamy paste of powdered pumice and linseed oil. Rub gently with the grain of the wood. When edges of burned area are smooth, polish.

If you do not have pumice and linseed oil, silver polish which contains a mild abrasive can be substituted. Rub an area three or four times the size of the burn. If the cleaning action of the silver polish lightens the area, finish by polishing with a colored wax or furniture polish.

Deep burns require complete refinishing of the piece, but then again you may learn to live with the blemish, even develop a small affection for it.

Alcohol. Whether such stains are caused by drinks carelessly set down, spilled perfume, or medicine, they are apt to dissolve varnish or shellac and make permament rings on furniture. Medicine may also leave a stain. Use your emergency dusting cloth or dusting paper in a drawer in the room to wipe up the spill immediately. Later, when you are cleaning, polish. If this does not clear up the spot try a paste made of powdered pumice and linseed oil.

Heat marks. White rings from hot dishes occur often on the dining-room table. To prevent them it is important to have asbestos pads the size of your place mats as well as one which can be extended to full table size when a cloth is used. Avoid table pads with fuzzy surfaces. If fuzz from a table pad does stick to softened varnish, the area may have to be cleaned off and revarnished.

Light blemishes may disappear with a furniture polish. For deeper marks rub the spot with a non-linting cloth moistened with camphorated oil. Let dry a few minutes, then rub briskly.

Water rings. These can be avoided by using coasters for glasses and flower vases or by building up a wax surface on all table tops.

If water rings do occur (a) rub with furniture polish; (b) use camphorated oil treatment; (c) if very stubborn, place two layers of clean blotters over the spots and press with a warm iron. If this doesn't work, try the pumice or silver-polish methods outlined under burns.

Bloom or fog. In humid or rainy weather, or in a house that has been closed for some time, highly glazed finishes often acquire a bloom or blurred look. If the bloom doesn't come off with furniture polish, make a solution of one tablespoon of cider vinegar to one quart of water. Dampen a cloth in the solution, rub, wipe dry, and polish.

Checking or crazing. This is another characteristic of highly glazed finishes, perhaps most commonly seen on pianos. It can usually be avoided by keeping such pieces out of the sunlight and away from radiators.

Checking cannot be eliminated without complete refinishing but it can be camouflaged by polishing with wax the color of the wood.

Small repairs. While cleaning and polishing furniture take care of minor repairs; loose chair joints and drawers that stick are annoying and can be easily corrected.

To repair joints, whether doweled or mortise-and-tenon type, first pull apart. Then, using a pocket knife, scrape off and out all old, dry glue. When joint is clean squeeze a small amount of glue (Elmer's or Sobo) on both parts and spread around evenly, leaving no excess. Finish by pressing the two parts together, wiping off excess glue that oozes out. If you have no furniture clamps, tie with rope or heavy twine; dry for twenty-four to forty-eight hours. On teak furniture use resorcinol instead of white glue.

Drawers. In damp weather drawers may swell or warp. If condition is not extreme, pull drawer out and rub on the runners and on the center guide paraffin (candle wax), paste wax, or even soap. Silicone spray is also effective. If sticking continues, the runners may have to be sandpapered, then treated with wax.

Pulls and fittings. In old furniture, hardware on drawers sometimes loosens. Inside the drawer, back of the knob, is a nut or screw. Hold the knob on the outside with one hand and, using pliers or a screwdriver, tighten the screw or nut on the inside. If still loose, remove screw and slip a washer on before tightening. In extreme cases it may be necessary to remove all hardware and fill in the opening around the screw holes with plastic wood. Let harden before replacing the screw.

UPHOLSTERED FURNITURE

Protective finishes which are used on a variety of weaves and fibers have simplified the maintenance of upholstered furniture. For family or recreation room and boys' rooms the total washability of vinyl upholstery is worth considering. In other rooms, balance the use of the room and the amount of air pollution against your potentials as a housekeeper and choose upholstery accordingly. Plain surfaces, light colors, and flat, linenlike weaves will show more soil than patterned fabrics, dark colors, and pile or textured weaves.

Protective finishes also are making the care of upholstery easier. Well-known ones are Scotchgard, Zepel, Syl-mer and Duraclean. Many fabrics and upholstered pieces come with these finishes or they can be applied by certain companies and will last through several cleanings. Fabrics treated with them resist soil but are not impervious to it. Liquids spilled on them are not absorbed as quickly as on untreated materials; they will "sit" on the surfaces until they are blotted up.

. . . *don't select fragile fabrics*

Good though these finishes are for longer-lasting freshness, upholstered furniture needs tender care: weekly dusting, deep cleaning and shampooing occasionally, and immediate spot removal. Weekly dusting can be done with a whisk broom or the brush attachment of the vacuum cleaner (except on down-filled cushions). Pay attention around the welting, the platform beneath the cushions of sofas and chairs, the top of the back, where dust settles, and the back. Check for spots and watch the arms of chairs and sofas; don't let grime accumulate; remove as quickly as possible. (See Chapter 24, "How to Remove Spots and Stains.")

Spot cleaning on upholstery presents special problems because of the filling. Use a minimum of liquid whether water or cleaning fluid. Do not use dry-cleaning fluids on furniture padded with foam rubber or upholstered with urethane, bonded or backed fabrics. Before cleaning or removing spots check fabric in a concealed place for color fastness. Never use ammonia water, as it affects dyes.

The three basic methods of cleaning upholstery are:

1. Detergent-and-water solutions. Whip one part detergent and four parts water to a stiff suds. Apply cautiously. Rinse with a damp sponge. This method will remove many food stains.
2. Absorbent powders. Use French chalk, Fuller's earth, or cornstarch. Apply liberally, leave on overnight, and then brush off. This method is effective for the removal of fresh grease stains. The powder is sometimes hard to brush out of deeply textured fabrics.
3. Dry cleaners. There are several excellent commercial cleaners for upholstery. The foamy type is absorbed less and is less apt to leave a ring on the fabric.

Upholstery will last longer if it has periodic professional cleaning. Results are better if the cleaning is done before the soil is ground in. To prevent fading do not leave furniture in direct sunlight for long periods. Use a steam iron to fluff and freshen pile fabrics such as velvet or mohair. Do not rest the iron on the fabric.

MISCELLANEOUS SURFACES

Leather. Leather table tops and furniture require dusting with a dry cloth and an occasional once-over with a damp cloth. Wash very soiled leather with saddle soap or any mild suds. Rinse with a damp cloth wrung out of clear water, dry, and buff with a chamois. To remove mildew wipe with a one-percent solution of peranitrophenol.

Metal furniture. Dust and sponge with soap and water occasionally. Never use scouring powder on chrome as plated surfaces, once scratched, may peel. Wax gives a good protective coating.

Most wrought-iron furniture has been treated for rust resistance.

Paint outdoor iron furniture so that rust doesn't start. Don't paint over rust. Scour it with steel wool and/or a liquid rust remover. Follow directions on the label. In bad cases the cleaner may be left on for an hour before being removed. Then wipe off all the loose rust with a cloth or steel wool and apply the paint.

Accessories of metal, lamp bases, vases, boxes, and candlesticks, will respond to dusting, polishing, and care. On silver, use a standard polish or a processed cloth.

Use the electrolysis method, in which an aluminum pan, aluminum foil, or an aluminum disk is featured only on plated silver you do not value. This method removes all shading and gives a white, institutional look.

Store silver in flannel bags processed to keep it from tarnishing. Lacquer only ornamental silver which is not used for food.

Brass and copper. For a hard, bright finish which removes all shading and aging use salt and vinegar. Standard metal polishes will give the same results and are more pleasant to handle. After using any of these cleaners wash metal carefully in soft water and soap. If allowed to remain the solution might pit the surface.

For a soft, antique finish use linseed oil and fine pumice powder. This polish is pleasant on fine old pieces of brass and copper. Rub occasionally with lemon oil. For longer protection spray with clear lacquer.

Iron. Scrub off rust spots with a stiff brush. Apply a coat of black varnish. When storing, coat with wax or unsalted fat.

Pewter. This is a soft metal and should be handled carefully to avoid denting and melting. Do not allow pewter to stand on a hot stove or in a warm oven. Use silver polish to develop a dull luster. Wash with soapsuds and clear water.

Marble. Unfashionable for some years, marble is again popular. It is used for the tops of tables and chests, for floors, walls, and windowsills. It comes in many colors and in both high-gloss and mat finishes and can be refinished if marred. It is completely waterproof and responds to routine care with warm water and a mild detergent.

Since marble does stain, use coasters for glasses and remove all spills at once, especially oily substances and organic stains, such as tea, coffee, tobacco, etc. Acids, vinegar, wine, and fruit juices will stain also and etch the surface of old marble. If metals come in contact with marble, as in a fireplace facing, it may show rust stains.

There are several marble cleaners on the market. Read the directions for using them. The poultice method is often recommended. The poultice is made of a paste of whiting and the proper cleaning or bleaching agent, and is often applied hot. After it has been spread thickly over the surface, it should be kept from drying too fast by covering with a sheet of plastic. After three hours or more, flush the dried powder from the surface with hot water, polish with a dry cloth. Repeat if stain remains. Use soft water to prevent insoluble deposits.

On organic stains use whiting and a bleach such as Javelle water or hydrogen peroxide.

On oil and grease use whiting and a solvent.

On a dirt-soiled surface use borax and hot water. Use ammonia sparingly as repeated usage eats the surface, and never use acid, lye, or caustic cleaners on marble.

When the surface is dull a high luster can be restored with the felt buffer attachment of an electric hand polisher.

12 How to Clean Underfoot

Cleaning underfoot would be reduced 50 percent if we could coax family and friends to take a tip from the Japanese and remove their outdoor footgear before coming indoors. This is a sensible plan and in the space of a brief few weeks in Japan I found that parking shoes at the door became a habit. However, there seems no likelihood of such an idea's prevailing here, so cleaning underfoot is a continuing major chore.

Floors are divided into three main categories: soft-surface floors, such as rugs and carpets; smooth-surface floors, or vinyl, vinyl asbestos, cork tile, linoleum and wood; and hard-surface floors, such as brick, stone, slate, terrazzo, ceramic tile, concrete, and marble. There is a different method for cleaning each type.

SOFT-SURFACE FLOOR COVERINGS—RUGS AND CARPETS

The 1960's have brought a revolution to the manufacture of rugs and carpets. Attractive pricing has made them attainable to everyone, while new ways of making them and new fibers have changed them completely. Once-famous carpet manufacturers now share the market with an army of newcomers. Instead of just a half-dozen well-known brand names, there are now two or three dozen worth knowing. Instead of always being wool, rugs and carpets may be synthetic fiber or a blend of several fibers. When synthetics were first introduced in the forties they were not good performers. Now nylon, acrylics, the polyesters, and polypropylene olefins are developed specifically for carpets and all of them should receive the same amount of care and attention. The polypropylenes are the exception; carpets of these fibers will not be damaged by water, as they are hard, nonabsorbent fibers recommended for kitchen and outdoor areas.

Carpets and rugs are among the higher-priced items that go into the home.

A completely carpeted house eliminates the need to scrub floors. A vacuum cleaner will do the entire floor-cleaning job. In a home with a combination of soft and smooth floor coverings, the smooth floors accumulate more fluff from the air than when there are no rugs or carpets.

You will never learn to identify all of the different fibers—even experts in the field fail—so, when you are buying a rug or carpet, get all available information about the composition, weave, and care. Make a note also of the date of purchase, the price plus the laying charge, and the name of the store. This is valuable reference data and will be useful if you sell the carpet with your house. There is a range of carpet prices. As a rule you get what you pay for if you deal with a reliable retail store.

Rug and carpet pads. Rug cushions, also called underlay and carpet linings, are desirable. They give a feeling of luxury to less expensive rugs and carpets and prolong the life of both expensive and inexpensive ones by acting as a buffer between the hard floor and the springy pile.

Rug cushions are made of foam or sponge rubber, urethane, and rubberized hair. Use thick ones for deep, luxurious effects and thinner ones where buffer and nonskidding action are the principal requirements. Roll back both the rug and the pad for occasional cleaning.

Use the right casters under heavy furniture; imperfect ones can chew up carpet pile. Use plastic wheels, not steel casters on deep pile surfaces. Rubber wheels may leave marks and the pile will impede the swivel action.

New carpets and rugs fluff or develop fuzz on the surface and the vacuum cleaner bag may be packed with fluff the first two or three times a new rug or carpet is cleaned. Don't be alarmed; all new rugs shed for several months when they are first laid; it's natural. There are three reasons for this: (1) When the pile is cut *some* fibers drop into the pile; the fuzz is not anchored and comes off when the pile is swept. (2) Carpet yarn is made up of both short and long fibers and some of the short ones are not caught during the weaving. (3) In storage, carpets are apt to lose moisture, which is regained when it is laid. As the carpet regains moisture there is less shedding. Some carpet specialists suggest not cleaning a rug for several days after it is laid. Adequate humidity will add to the life of pile rugs and carpets. Overheated rooms and dry air cause continued fluffing, crushed pile, and a lifeless fabric.

Sprouts. These are threads which are longer than the rest of the pile and are frequently found in a new rug or carpet. They are tufts which escaped the cutter, loops in a twist weave which have unraveled for some reason, or pieces of the backing which have worked through. Never pull them out; clip them level with the pile surface, using scissors.

Missing tufts. Notwithstanding rigid inspections, occasionally a carpet will turn up with a patch of missing tufts. Just notify your dealer, who will secure matching yarn and burl-in or retuft in your home.

Pile crushing and shading. This is another problem. It, too, is natural. Originally the pile stands straight up and down. As the rug is used it is pushed one way or another. When a mass of fibers all fall one way, like a well-brushed head of hair, they look glossy and light in color. The contrast or shading usually shows between traffic lanes and unused areas.

A rug cushion will soften shading by reducing the sharpness of the pressure. Place rugs so that the light goes into the pile, if you want the rug to appear darker. Turn the rug around and it will look lighter and more lustrous. This is especially true when placing oriental rugs. Reverse a rug occasionally to distribute wear. Occasional stroking with a vacuum cleaner or a broom will also tend to correct slant of tufts. However, since shading is natural don't worry about it.

Use a whisk broom or the nozzle of the vacuum cleaner on rug or carpet around feet of a grand piano, sofa, and other hard-to-move pieces. Macy's New York department store reports that they vacuum their carpets three times a week and despite all the traffic—thousands of feet daily—Macy's rugs last six to ten years.

It is sometimes a shock to compare the original color sample with a rug or carpet that has been down on the floor for several months. The color won't match, but the rug isn't fading. The color change is due to dust, dirt, and grease-laden air. Delicate colors fare worse. In a year's time a delicate rose may appear taupe, a light blue may become dull gray-green. The original color may be restored by a professional cleaner.

Curling corners. Sometimes the corners of a carpet buckle or curl. To correct, apply a hot iron to a damp cloth on both back and front as though you were steaming trousers. Another method is to sew cardboard triangles in the corners with heavy thread.

Tautness is important for long carpet wear. Good carpet layers use a stretching machine to insure a tight installation. Have your carpet checked two or three months after it is laid if you feel that restretching is needed.

When a room is to be closed for any length of time, thoroughly vacuum the rug or carpet. Wool rugs or carpets should be sprayed with moth repellent or sprinkled evenly with naphthalene or paradichlorobenzene crystals. Allow about one pound of crystals to a nine-by-twelve rug, roll, and seal with gummed tape or wrap in brown paper.

If there are dogs or cats in the house, special moth prevention should be taken as the hairs become embedded in floor cracks and under the baseboard and offer a breeding place for moths. To prevent moths, particular care in vacuum cleaning under the rug and around the baseboard is essential. Use a damp cellulose sponge mop to pick up hard-to-remove hair and lint from rugs and upholstery. Hair visibility can be reduced by selecting carpets to match your pet's coloring. A Dallas family selected a black-and-white carpet to go with their Dalmatian, a Westchester family favors rust-red carpets to blend with their Irish setter, and an elderly woman in Chicago always has white carpets to avoid complaints from her maid about her white poodle!

Area rugs. These rugs are smaller than room size and larger than scatter rugs and are used to define certain areas in a room. Even when these rugs are small, don't use the old-fashioned method of hanging them on a clothesline for a beating. Even shaking is not too good for them; it tends to break the threads in the backing and weakens them. Small rugs can be washed and shampooed at home. Those with soft cotton backs can even be put through the washer. However, do not wash or dry clean or use solvents on rugs with rubber backing; it will damage the rubber and may stain the pile.

Fur rugs. Fur rugs are staging a revival. Clean with a vacuum sweeper. Spray occasionally for moths, especially if the house is to be closed. Just as you have your fur coat reconditioned occasionally, send the rug to a reliable cleaner once a year for cleaning and glazing.

Summer rugs. Fiber, sisal, rush, and grass rugs require very little surface cleaning. An occasional top brushing with broom or electric sweeper is enough. But remember the dust shifts through these rugs and the floor underneath may really need the cleaning.

Rush and grass rugs. Such rugs have a tendency to dry out; this makes them split. In a dry climate hose them down outdoors once in a while.

Fiber rugs. These are made of tightly twisted paper and do not require humidity although they can be shampooed. If they are faded, they can be painted, preferably in the garage or outdoors. If painting must be done indoors, protect the floor underneath with newspapers as the paint may go through. Use a spray paint for best results.

. . . use nonskid pad

Care and Maintenance. Resistance to soil is built into better carpets. Nevertheless, soil is inevitable and even with regular care carpets and rugs will need a deep cleaning every twelve months or two years depending on the use they get.

Ideally areas which get the most use should have a surface cleaning daily and a deeper cleaning once or twice a month. Daily removal of litter and a weekly cleaning should be given whether the carpet *looks* dirty or not. The air-borne dust which settles on tables, window-sills, and other surfaces also settles on carpets. If the dust is not removed from the surface, it sinks into the pile; when the soil has penetrated the pile one-third of its depth professional cleaning is needed.

Since the presence of dust seems to be eternal, a regular schedule for carpet care will preserve a fresh look and delay the labor and expense of shampooing. To freshen a carpet between professional cleanings, dry clean with a special absorbent powder such as Powderene. Scatter it on the rug, distribute evenly with a broom, let it stand, perhaps overnight, then remove with the vacuum cleaner. It may take an hour to remove the powder completely from a nine-by-twelve rug. Empty the bag or put in a new one several times if you are cleaning a large area.

Shampoo sweepers that use a special detergent suds also are used to clean and brighten pile rugs and carpets. In some areas the equipment can be rented from supermarkets. After sudsing and rinsing, dry thoroughly as quickly as possible in an airy place, using quantities of clean cloths. If floor is uneven, this method is advisable, as it will reach into the troughs or irregularities in the floor.

A third method for brightening dulled color is to sponge the surface with a liquid cleaner such as carbon tetrachloride. Apply carefully, quickly, and evenly to prevent rings and streaks. Keep windows open. Read the directions before starting. Don't smoke, as these cleaners are flammable.

Spots and Stains. Speedy action is the most important factor in caring for spills on rugs and the unforeseen accidents that will occur. Keep on hand a supply of clean, absorbent cloths. Even if there are guests, don't stand on ceremony; mop up spills before they dry and set. If the spot still lingers after patting with a cloth, add a little cleaning fluid to cloth. Repeat. If it still shows, try a clean sponge dampened with water but avoid water spots and never use soap solutions. For instructions on specific stains see Chapter 24 on stain removal.

If rain comes in a window, or a pitcher of water is spilled, blot up as much as possible at once with a clean, unstarched cloth or paper towels. Then place a bath towel over the wet area as a final blotter. Weight with magazines. Repeat with fresh towels until area is dry, then remove the weight. A fan may be directed at the back of a rug to speed drying.

SMOOTH-SURFACE FLOORS

Floorings come in infinite variety but, regardless of the surface, care is the secret of having really attractive floors. In addition to daily dusting and weekly polishing all floors call for a thorough treatment at least twice a year. Such cleaning means moving furniture and rugs out of the room so that every corner can be vacuumed or brushed with a fine dry dust mop. If there are spots and soil, the floor must be washed. Whether floor is wood, vinyl, or other material, never flood. Use water sparingly. Use a cloth wrung out in mild detergent suds. If soil is heavy, use a packaged cleaner, following instructions carefully. Carbon tetrachloride or turpentine may be used to remove a wax build-up, but be sure to use only in a well-ventilated room where there is no flame, fire, or burning cigarette, since both are flammable. Apply with a clean cloth and then remove softened wax. Wipe floor with a cloth wrung out in detergent suds; follow with another of clean water. Electric scrubbers are available and like carpet cleaners can often be rented from supermarkets.

Apply fresh wax only after surface is clean and dry. The type of wax used will depend on the floor material and the use of the room. Paste and liquid waxes require polishing with a hand-operated or electric polisher. These also can be rented from the local hardware store or the supermarket. Self-polishing wax and liquid self-polishing-cleaning wax should be reserved for daily and weekly floor care. They dry to a gleam without rubbing but are shorter-lived.

Wood floors. Keep wood floors clean by sweeping, dry mopping, and vacuum cleaning. More detailed care depends upon the finish. Popular finishes include wax, varnish, shellac, paint, and oil.

Waxed floors are usually hardwood and nine time out of ten they are oak. In old houses maple, cherry, and even teakwood may turn up. Wax brings out the beauty of the wood and results in a handsome floor. But waxed floors, like a good lawn, require attention.

A wax finish is built up on a floor with two or three applications of paste wax. On an open-grain wood like oak a filler should be used first. A wood filler is a paste preparation used to fill the small crevices in coarse-grain woods so that the surface will be smooth. Each coat of wax is buffed to a hard finish before another layer is applied. If the floor is light, use a wax and stain combined. Select a walnut brown stain. Nothing makes a room seem as cheap as the light yellow oak floors so often used in development houses. Waxed floors should be rewaxed with a mechanical waxer and paste wax applied at least twice a year. If for any reason the wax is tacky or grimy, remove all wax with a commercial wax remover and start over.

Do not use a broom on a waxed floor.

Do not scrub with water.

Do not rub, wipe, or mop it in a circular motion. Always move with the grain of the wood.

Do not let water stand on waxed floors. If it rains in a window, if water is spilled, or if there is another kind of accident, wipe up the moisture or a white blush will develop. If waxing does not remove the spot, rub it with turpentine. This will also take off the wax so that a patch job of waxing will have to be administered.

Liquid wax that requires buffing may be used on a wax floor once a month. But do not use self-polishing waxes that have a water base. They are apt to raise the grain of the wood.

When the liquid wax is dry, buff it with a long-handled polisher with a lamb's wool or fine steel-wool head. Some vacuum cleaners have an attachment for this job. If wax is not applied frequently enough, wood takes on a porous, starved look.

A waxed floor should be kept clean with a vacuum cleaner or a dry mop. Do not use an oiled mop or a wet mop.

Both shellac and varnish offer a quicker way of building up a finish on a floor. Shellac dries overnight but is not quite as durable. Varnish should be allowed to dry several days before the floor is used. Both methods form a hard skin over the surface of the wood that makes the floor easier to care for. The hard shine of the finish that they give can be reduced by waxing. A thin coating of wax which is never allowed to wear off will keep a shellacked or varnished floor in condition for years. Self-polishing wax may be used but it is not as satisfactory as either paste or liquid wax. Clean the floor with a dry mop; never use a wet mop. The cleaner the floor is kept, the longer the wax and shellac or varnish will last.

To refinish, every trace of wax must be removed. Follow method described on page 111 for removal of ingrained soil.

Before refinishing old floors fill in all the cracks. First clean the cracks with a vacuum cleaner. Then force in crack filler tinted to match the floor. Smooth top with a putty knife. An oil-base filler works up like putty and is easy to use. It will harden overnight and be ready for finishing with the rest of the floor.

Oiled floors are not easy to do because of the time involved, but in the hands of an expert nothing is more handsome. One of the finest cabinetmakers in New York uses boiled linseed oil on the floors in his home, and they glow like satin. The oil is applied and allowed to stand overnight; then the floor is rubbed down until not a trace of oil remains. This is done at three-month intervals the first year until the finish is built up. After that oiling is done only once a year. Both oiled and dry mops may be used on oiled floors. Oil darkens wood and may eventually turn it almost black.

Painted floors may be vacuumed or brushed with a dry mop. Use a damp mop if floor is soiled. When dry, protect the paint with any one of the three types of waxes mentioned above. If the surface is constantly coated with wax, the wear will come on the wax, not on the paint, and the floor will not have to be repainted for years. For added protection use a runner or small rug in the traffic areas.

To camouflage wear on a painted floor, spatter it. Spattering is an art which seems to have originated on sand-ridden Cape Cod, where it is almost impossible not to track sand into the house from the beach, but if a blue or sea-green floor is spattered in gray, white, red, and yellow, for instance, the sand doesn't show so much. Who said those early New England housewives weren't practical?

Odd fact: If your wood floor squeaks put talcum powder in the cracks; this will often cure it.

Vinyl floor covering. No smooth surfaces, tile, or flooring that comes in a roll should be cleaned for seventy-two hours after installation. Protect floor with building paper if there will be traffic over it.

Vinyl floors may be either waxed or polished with a buffer. Use the wax recommended by the manufacturer of the flooring. Ask a dealer for advice, or make a survey of the types available yourself. You will find high-gloss and heavy-duty ones recommended for traffic areas, as well as milky-white waxes for use on white or colorless floors.

To prepare floors for waxing and polishing follow instructions given at the beginning of this section. When surface is completely clean, apply the polish. Pour it into a shallow pan large enough to accommodate a felt, lambswool, or cloth applicator. Apply a thin layer without streaks over the entire floor. Let dry for about thirty minutes, then polish. For new floors or annual cleaning, apply a second coat and polish again.

Oils, grease, or treated mops should never be used on vinyls. Also avoid gasoline, kerosene, naphtha, or other solvents for removing spots. Never use paint, varnish, lacquer, or shellac on vinyl.

As pure vinyl melts at 350 degrees, avoid grinding burning matches or cigarettes into vinyl floors. If hot grease spills on a vinyl floor, it may make holes.

Cork and linoleum floors. Though entirely different in composition from vinyl, these may be cared for in the same way. However, cork floors may be oiled instead of waxed.

Rubber floors. After cleaning, apply only self-polishing wax. Avoid grease spatters, oil, solvents, strong cleaners, and abrasives that may rough up the surface.

Vinyl-asbestos and asphalt-tile floors. These are less expensive than vinyl or linoleum. Dampness does not affect asphalt tile and as a result it is used for basement recreation rooms and for surfacing floors in new houses with concrete slab foundations. In the kitchen a grease-resistant type should be specified.

Asphalt tile is a composition of asphalt and other ingredients. It can be dissolved in oil, so do not use an oiled mop on it and never use liquid wax which contains an oil solvent. Use either the wax the manufacturer recommends or a self-polishing wax. Self-polishing waxes in contrast to liquid waxes have a water, not an oil, base.

Keep clean by sweeping or brushing with a dry mop daily. In the service sections of the house wash once a week with a detergent and water or a combination cleaner-waxer which cleans as it waxes.

HARD-SURFACE FLOORS

ceramic tile	terrazzo
brick	concrete
stone and slate	marble

These floorings offer several problems. Even though they are impervious to moisture, the concrete between the stones or tile is porous and should be sealed.

Brick, unglazed tile, concrete, and terrazzo should be treated with a penetrating sealer, such as clear polyurethane, then waxed to bring out the luster. Concrete is sometimes painted with concrete floor enamel; this seals, stops dust, and gives color. If kept waxed, the painted surface will wear well.

Since such floors have slight irregularities, a brush attachment on the vacuum cleaner gives best results. All can be cleaned with detergent and water. A mild abrasive can be used when needed. Don't use an oiled mop except on brick where an antiqued oil finish has been built up.

13 How to Groom a House

So the house is clean, is it? But being clean isn't enough.

A house can be:

clean—but not neat
clean—but cluttered
clean—but bare
clean—but forbidding
clean—but not colorful

You know women who have that scoured look. Their clothes are immaculate, but they have been chosen with an eye to durability rather than taste. Their nondescript hats are suitable for any season, and their sensible shoes make no concession to style. These women have stout hearts and are hard workers, no doubt, but they seem to be missing some of the fun in life.

On the other hand, there are women who start out in the morning with every hair in place in beautifully arranged coiffures, their make-up is right, their clothing attractive, and you know that each button and zipper is in working order. These are the women who go through a trying day and arrive home looking as cool and well groomed as when they started. Such perfection may be too much to aspire to unless it comes naturally, but we should at least aim for some point in between these two extremes.

Good grooming in a room and good personal grooming are closely related. Good grooming is rooted in good design, appropriateness, and upkeep. Overdressed hair, a costume too dressy for the occasion, too much or too little make-up, too much costume jewelry, high-heeled, fancy shoes, and a generally overdone or inadequate costume won't endure the rigors of a hard day. Surprising as it may seem, a poorly designed room will fall apart in the same way.

A woman in Connecticut whose living room I had just decorated wrote to me: "I love every part of my new room, but there is a plus which I hadn't anticipated. We do all the things we used to do, yet the room never has that disorderly look. Even the Sunday papers don't upset its calm spirit."

It is true that a well-decorated room, one that is planned, one that has a simple color scheme to hold it together, will look neat longer than an unplanned room that just happened.

CLUTTER VERSUS COMPOSURE

Many rooms are launched with some empty spaces on tables, mantels, and shelves which give a sense of freedom, but as time goes on a clutter of objects appears. This is added to on holidays and anniversaries by gifts from well-meaning friends and relatives. Some of the boxes, vases, and figurines received are pretty. Others are neither pretty nor useful, but are kept for sentimental reasons or just plain lethargy, an unwillingness to decide what to do about them.

The stuff clutters the mantels, crowds table tops, overflows from shelves. It creates confusion, requires constant dusting, and makes no decorative contribution. Usually 90 percent of this clutter is too small to require a second thought. Having it on display is like wearing all the costume jewelry you own at one time. So, unless you want to develop a serious case of bric-a-brac mind, the frivolous, petty, small junk must be cleared out. If you want to keep it, store it in boxes and then it can be looked over occasionally as one visits a museum. But don't keep clutter on display if you want a well-groomed, attractive house.

What technique should be used for unscrambling the essential from the nonessential? The first step is to remove every accessory in the room. Clear off the mantel, the tables, the shelves. First put aside all empty vases. They should appear only when they are holding flowers. Select one pleasing ash tray for each table and possibly two cigarette boxes for the room.

Discard or pack up all small, meaningless figurines—cats, dogs, ducks, and what-not. Now consider the mantel, usually the most important spot in a room. Select three or four of the largest objects you have and try them out. However, when it comes to arranging the mantel in most cases there will be nothing large or dramatic enough to use there. Seldom can one depend on haphazard gifts. Usually only study and shopping will produce the object with flair. Rather than use dinky little candlesticks and doodads on the mantel, get a big fish tank and fill it with green leaves such as rhododendron or laurel. Such a mass at least has size and color importance.

In the houses I have stripped of useless ornaments and bric-a-brac, there was general agreement on the improved appearance of the rooms as well as on the time saved in cleaning them. But sometimes there

. . . discard meaningless objects

are groans. I recall the case of a young bride. About two months had elapsed between the time we had decorated the house and the date for photographing it for a magazine. When we returned to take the pictures, the living room looked like a gift shop. Every nook and cranny held a wedding present, most of them puny silver things or bits of crystal—and all this against a strong modern background. We made a clean sweep and substituted large pottery ash trays, wooden cigarette boxes, and plants that we had brought with us.

As the bride admired the effect she whispered, "Bill will never forgive me. I kept him up until three o'clock last night polishing this silver and now you aren't going to use it!"

Storage. One reason rooms have clutter is lack of convenient storage space. If there is a place for extra vases, bric-a-brac, books, magazines, sewing, game equipment, sheet music, records, scrapbooks, gifts, collectors' paraphernalia, and desk accessories, they aren't so likely to be left lying about.

A woman in New Jersey who enjoys arranging accessories has built a storage wall fifteen-inches deep along one entire side of her dining room. It looks like a wood-paneled wall, but in it she keeps her stock of accessories. Whenever the mood comes she changes accessories so that she can see her "playthings" as she calls them, and still have no clutter.

In a home in northern New York State a room in the basement has been set aside for accessories. It is at least twelve by fifteen feet and has tiers of shelves placed at right angles to the wall like the stacks in a library. In that household accessory changes are made seasonally, four times a year.

Without question there is inadequate provision for closets, cupboards, and other storage space in most houses. Few of us have strong enough powers of concentration to just sit and contemplate life or the wonders of nature. To pass the time we need books, notepaper, games, sheet music, or other leisure-time materials. The house which really serves the family, and which is at the same time easy to care for, should have storage space in every room for the things that are used in that room. If such storage is not provided, an active household will gradually be submerged in debris. The family with a tendency toward inactivity will gradually become duller and more lifeless, and no doubt spend all of its waking hours watching television.

There isn't a room which won't produce storage space for necessities if you study the problem. Provide storage and the family will fill it. Provide storage and you will have less dismal dusting to do and life will be more orderly.

As an example, in a small apartment I visited recently two office files had been put in the big old bathroom! It was an odd place for files, but they were sprayed the color of the walls and the extra storage drawers thus provided had revolutionized the household.

Little things. Planned interiors and adequate storage are basic necessities in good grooming for a house.

After a room is cleaned is the time to twitch it here and tune it up there for perfect grooming. This final adjustment requires almost no time. What are needed are a desire for perfection and an interest in exquisite detail, some fussiness, and a creative instinct.

Windows. Assume that the windows are clean and the curtains and draperies fresh. Adjust the shades or blinds evenly at the top of the window. Shake out the curtains and draperies and arrange the folds neatly. See that the outside of the draperies is drawn tight from floor to ceiling. Tack the hem line of the draperies to the baseboard or, better still, use a ring and cup hook to hold it in line. This weekly action will help keep the draperies fresh and will discourage ugly tight folds. Often draperies look so sad and discouraged I'm sure they haven't been touched by human hands in years. Love things around the house just a little bit and they will put on a better performance. Neglect them and they will get back at you.

Pictures. These should be frequently straightened and dusted.

Mantel tops. The mantel top is as important to the appearance of a room as a hat is to a costume. See that it harbors no nonessentials and that the objects on it form an attractive still life.

Fireplace. The hearth must come in for attention whether you use it or not. When it is not in use, keep the damper closed so that ashes won't blow into the room; in winter this will conserve heat. Whether you clean the fireplace after each use depends on your own wish. Meticulous housekeepers like to clean out the ashes each time the fireplace is used. I rather like a nice pile of ashes. They form a base for the next fire. In any case you can't escape the Cinderella job of sweeping the hearth. If brushed back in the firebox, ashes look fine. Finish by assembling and laying paper, kindling, and logs for a fire. Discourage the use of the fireplace as an incinerator. Matches, cigarette stubs, scraps of paper, strings tossed on the hearth are as slovenly as a run in your stocking. Guests may be the worst offenders, but polished andirons and an air of neatness will discourage all but the most insensitive.

Books. Books are essential and a good decorative feature. Keeping them in orderly ranks on the shelves is a simple task that can be done almost automatically at any time of day. It's bad for books to lean against each other in a drunken fashion. Keeping them straight is not only good for books, but it gives a room a cared-for look.

Magazines. These might be called a mounting problem in many households. Far be it from me to suggest throwing them out. Some of the most delightful hours of my childhood were spent in our enormous attic with old magazines. They were our source for paper dolls, for scrapbooks, and for paste-up material for dummy magazines. We collected and read old continued stories and used the *National Geographic* for schoolwork. What to do with old magazines in this era of apartments and atticless houses is a problem which has to be worked out individually. In any case, they cannot be kept on display forever if you want a well-groomed, easy-to-care-for, sleek-looking room.

Keep weekly magazines out not more than two to four weeks and monthly magazines not longer than two months. Arrange your supply of magazines neatly, either piled up on a table or spread out if space permits. A magazine rack on the back of a door helps, or plan bookshelves with a magazine shelf. If back numbers are weeded out regularly, it is easy to keep the current ones available and in good order.

Lamps. Lamps are sometimes called the costume jewelry of a room, but this idea does not convey their true importance. It might be more accurate to compare lamps with spectacles which help you to see better. The main function of a lamp, like glasses, is to improve vision. The secondary function of a lamp is to add to the attractiveness of the room.

Lamps are a source of light and a center of attention. See that lamp bases and bulbs are immaculate, that shades are fresh and clean and straight.

Flowers and plants. It is important that they be fresh and vigorous if they appear on parade, and they should be placed with intelligence. Just because flowers are attractive in a room is no reason for overdoing it. A dozen bouquets will give an otherwise well-ordered room a funereal air.

Plan one large bouquet for the mantel, a piano top, or a bare corner. All other bouquets must be definitely minor. Place a low arrangement on a coffee table and perhaps another bouquet on a lamp table. As a rule three flower arrangements are enough for any room. Cut the stems shorter each day and transfer them to containers more suitable to short stems. Change the water every day and when the flowers are discarded remove the container entirely. Put a piece of charcoal in large vases that are difficult to change daily.

Ash trays, cigarette boxes, and bibelots. Such things should be kept shining. It's worth being fussy with them for they are things which are seen at close range and are frequently handled.

As you check the small accessories, see that all clocks are running and on time. Review the desk and its contents. Note whether ink, stamps, clips, or notepaper are needed.

Chair cushions and pillows. These should be plumped a couple of times a day as you walk through the room, just as you powder your nose as a pick-me-up. Such plumping does wonders in creating an orderly room, especially if there are down cushions to cope with.

Sheet music and records. If not in their own drawer or shelf, they should be neatly stacked.

Drawers. Even though these come last, they are definitely not an afterthought. Drawers upstairs and downstairs, drawers in desks and in bedrooms, wherever they are, are an eternal problem. Attention should be applied each time a drawer is opened. If daily upheavals are avoided, the final day of reckoning can be postponed. But the time will come when the entire contents will have to be emptied, lining paper replaced, and an organized reloading negotiated.

There is a tendency nowadays to smile superciliously at the mention of a fussy housekeeper. Smile if you want, but acquire the habit yourself. There is a lasting satisfaction to be had from doing things precisely and nicely, in preserving so-called old fashioned amenities. Actually, they are no more old-fashioned than cleaning behind your ears and washing your hair occasionally.

Establish your household as one that is loved, one in which efficiency is a watchword, and one in which standards count.

If you are an immaculate housekeeper, be proud of it but don't brag about it. Just remember that Michelangelo once remarked that it is the trifles that make perfection—and perfection is no trifle.

14 How to Make a House Smell Good

The olfactory nerve has a long memory. The impact of an odor may last a lifetime. I shall never forget either the noisome smell of fish canneries or the pungent aroma of evergreen forests in the Pacific Northwest. Then there is the memory of the fustiness of snow-banked houses in Canada sealed against fresh air, the moldy scent of old English inns, and the musty chill of ancient French cathedrals. Take me blindfolded to any one of a dozen sections of New York City and its characteristic odor will tell me where I am.

Sweet in my memories of childhood are the heady bouquets of mincemeat bubbling on the back of the stove, the warm yeastiness of bread hot from the oven. There linger also the lavender scent of the linen closet and the haunting odor of sandalwood in my mother's dressing room.

After years of neglect the subject of fragrance is being reintroduced both in the home and in the factory. Air pollution is becoming a number-one problem owing to the wide variety of nose-ruffling industrial smells which disturb workers, the surrounding neighborhood, even whole cities.

Sometimes these so-called industrial odors persist in the product being made. Customers shy away from some synthetic rubber and plastic items because of their strong chemical smell. Most liquid detergents have to be deodorized to make them acceptable for kitchen use.

Even though, generally speaking, the sense of smell may be the oldest of human senses, very little is known about how the human nose works or why some smells are pleasant, others objectionable. Moreover, no instrument yet devised can take the place of the olfactory nerves. There are devices for detecting and measuring the presence of certain more or less volatile chemicals—osmoscopes.

The fact is that there are 600,000 cells in the human nose connected with the olfactory center so that with training and conscious effort man's scent range would be almost without limit. In a current survey 17,000 different odors were distinguished by human noses. It is said that Helen Keller, blind from birth, could identify her friends by their individual odors!

It's quite true that everyone has a sense of smell. Like any of the other senses, it becomes a sensitive and sure instrument only when it is cultivated. The French say that a nose is a gift, but even though you are born with one, years of training are needed to become a "nose" or perfume creator. The fact that there are only twenty recognized "noses" in France indicates how limited is the professional field. But, in a country like this, where perfume purchases run into millions of dollars, there must be a large group with at least amateur standing as "noses."

Most fragrant smells are highly complex. The odor of roses is made up of twenty or more aromatics, and the tantalizing odor of coffee is a blend of thirty-five different ingredients. Unpleasant odors, on the other hand, tend to be rather simple; in fact, that may be the reason we don't like them. Human noses, even uncultivated ones, have become accustomed to nice, rounded-out, complicated odors.

Repeated surveys show that houses often do not smell good. A friend of mine conducts field surveys in all sections of the country. Her calls on women take her into the better houses in pleasant residential sections. When I questioned her on odors she exclaimed, "I'll never forget the smell of those houses! Even in the cleanest houses the air is often as stale as in a dungeon. I can tell whether they have had fish, cauliflower, or lamb roast, if there is a chain smoker in the family, if they always burn the toast, or if they wash the babies' diapers at home."

Another home was described as big and comfortable with a pleasing fragrance. There was the smell of trees and leaves, of shined shoes and riding boots, of sun and pungent wax in rooms filled with eighteenth-century furniture.

The subject of odors sometimes turns up in court. In a six-family apartment house near Stuttgart, West Germany, a complaint was leveled at one family who made sauerkraut at home. The judge himself is said to have sniffed the building and ruled that sauerkraut does not smell bad!

In another "smells case" in a Malay legend, two beggars are said to have managed to exist for a year by camping next to a restaurant and living off of the delicate odors emanating from it. Eventually the restaurateur took the two beggars to court. The case was settled against the beggars, who were ordered to settle the case for fifty dinar. But the payment was to be made in court by ringing the coins loudly on the counter without their being handed over. Thus the *sound* of the coins paid for the *smell* of food!

The best and most basic method of getting rid of unpleasant odors is to have a clean house that smells clean. But just as a newly laid egg has no taste, so really clean air is marked by an absence of odor which takes us right back to the chapter on cleaning house.

First, air every room every day, summer and winter. Air mattresses, pillows, blankets, and clothes. Perspiration, according to recent studies, is rated as the most annoying odor in the catalogue.

Second, clean everything thoroughly. Clean blankets and pillows, clean cloths and rugs, clean upholstery, curtains, draperies. Clean water in flower vases and clean ash trays have no odor.

Third, watch cooking operations. Keep the kitchen windows open or the ventilating fan going while baking, broiling, or cooking smelly foods. Don't burn toast or bacon—or anything else. Cook cabbage, cauliflower, and other strong-smelling vegetables by the short process —in a pressure cooker. Wash utensils and plates that have been used for fish at once, using first a salt-water solution as a deodorizer before soap and water. Remove every trace of burned fat from the oven and broiler after each use and do not tolerate partially decayed apples, onions, and potatoes in kitchen bins.

Fourth, install an electric ventilator in the kitchen and use it. Be scrupulous in the care of the bathroom and the kitchen. Use antiseptics for washing floors, walls, fixtures. Use drain cleaners. Keep range, refrigerator, and garbage can immaculately clean.

Fifth, don't overlook the attic and basement. They should be clean, dry, and well ventilated.

Getting rid of odors is only part of the problem. Occasionally, the need may be to mask a bad odor with a pleasant one. Accordingly, there are now commercial agents or reodorants, as they are called, which cover or mask less pleasant or objectionable odors, as opposed to deodorants that neutralize odors. There are fresheners in automatic spray cans and plastic bottles that need only to be squeezed to send out an odor-masking mist.

Individuals with especially sensitive noses will appreciate the little electrical contraptions that look like table radios which clean and humidify the air.

Reodorants are also used in soaps, in polishes for the care and preservation of wood, metal, glass, and leather surfaces, and in the moth-and-larvae-fighting chemicals. Formulas are being developed for the odor improvement of such commonly used items as facial tissue, lingerie fabrics, and insulating materials. Plastics are now being scented by the addition of highly aromatic polyethylene pellets to the mix before it is extruded or molded. Scents are now available for almost everything from plastic flowers to cedar-scented garment bags.

These commercial solutions may satisfy the majority, but it is still a delight to turn back to some of the old-fashioned ways of reodorizing. Perhaps the most down-to-earth suggestion comes from a home economist: Clean the house thoroughly, air it well, and then bake buttery cinnamon buns!

Injecting a trace of perfume here and there through the house takes almost no time and it gives great pleasure. Once established, many fragrances are self-perpetuating; others will endure for years. So here again it isn't so much the time or expense involved as the wish to have an aura of fragrance and the interest in the details and the amenities of the house that are important. Many people will say that to worry about fragrances in this upset world is silly. But perhaps there would be fewer upset individuals if there was more indulgence in such simple pleasures.

There are six fundamental groups of odors. A study made on the reaction of one thousand people indicates that the most favored are flowery scents and fruity or spicy ones. However, resinous vapors are popular, whereas burnt or putrid smells are as a rule outlawed, though burnt coffee or maple, tobacco, and tar are actually liked by some people.

The most popular fragrance is the rose, closely followed by lilac and pine. Next in order are lily of the valley and violet, coffee, balsam, and cedar. Sixty-seven percent of the group studied liked wintergreen, with the young group bringing up the vote for chocolate. Then in close succession come carnation, orange, and vanilla. Among popular resinous scents are camphor, cedar, balsam, pine, witch hazel, menthol, and turpentine.

The rose garden. Each season has it own fragrance. I'm sure that

Rip Van Winkle, before opening his eyes after his long sleep, knew that it was fall from the haunting, winy odor of mingled dried leaves, chrysanthemums, and ripe fruit that perfumed the air.

The garden then is a natural place for introducing fragrance in a house. Plant aromatic shrubs and vines near windows which can be opened. For spring there are lilacs, spring-flowering witch hazel, and sweet shrub. Climbing roses can be trained about windows, porches, and arbors. Honeysuckle is another delicious perfumer. A blossoming linden tree will make the month of June perfumed perfection. Such strategy was common in planning eighteenth-century gardens and is recommended today.

Fireplace scents. Aromatics were originally burned over an open flame, thus giving off a strong, quick-spreading perfume. Oriental incense is also carried on smoke. The fireplace offers a wonderful source for adding smoke fragrance. Such an idea is not unfamiliar to the countryman who each fall savors anew the first whiff of wood smoke on cool clean air.

A friend of mine actually collects aromatic woods to burn in her fireplace. One evening she uses apple wood. On special occasions a hickory log is produced, while on deluxe evenings driftwood from the beach, salt-soaked and bleached, inevitably brings comment for its fragrance and the added excitement occasioned by the spurts of blue, green, and yellow flames when a mineral-loaded pocket in the wood burns. She also uses pine cones and aromatic cedar chips, and once she brought back from Phoenix, Arizona, a suitcase full of desert-growing mesquite wood to burn on occasion in her New England fireplace!

Sophisticated scents originally used in burnt offerings by religious cults were myrrh, sandalwood, benzoin, and labdanum, the resinous juice of rockroses.

The Japanese are exceptionally cultivated in the area of burned fragrance and consider the discovery of a new scent or odor the occasion for a scent-savoring party. Each guest brings his own incense in a small container. They sit in a circle and each of the guests passes his scent around the group. The container and the scent are both admired and the experienced ones try to guess its source. Finally, the host brings out his rarity. Again the container and the scent are admired and its source explored. All this makes a simple and delightful evening of discovery as well as exploration of the minds and interests of friends.

There are more usual methods for pursuing aromatics but, if you adopt any, remember that too much of anything can be irritating. To give pleasure, scents must be subtly used; they must have a surprise character and not completely pervade the house. To enter the living room and find the delicate perfume of potpourri there, to open a bureau drawer and receive a pleasant whiff of vetiver, to slide in between clean, lavender-scented sheets—that's using scents knowingly. These sources of house perfumes are possibilities:

Put vetiver packs in the linen closet. (Order from D. H. Holmes Co., New Orleans, Louisiana.)

Keep fresh lavender bags in your lingerie.

Bring pine pillows back from Maine.

Unwrap scented soap and store between bath towels.

Hang a pomander ball in guest-room closet and a pine cone in your husband's closet.

Brush clear, scented lacquer on unpainted surfaces, under closet shelves, on hangers, under chair seats, in drawers. (Lacquer scents are made by Mary Chess in white lilac, gardenia, and carnation.)

Line dressing-table drawers with fitted pads, which are scented, or use the scented drawer paper now available.

Place a bowl of potpourri on the coffee table in the living room or on a hall console.

Experiment with air deodorizers.

Use a trace of pine-scented disinfectant in kitchens and bathroom scrub water. Clip a deodorizer cake to the lid of the garbage can. It not only will deodorize but also will ward off pests.

Install a portable electric air cleaner and purifier.

An old household book published by Lord and Taylor recommends as deodorizers, "Coffee pounded in a mortar and roasted on an iron plate . . . sugar burned on hot coals, and vinegar boiled with myrrh." Another source suggests as a party preparation that a deep-bowled iron spoon, heated red hot, then filled with aromatic oil such as rose geranium or lemon verbena, be carried through the house just before the guests arrive. To dispel cooking odors the leaves of southernwood (*Artemisia abrotanum*) thrown into a hot pan or open fire, is also recommended.

A less extreme method of ridding a room of tobacco smoke and sweetening the air is this: place a bowl containing two tablespoons of ammonia and one cup of water in a room overnight. It will clear away odors.

HOW TO MAKE POTPOURRI

If you have a garden you can make your own potpourri just for fun. As a teenager I made it for sachets for Christmas gifts. My mother's rose garden was my source of supply. To complicate the project I felt that the flowers should be picked at sunup. Actually this was not necessary, even though it is desirable to pick flower heads in a dry spell before the heat of the day. Select flowers before they are full-blown; loose buds are most fragrant.

Clip off the whole flower head with shears, then quickly, before they begin to sweat, pull off the petals and spread them to dry in a ventilated, dark place. Keep each variety of flowers in a separate pile. After the petals are thoroughly dry, they are ready to pack in screw-top jars in alternating layers of petals with sprinklings of orrisroot. Store in a dark place to preserve the color. Some formulas also recommend a sprinkle of uniodized salt but use cautiously in damp climates as salt takes up moisture and may mold the mixture. All summer dried petals may be added to the jars. When the year's crop of petals is collected it is time to mix the brew.

Choice of ingredients. There is no one formula for preparing potpourri. The mixture may consist of just rose petals with an assortment of other flowers available in your own garden—lavender, geraniums, pansies, calendulas, bee balm, heliotrope, mignonette, lemon verbena, violets, bachelor buttons, pinks, orange or lemon blossoms; herbs such as basil, rosemary, thyme, marjoram, mint, wormwood, sweet pennyroyal, orrisroot; spices such as cloves, mace, allspice, cardamon seeds, coriander, bay leaves; oils from rosemary, lemon verbena, peppermint, eucalyptus, attar of roses, geranium.

Never include all of these ingredients in any one formula. The odor would be confusing. Several recipes are given on page 130. You will see that most of the formulas include a combination of three to five flowers, two or three herbs and spices, and one or two oils. Rose petals and lavender are usually the principal ingredients. The variation comes in the addition of the herbs, spices, and oils. Delicate mixtures include only floral scents; others favor spices or herbs. Use strong-scented ingredients in scant measure. Keep a tight hand on cedar and balsam needles, all mints, and the oils of peppermint and eucalyptus, or they will dominate the mixture.

A pleasant fragrance is the principal aim, but at no sacrifice it is also possible to have an interesting texture and pretty color effect. Lavender and herbs build texture and contrast and unscented flowers like yellow calendula petals and blue bachelor buttons do nice things for the color.

Gum benzoin and gum storax are added to preserve the petals and to act as a fixative. To approximately one quart of petals use two tablespoons of preservative. Occasionally, a dash of brandy is added as a blender. Eau de cologne may be substituted. Herbs and spices can be found at the grocery store, if not on your kitchen shelves, and the oils and fixatives are drugstore supplies.

It is possible to make up your own formula, using what you have. For instance, to one quart of rose petals and one cup of lavender add one tablespoon of three herbs and two or three tablespoons of crushed spices. Follow this with twelve drops of one or two oils, added a drop at a time; then stir well. Last, put in two tablespoons of fixative and several drops of brandy. After mixing thoroughly with a wooden spoon or glass rod, store tightly closed in china, pottery, or glass. If in glass, keep in a dark place. Stir occasionally and in a few weeks the potpourri will be blended and ready for use.

POTPOURRI 1

1 quart rose petals
1 cup lavender
1 tablespoon rosemary
1 tablespoon nutmeg, cinnamon, and cloves
2 tablespoons powdered gum benzoin

POTPOURRI 2

1 quart rose petals
1 tablespoon lavender
1 tablespoon crushed cinnamon and mace
pinch of calendula petals
2 or 3 bits of dry lemon peel stuck with cloves
2 tablespoons gum storax

POTPOURRI 3

1 quart rose petals
1 cup mixed mignonette, pinks, heliotrope, lavender, or any other flower combination
1 pinch (a few leaves each) of bay leaf, marjoram, cedar, and balsam
1 teaspoon each of powdered cloves, mace, and cinnamon
½ teaspoon crushed coriander and cardamon seeds
1 tablespoon each of powdered gum benzoin and gum storax
Few drops of brandy and attar of roses

Potpourri mixtures are used in sachets, in padding on hangers, and in either closed or open porcelain jars. In a closed jar, potpourri will keep for years. The jar, of course, stands open when fragrance is wanted.

HOW TO MAKE A POMANDER BALL

Pomander balls are as ancient as potpourri jars. They are hung in closets or put between linens and towels. They are tedious to make and require real patience to finish but they last for years. It's fun to have a pomander party. With a group all doing the same thing the work goes faster. It is also interesting work for invalids and they make charming gifts.

The ingredients are simple. You will need:

a pretty apple or
a small fine-skinned orange
a big box of cloves—long perfect ones
a ribbon for a bow
a sheet of cellophane

Note: For an orange pomander, add two teaspoonfuls of powdered orrisroot and powdered cinnamon.

Wash the fruit carefully. Wipe apples with an oiled cloth. Next, starting at the stem end, add row after row of cloves, putting them as close together as you can until the fruit is completely covered. Let stand until all the juice is dried. Wrap in cellophane until seasoned and ready for use. Then tie a bow of red or green ribbon to the stem.

An orange is handled in the same way, although you may find it easier if you use a pin to prick the skin before inserting the cloves. When it is full of cloves roll the orange in orrisroot and cinnamon. Wrap and let stand two weeks, dust off powder, and tie it up with ribbon as you would a package, with a loop to hang it.

FLOWERING QUINCE

A famous landscape gardener uses the fruit of flowering quince for pomanders. They have a delightful lemony aroma. These can be studded with several cloves and rolled in orrisroot. Put them in gauze bags and place in linen closets and drawers. This is as easy a process as can be imagined, but in most gardens quinces are left to rot or for the rabbits to eat.

3 ❦ *About the Kitchen*

15 How to Plan a Kitchen

A kitchen may be the heart of the house but it is also the work center. Four hours a day is about the minimum time that can be spent in the kitchen, cooking and cleaning up after three meals. This adds up to 28 hours a week, 126 hours a month, and 1,512 hours a year. No extra time is allowed in this figure for special meals such as Thanksgiving and Christmas. Menus for such festive occasions may require three, four, or more hours to prepare.

Faced with these pyramiding hours, the place to tackle the care and upkeep of a kitchen is in its basic organization and equipment. Efficient arrangement of major and minor appliances and adequate storage result in many hours and much energy saved. Four hours spent reorganizing a kitchen could save 50 to 75 hours a year.

Too many architects and builders, and even women who should know better, have a false idea about what constitutes a modern kitchen. If it looks handsome and has cabinet-lined walls they think it is good. As a result most kitchens, new and old as well as those still in blueprint form, are not as efficient as they could be. The fact that a kitchen is a show place and is linked in color and decoration with the family room or back terrace, or that it shares the period feeling of the rest of the house, does not make it efficient.

All of this is fine; it helps us whistle while we work. But efficiency in the placing of appliances and cupboards should not be sacrificed to decoration. Since the kitchen is a work space, a scientific approach should be taken toward the location of storage, equipment, and work counters.

Kitchen planning is a complicated business even for experts. The cost of installing equipment is also somewhat stratospheric. If by chance you are to have a new kitchen, study plans, look at new equipment, make a scrapbook of these, and play with the idea for a year. Then you will know what you want before you approach an architect or a kitchen planner.

Getting breakfast is a trial to a great many women. As one woman said, "There is always so much confusion. The toast burns, the coffee pot boils over, and the eggs are ready before the orange juice is squeezed." By analyzing every step of breakfast preparation this woman now confesses she can save fifteen minutes and the whole procedure is more or less peaceful. A time-and-motion study will help analyze kitchen procedures. Select a simple operation such as making coffee.

The steps are these:

1. Make the coffee as you always do. When you start, write down the time. Then get the coffeepot. Where do you keep it? Go to the sink; measure the water. Where is the coffee kept? How do you measure it into the pot? Where is the measure kept? Now put the coffee on the range or if you use an electric coffee maker, plug it in. How long did it take you? Perhaps only a few minutes. But a few minutes lost on every operation means hours lost in a week.
2. Next rearrange the coffee-making equipment to save steps. Move the coffeepot to a shelf near the sink and place the coffee can beside it. Keep a short-handled coffee measure in the coffee can. If you usually use four tablespoons of coffee, try to find a one-fourth cup measure (four tablespoons) so that one movement will produce the correct amount of coffee. With a measuring cup fill the coffeepot with water. Note on the side of the pot how full it is. It should not be necessary to measure the water in the future.
3. Now make another pot of coffee. Time yourself and concentrate on economy of motions. Go to the sink, reach for the coffeepot, fill it directly from the tap with the right amount of water, add coffee, apply heat to the coffeepot. Compare the time with that for the original operation.
4. Finally consider major changes such as (a) using an automatic coffee maker plugged in near the sink; (b) changing to instant coffee—though for some people this is heresy; (c) enlisting another pair of hands to make the coffee. Even if you still use ground coffee, regularly, have instant coffee on the shelf for emergencies.

The coffeepot problem is a simple one. Try another time-and-motion study that is more involved. To make such studies of every operation in the kitchen would be an eight-hour-a-day project for twelve months. Fortunately, the stop watch has already been held on most of them from making an angel cake to washing the dinner dishes. Here are some of the ideas resulting from such studies:

Use a table with rollers as an additional work table in the kitchen.

Place a serving table in the dining room close to the kitchen door.

Use more trays for setting table, clearing table, and serving.

X Separate glasses and dishes used daily from others; keep most frequently used items within arm's reach of the sink.

Rearrange kitchen cupboards, putting pots and pans used most frequently where they are most easily reached. Those used only occasionally may be stored in a separate closet.

Store pot lids and pot lifters and skillets by range and other equipment where it is first used.

THREE WORK CENTERS

Kitchen activities can be divided into the following:

meal planning and marketing
food storage
food preparation
table setting and serving
cleaning up after meals
storage of dishes and pots
overall kitchen cleaning

Each of these operations centers around a major appliance. But work counter and storage facilities for tools and supplies are needed for most efficient use of each appliance. A clear understanding of the work of the three centers gives a good start toward basic efficiency.

1. *Refrigerator-preparation center.* In a recent time-and-motion study made by a manufacturer of kitchen appliances the operations involved in the preparation of eighty-four meals were charted. It was found that the refrigerator and the preparation center beside it were used more than any other combination of equipment. The chart below shows where the work needed to prepare the eighty-four meals was done.

Location	*Number of Operations*
Refrigerator and preparation counter	2,806
Sink and drainboards or counters by sink	1,057
Range and serving counter	801

By actual count more steps can be saved by having a work counter (a minimum of thirty-six inches long) beside the refrigerator than by any other combination of appliances and work surfaces. The refrigerator should open toward the work counter. Without a step, raw foods can be transferred from cold storage to work counter. Dry staples are stored in cupboards above the counter and pots, pans, casseroles, and salad bowls below, so that no rushing around is required to collect the wherewithal to mix a cake, prepare a roast for the oven, or make a salad.

For maximum efficiency the following tools and staples should be stored at the preparation counter.

DEVICES ON COUNTER FOR READY USE

mixer and blender
serving trays
cutting board
sugar and flour canisters

CUTLERY IN DRAWER OR HANGING AT BACK OF COUNTER

pastry blender
egg beater
cookie and biscuit cutters
knives (paring, slicing, chopping)
graters, scissors
can and bottle openers
spatula
spoons (measuring, mixing, wooden)

DRAWER AND CABINET BELOW COUNTER

cake, muffin, pie pans
cookie sheet
casseroles, custard cups
salad bowls
flour sifter and rolling pin
salad, dessert molds
plastic bags and foil for refrigerator freezer

CABINET ABOVE COUNTER

mixing bowls
measuring cups

DRY STAPLES

spices and salad herbs
vinegar
cornstarch
nuts
salt and pepper
baking powder and soda
cream of tartar
raisins
paprika
chocolate bits

2. *Sink-dishwasher center.* Since water is needed at both preparation counter and range, the sink should be placed between them. The greatest abomination is a sink with only one drainboard or counter. It makes dishwashing a most difficult operation. Without question there should be an eighteen-inch counter or drain on each side of the sink well. The ideal sink-dishwasher center includes:

sink, two-well preferred
electric waste disposer
two counters or drains
storage above and below
automatic dishwasher
drawer and door storage
good lighting

If there is no dishwasher, a double-well sink with a spray device is a convenience.

If an automatic waste disposer is out of the question, a garbage can under the sink is standard equipment. Also have a wastebasket. In one kitchen that is full of special gadgets there is a metal-lined shoot to the basement under the sink for disposing of paper.

The following small appliances and staples should be stored at the sink-dishwasher. Several items have duplicates at the preparation counter. If the counters are side by side, as they should be, the cutlery drawer may be shared, thus making duplication unnecessary.

HAVE EASILY AVAILABLE AT SINK

soap and detergent
metal cleaner and silver polish
cleaning sponge
soap pads
scouring powder
nylon scrubber
paper towels

IN DRAWERS

paring knives, butcher knife
vegetable brush
hand towels and dishcloths
plate scraper
chopping board
rubber gloves

IN CUPBOARDS

coffee maker
strainers and colander
double boiler and saucepans
dishes and glassware

3. *Range-serving center.* If any piece of equipment has to stand against a wall by itself, the range is the one to isolate. It is possible to manage without an auxiliary counter for serving with a flat-topped range and/or a wheel table.

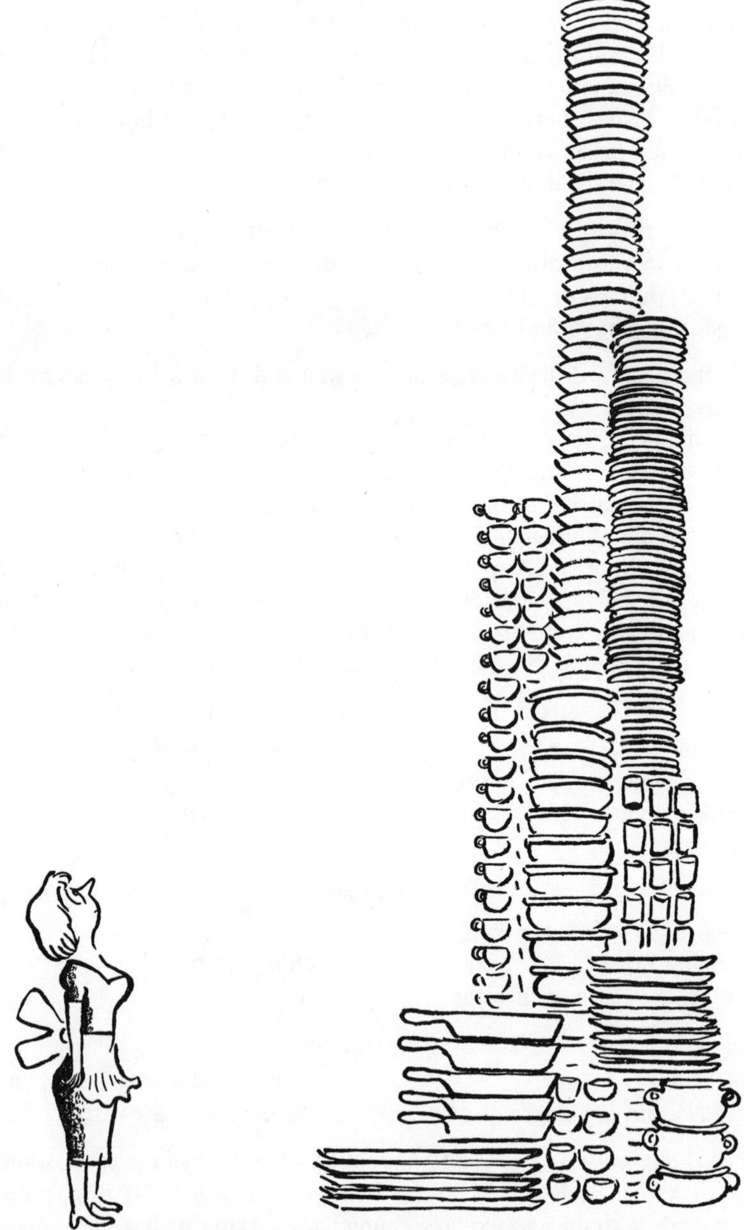

. . . when married five years, you have washed 135,000 dishes

The ideal plan includes a range, a serving counter, and a pot cupboard as well as shelf storage near the range. A great many steps are saved by duplicating seasonings and cutlery at the range center. Also think through every operation and store at the center all equipment and supplies which are first used there.

STORE NEAR RANGE

toaster	electric broiler
waffle iron	electric coffee maker

CANISTERS

flour	sugar
salt	pepper

SEASONINGS

herbs	bouillon cubes
meat sauces	gravy mixes

BEVERAGES AND CEREALS

tea	chocolate
cocoa	cereals
coffee	crackers

TOOLS

spatula	pancake turner
egg poacher	forks and tongs
stirring spoons	cooking thermometers
ladles	paring knives

UTENSILS

frying pans	saucepans and lids
soup kettles	teapot
serving dishes	trays and wire racks
platters	pot lifters
vegetable dishes	potato masher, rotary beater
dinner plates	

ARRANGEMENT OF THE THREE CENTERS

An understanding of the use of the three centers is the first step in kitchen planning. The second step is the actual arrangement and selection of the equipment of the three centers.

The ideal kitchen or rather the most efficient plan is to place the three centers around the sides of a room or space in an unbroken U shape. The refrigerator center is located on one side. The sink is located on the end wall and the range comes to rest opposite the refrigerator. The three major appliances are linked continuously with cabinets twenty-four inches deep, having counters and twelve-inch-deep wall cupboards above.

The width of the floor space between the arms of the U should vary with the number of people who use the kitchen and the number of people who are served. A good minimum work area for one or two workers is eight by ten feet. For several workers and a larger family the work area could be increased to ten by twelve feet.

In a U-shaped kitchen a dining area may be developed against the wall opposite the sink.

An L-shaped kitchen, though not quite as efficient, is equally popular and makes possible a more generous dining area in the corner opposite the L. In this type of kitchen two centers may be on one arm and the third center on the other.

Still another plan is referred to as the parallel wall plan. For many small kitchens this arrangement works out nicely and sometimes the two walls are only an arm's length apart so that you can sit on a stool in the middle and almost touch all points. The refrigerator and preparation center are located on one side and the sink and range opposite.

Endless variations are possible using these three basic plans. Doors and windows may interrupt the smooth flow of cabinets around the room, but nothing should interrupt the sequence of equipment. Rooms which are too large may be reduced by introducing a peninsula or island arrangement. A peninsula can be made by placing the range and/or cabinets at right angles to the wall so that they jut into the room, thus reducing the work area. A snack bar or serving counter may be located behind the range, thus creating an area for laundry equipment or a breakfast table. In an island plan one work unit is completely free standing.

Storage analysis. It is clear from reviewing the lists of required equipment that a lot of storage in the right place is a part of kitchen planning. Storage requirements are usually calculated in relation to the normal occupancy of the house or by the number of bedrooms.

In planning a kitchen, place doors at least thirty inches from corners of a room so that storage units can fit into the corners. Since splash backs on counters are three to eight inches high and counters are thirty-six inches from the floor, windows in the work area should be placed at least eight inches above the counters or forty-four inches from the floor.

Wall-cabinet storage space. This refers to the twelve-inch-deep cabinets placed above the counter surfaces. Six square feet of shelf space should be allowed for each normal occupant of the house, plus an additional twelve square feet for entertaining and accumulation.

As a rule, a space of fifteen inches is allowed between the counter and the wall cabinets. If you are under five feet four inches, allow only twelve inches between counter and wall cabinets and you will be able to reach three shelves. Above one twenty-four-inch counter install shelves only six inches wide. Use this counter for small appliances, such as coffee makers and blenders that may be more than twelve inches high.

Base-cabinet storage. This refers to the twenty-four-inch-deep cabinets beneath the counters. Base cabinets occupy all of the space beneath upper wall cabinets not occupied by the range, refrigerator, dishwasher, and laundry equipment. Special features which add to their convenience are revolving shelves in hard-to-reach corner units, cutlery drawers, slide-out cutting boards, a file compartment for large platters and trays.

Pantry. A major kitchen necessity today is a pantry, preferably a walk-in closet lined with shelves. If space is lacking for this, twelve-inch shelves behind double doors is a satisfactory substitute. The contents are visible and it is possible to allow greater space between shelves for oversize packages and equipment. Ideally pantries are located in the kitchen, but any space in the service area may be used.

Broom closet. It is convenient to have a broom closet and mop closet right in the kitchen area. The space should include shelves for the many special cleaners used today, as well as the usual cleaning equipment. If the walls and doors are lined with peg board, there may also be space for a basic repair kit, including hammers, screwdrivers, pliers, nails, and tacks.

OTHER CONVENIENCES

Ventilating fan. For eliminating odors a hood over the range or a fan is desirable.

Electric clock. A wall clock is convenient and inexpensive to install.

Radio. A radio or television in the kitchen leaves no excuse for not proceeding with housework during a program you want to see or hear.

Convenience outlets. Install a double outlet at each counter and one or more near the dining area, or better still use a continuous outlet strip or a special appliance center above the preparation counter or by the range center. The latter consists of four regular convenience outlets, each with a circuit breaker and timer.

Intercom systems and telephones also are often installed in kitchens. Women who have them say they reduce running around the house, up and down stairs, 50 percent.

Light. Plenty of light makes the hand quicker and all jobs easier. Never neglect this point. One young couple, after working in their remodeled kitchen until midnight, wrote, "We adore the beautiful lighting in our new kitchen. Believe it or not, Dick and I canned fruit last night until midnight without getting tired. We really think it was because we had plenty of light."

MAJOR APPLIANCES

The range, refrigerator, and dishwasher are the heart of the kitchen. The difficulty is that most women do not take the time or trouble to learn the full possibilities of these modern marvels.

If you are buying appliances weigh your needs, shop carefully, and get the type that will serve you best. Arrange for a demonstration. Get all of the literature available. Understand the appliance and keep the book of instructions.

See that the appliance is properly installed on a level floor. Keep it clean and operate it according to directions, and the number of years of good service it will give without the need for resorting to the service man is remarkable. Buy not only a well-known brand, but also from an established store that will stand behind its merchandise and service it.

The range. Consider whether you want a built-in unit with wall oven and surface units countersunk, an eye-level oven, or two ovens, or a free-standing range, complete in itself. Check on the broiler. Is it easy to use and to care for? Is the oven easy to clean? There are self-cleaning ovens, ovens with teflon-coated linings, and others with walls which can be removed for cleaning. Do you want four or six surface units? Would you use a well cooker or a built-in griddle if you had them? Would a heat-control surface unit with a timer be useful? Do you want a window in the oven door? Of course the extras all add to the cost of the range.

Another decision to make is the type of fuel, electricity or gas. Do some research on both fuels, consider the advantages and disadvantages of both before you decide.

The refrigerator. The new refrigerators are a joy and by careful shopping you can find one that exactly suits the needs of your family.

For most households the largest size that will fit into the kitchen as well as the budget is the best. In considering size, cost of operation must be considered as well as original cost. If you do not own a separate freezer, your new refrigerator should have a freezer compartment for the joy of it and to avoid feeling underprivileged. Moreover, a frost-free refrigerator is worth the extra cost. This advance is another step in freedom from bondage, which started when the electric refrigerator eliminated the water pan under the ice box.

Frost-free refrigerators are priced higher and may cost twice as much to operate as models that have to be defrosted. However, a frost-free refrigerator section with a manually defrosted freezer compartment costs considerably less to operate than a frost-free refrigerator-freezer.

Lack of frosting is made possible by a fan which circulates air out of the refrigerator and freezer onto coils at the back. The coils pick up the frost and the condensation then flows to the lower part of the refrigerator, where heat from the compressor dissipates it.

Another tempting but not so important extra in a refrigerator is an automatic ice maker, which is needed only by a family that uses quantities of ice cubes. This extra will include not only original cost but added operation cost, as well as an installation charge since it must be connected with the plumbing.

The dishwasher. In today's household dishwashers are fast becoming a necessity. There are free-standing and portable models as well as under-counter models connected to water, drain, and electric lines.

The capacity of a dishwasher is usually keyed to a standard place setting. For a large family, the dishes may be washed after each meal but for a small family, once-a-day washing is common. The dishes are loaded in the washer after each meal but washing is delayed until washer is full.

Waste disposer. Almost all building codes now permit the use of an electric waste disposer. It may be a part of a combination sink-dishwasher unit or may be installed in most standard sinks. It may share the dishwasher drain or have a separate line.

Used properly, it will save many steps and solve the problem of coping with kitchen waste. A garbage disposer does not handle paper, glass jars, cans, or large bones; it can dispose of all other kitchen refuse.

SMALL APPLIANCES

Space for storing small electric appliances should have special attention. An automatic blender has become almost a necessity. Other appliances such as an electric casserole, skillet, and rotisserie can improve the efficiency of a kitchen. However, it is expensive to buy small appliances that are never used, so buy only those which fit into your food preparation and serving pattern.

POTS, PANS, AND CUTLERY

A good housewares department is as exciting as a circus. The sideshows may include Danish casseroles, French lettuce baskets, Swedish cutlery, and colorful American pottery and plastics. Today cooking equipment can be as handsome as it is efficient and have an international flavor. Buy each piece with care. Consider what it will do, how often it will be used, and where it can be stored. Good pots and pans will last for years and handling them can give real pleasure.

Pots, pans, casseroles, and mixing bowls are available in a variety of materials.

Stainless steel. An ideal material for pots, it is easy to clean, is light weight, durable, and resists corrosion, pitting, and staining.

Aluminum-clad stainless steel. This combination of metals gives rapid heat distribution, provides even heat, reduces hot spots, and is easy to clean.

Copper-core stainless steel. The copper layer is sandwiched between two layers of stainless steel. This combination has good heat conductivity.

Copper-clad stainless steel. Especially good for low-heat cooking, reduces hot spots. Copper bottoms are decorative but require care.

Copper. Must have lining of tin or stainless steel for use in cooking; good heat conductor. Old pieces make interesting kitchen decoration.

Stamped aluminum. Second to copper in heat conductivity, lightweight, low priced. Dents, loses its shape, seldom well styled.

Cast aluminum. Heavy weight, durable, holds the heat better than stamped aluminum. Colored exteriors have eye appeal.

Cast iron. Durable construction, holds heat best of all metals, recommended for slow, even cooking, low priced, often seen in old-fashioned kitchens. Used for popover pans, griddles, and frying pans.

Porcelain enamel on steel. Nonporous and easy to clean, even heat distribution. Comes in a variety of colors and decorations. As it may chip and craze, avoid rapid temperature changes. Use for acid foods.

Porcelain enamel on cast iron. Heavier than porcelainized steel, more durable, higher priced, easy to clean, holds heat, well styled. Cook, serve, and store food in same dish.

Glass. Casseroles, pie pans, and custard pans are oven-proof. Specially processed glass can be used for range-top cooking. Moderately priced. Good for baking, serving, and storing.

Glass-ceramic. Dense, not clear like glass, is both oven and flame resistant, holds heat, is easy to clean, can be taken from the freezer and put in the oven without danger of crazing or cracking.

It is hard to imagine a well-equipped kitchen without several of these materials represented.

When buying pots and pans, know the size of the heating units on your range. For greatest efficiency the pots should always cover the units completely. On electric ranges, especially, select utensils with flat bottoms and straight or curved sides rather than sloping sides to avoid loss of heat. All pots should have tightly fitting lids and easy-to-grasp handles, and be easy to clean.

Use medium-weight utensils that are quick conductors of heat for quick cooking and heavier cast aluminum and iron for slow, long-cooking processes. The latter will not develop hot spots, are less likely to burn food, and prevent drying out and scorching. If you are careless and frequently burn foods, you may want to pay extra for pots with one of the nonstick finishes.

Nonstick finishes. To buy or not to buy nonstick finishes for pots and pans is a question of price. When they are finally perfected, these easy-to-clean finishes may be worth the greatly increased cost. Until that day it is important to know exactly what you are buying.

Teflon is the best-known nonstick process, but there are others. Wayne-clad, Descoflon (English), Colorcast (Irish), and Halon. There are two kinds of nonstick finishes. One is a superficial finish like paint; the other is referred to usually as a "hardlock" process and is guaranteed not to peel, flake, chip, wear, or wash off. For the latter, a steel-hard porous metal is impregnated with Teflon or similar material, then they are permanently fused with high heat.

The secret of all nonstick materials is a durable, glass-smooth, slippery surface. With most nonstick finishes you can cook without fats, but a little fat in the pan improves flavor and makes foods with high sugar content, like muffins, much easier to handle. Always season a nonstick utensil the first time you use it by wiping it with a cloth saturated with salad oil. Read all labels and instructions before using. Then, after several days of use, read them again; you may find details you missed on the first reading.

Contrary to common belief, food will burn in coated pans; in fact lower heat is recommended to prevent burns, even though burns clean easily. Stains are common. These can be removed with a solution made of two tablespoons of baking soda, one cup of liquid household bleach, and a cup of water. Put the solution in the stained utensil, boil for five to ten minutes, wash thoroughly, dry, and rub with salad oil. If this process is used too often the surface of the coating may be damaged.

Use wooden spoons for stirring. Scraping with sharp-edged tools can scratch the surface. The damage is aesthetic rather than functional.

EATING AREA

No kitchen is complete without a place for a dining table and chairs. Whenever I visit a house with a kitchen too small for even a snack bar, there are complaints about it.

Statistics show that 85 percent of the families in this country eat one or more meals in the kitchen area every day and 50 percent eat all but an occasional company or holiday meal in the kitchen or family room. To maintain standards and the amenities of meal service, the kitchen-dining area should be made as attractive as possible, having, perhaps, big windows, a bay arrangement, or even a fireplace.

16 How to Use a Kitchen

Even an ideal kitchen, equipped with all the latest gadgets arranged for maximum efficiency won't run itself. It still requires a guiding hand and good management. Many things can be done in a kitchen, but the main business is preparing three meals a day.

Dealing with food takes more hours each day and each week than any other household activity. There are two approaches. One is to hate it, resent it, and make short shrift of meals. The other way is to enjoy it, have fun at it, and create dreamy dishes to delight the family.

Many creative jobs have been taken out of the house, but cooking remains. If you have the right point of view, cooking can be an exciting adventure, that will last a lifetime. Everything that concerns food can be a pleasure, from collecting the raw materials to their final appearance at the table.

To get satisfaction out of cooking, know-how is necessary. Show me the woman who doesn't like to cook and you have shown me the woman who doesn't cook well. To be a good cook means study, observation, and practice. But once you have acquired a sure touch you are an artist. You have an accomplishment to be proud of and one that will give pleasure to others.

Cooking is comparable to composing music or painting. A good concert is a symphony of sound and may be stimulating or soothing. A good casserole is a symphony of flavors and can smooth troubled brows. A delicious angel-food cake pleases the eye and stimulates the palate.

Good cooking stimulates good conversation. It adds to the pleasure of travel. It is linked to an understanding of dinnerware, service, and table setting. It inspires the acquisition of a special library of books about food as well as scrapbooks. It is considered smart in sophisticated circles to be a gourmet, and after a hard day cooking can be as relaxing as reading a murder mystery.

Start studying, practicing, composing in the kitchen and before you know it you will be fascinated. Shun the marshmallow-whipped-cream school of cooking as a good decorator avoids insipid pink and blue. Learn to use herbs, a touch of wine, a bit of garlic. Pick up ideas for combinations, for garnishes and seasoning in restaurants, in books, on trips.

. . . create dreamy dishes

Acquire interesting table props. Don't select flower-dabbled, sentimental sets of dishes, but rather clean, simple china and crystal, or hearty, bold pottery, and don't overlook a plastic service if the children help with the dishes.

Collect interesting salad and dessert plates. Have some fine linens but don't fail to get some raffia, split-bamboo, or even plastic mats for practical purposes. Don't overlook centerpieces. Acquire an assortment of flower and fruit containers but also consider a covered tureen or two for use when flowers are not to be had. Candles and holders for them should be a part of your table inventory. Silver, of course, is important; its sparkle and sheen are a part of any well-laid table. But you may also want a set of stainless steel for kitchen meals and barbecues.

Really work at this food thing, develop a cultivated taste, and you'll love it. What better defense have you against the inevitable hours you will have to spend in the kitchen? Love it and grin at the hours. Hate it and glower at them. Take your choice!

THE NEEDED SEVEN

If you include in your menus a wide variety of interesting foods that are varied in texture, color, and flavor, and your family enjoys gathering together at mealtime, nine times out of ten nutrition will take care of itself. Nevertheless, if you are responsible for a family's food and you haven't read a book on nutrition, set about doing it immediately. The public library in your town will offer a selection of books which will supply the serious side of meal planning. Instead of fun, excitement, and adventure, nutrition books present food in terms of teeth, skin, hair, bones, blood, and vitality.

There are seven kinds of food needed in the daily diet; these supply not only the primary food substances—carbohydrates, proteins, fats, inorganic salts, and water, but they also supply accessory or additional factors called vitamins, which promote necessary chemical reactions in the body. The needed seven are:

1. Leafy, green, and yellow vegetables for inorganic salts and vitamins A, C, and E.
2. Citrus fruit, tomatoes, raw cabbage for vitamins A, C, and B complex.
3. Potatoes and other vegetables and fruit for carbohydrates, minerals, and vitamin C.
4. Milk, cheese, and ice cream for proteins, inorganic salts, and vitamins A and D.
5. Meat, poultry, fish, eggs, and dried beans, peas, and nuts for proteins, fats and vitamins A and B.
6. Breads, flour, and cereals, whole grain or enriched, for carbohydrates, minerals, and vitamin B complex.
7. Butter, fortified margarine, and salad oils for fat and vitamin A.

Avoid fad diets; don't serve the family food because it's good for them. Serve these seven foods attractively and your family will respond. When you first think in these terms it may seem like a puzzle to include a representative of all seven foods every day, but soon the seven will appear almost automatically in well-rounded menus.

MARKET PRELIMINARIES

Today the shelves of a store are our principal source for food. Seldom do we go to the garden and pick fruit, gather vegetables, slide eggs from under a hen, cast for fish, or dig for clams. Food production is a specialized field and most of us live miles from the source of supply. The compensation lies in the great variety of foods from around the world that are available to us. It's nice to know these foods exist, even if your family menus will never equal the one served to the Explorers Club at the Biltmore Hotel where the hors d'oeuvres included jellied cherry blossoms, sea urchin paste, lily bulbs sukoshi, rooster comb au vin, lava worm glacé, ants takusan, baby snakes blanche, pickled whale skin—and so on.

Nevertheless the products on the shelves of a big food market are almost as exciting and as representative of the world as the United Nations and are a lot more harmonious. Curry from India snuggles down comfortably with shrimp from Louisiana and olive oil from Spain. Coconuts from the Pacific islands smile blandly at tea from Formosa and dates from Iraq.

Be careful, though, when you are shopping. There are whimsey and mystery on those shelves, too. Read the small type on labels and you may discover that the Swiss cheese is from Wisconsin, not Switzerland. The Long Island ducks may have first seen the light of day in Connecticut. The Idaho potatoes may have been hoed in Alabama.

See food for what it is and marketing can be as exciting as going to a movie. It's worthwhile to squeeze the maximum adventure and entertainment out of marketing, because, after all, your weekly shopping bill runs to a fairly handsome figure. If marketing is done intelligently the results benefit your family's health and conserve your financial resources. Done with imagination and forethought marketing is the first step in the construction of interesting and nutritious meals.

In one household I'm familiar with, it is standard practice to make up the week's menus after the Saturday marketing. These menus are made by the man of the family, who was formerly a restaurant manager. The meals in that family are never flurried and the makings are always on hand.

Usually, planning menus before shopping is recommended, especially if you have an enormous family to feed or are planning very special guests or holiday meals. But it is seldom necessary to make exact menus from soup to dessert, and studies show that few women accomplish this dream.

One study made by a magazine showed that the great majority of women when asked the question, "What are you going to have for dinner tonight?" answered, "I don't know." Food specialists were horrified at this apparent lack of planning. Offhand it does seem somewhat careless. But if you have done a good job of food shopping the makings for several dinners are always in the kitchen. Often in my own household there may be no more than thirty minutes between the time a menu is conceived and when it is served, though the rough idea may have been running around in my head for several days.

Such last-minute planning is possible only when there is a large and well-stocked larder. There must be a balanced assortment of foods in the refrigerator or frozen-food compartment and on the shelves. To maintain such a stock requires experience and knowledge.

Even though you may not plan definite menus before marketing, there is homework to do. Check over the food supply, list all items that are low. Study food advertisements in the paper to get an idea of weekly prices. If there is a food page or column in the local paper, it may list vegetables and meats which are in good supply. If your store sends out weekly lists of specials, check off items worth stocking up. Perhaps there is a special on stewing lamb and you decide to get some. Check through the ingredients used in ragouts and stews in several cookbooks or service magazines. Look for interesting variations. Then add any special ingredients that may be required to the market list.

Whenever possible, buy your principal food supply on weekends when most stores run specials. In my area the specials are on Thursday, Friday, and Saturday. Food advertisements are plentiful in the Wednesday-night papers. This argues for Thursday and Friday shopping, after the announcements are out and before the crowd appears. Supermarkets report that the real crush doesn't arrive until Saturday afternoon.

A well-planned weekly supply of groceries may not have to be supplemented more than once during the week. Women who run to the market every day are time wasters. An exception must be made of the poor dears who cook in a kitchenette on two burners. They hardly have space to store a pound of bacon, to say nothing of a whole ham.

The problem of small kitchens with inadequate storage is being partly met by prepared mixes. The ingredients for an apple pie: shortening, flour, sugar, and apples could take up to a whole shelf in the cupboard. Compare their bulk with the tiny, two-by-four package which contains the complete makings for an apple pie. When the pie goes in the oven, the shelf is clear. Then there is gingerbread. It requires flour and sugar, ginger, baking powder or soda, sour milk, and a messy can of molasses. Forget all that. Buy a small package of mix and you are just forty-five minutes away from the rich fragrance of gingerbread ready to serve, and the cupboard shelf is empty.

Old-fashioned cooks have a way of looking down their noses at

. . . shop once a week

these mixes. As a matter of fact I came slowly to them. But now I think they are a wonderful modern invention. Mixes of all kinds belong on your kitchen shelf with other staples. It's wise to try new brands as they come out to see which you like best.

Pantry supplies. Staples on your shelves should be checked each week. My inventory looks like a young grocery store.

DRY STAPLES

crackers	mixes:
assorted cereals	biscuit
macaroni and spaghetti	pancake
rice, polished and wild	gingerbread
breakfast cereals, assorted	pastry
dried beans, peas, lentils	devil's-food cake
flour, cake, and bread	white cake
tapioca	chocolate frosting
cornstarch	muffins
baking powder	popovers
soda	cornbread

CANNED, DRIED, OR FROZEN FOODS

soups:	vegetables:
tomato	tomatoes
mushroom	mushrooms
black bean	corn, peas and beets
chicken and rice	beanhole baked beans
split pea	mashed, cubed, and scalloped potatoes
consommé madrilène	
gravy mixes	
New England clam chowder	

Fish: red sockeye salmon, minced clams, smoked herring, crab, tuna, lobster, shrimp
Meats: corned beef, dried beef
Fruit juices: grapefruit, prune, lemon, tomato, orange
Fruits: pears, figs, apricots, black cherries
Jellies, jams, and marmalades
Pickles and relishes

SEASONINGS

Salts: plain, celery, onion, garlic
Sugar: granulated, confectioner's, light brown

Pepper: peppercorns, black, cayenne, paprika
Spices: cinnamon, nutmeg, mustard, cloves
Extracts: vanilla, lemon, almond
Herbs: rosemary, marjoram, basil, thyme, dill
Sauces: Worcestershire, Kitchen Bouquet, chile, catsup
Bouillon cubes or essence of beef and chicken
Powders: chili, curry, mustard

MISCELLANEOUS

salad oils	raisins and currants
shortening	cocoa and chocolate
vinegars	shelled nuts in tins
tea	chocolate bits
coffee, regular and instant	cooking sherry
powdered milk	peanut butter

With this assortment in the cupboard and meats in the freezer, a meal can be expanded to include six extra people at a moment's notice. If your weekly shopping runs short there is always a meal waiting on the shelf. The truth is such meals can be delicious and inexpensive. On a cold Saturday night mushroom soup from a can, baked beans reheated in a bean pot with an onion and an apple and a dash of this and that, cole slaw, and a fruit tart can add up to a great success. A meal can be made of a large bowl of clam chowder or black bean soup, a big mixed green salad, and a hearty dessert. For an unexpected late supper there are scrambled eggs and a tin of smoked herring. The canned chicken soup with rice will be the base of endless soups of your own contriving. The shrimp and crab are first-course accessories for company meals and for curry or other specialties of the house.

AT THE MARKET

Forearmed as you are with your list, price information, and ideas for next week's meals, you are ready to forge ahead getting supplies which fit into the seven classifications of food needed every day. Buy by weight and for flavor, and buy things in season. In the late spring, stock up on close-outs at special prices. Just before the tomato crop comes in, canned tomatoes will go on sale. Canned asparagus may be closed out in May and canned salmon may be on sale in July. Stock up on these specials. Play the market like a stockbroker. Buy just enough for your needs in a falling market. Stock up on canned and frozen foods when prices are low against a rising market. Such buying isn't just a game; it has a salutary effect on the food budget and adds to the importance of your job.

In a sense buying is as much of an art as cooking. A knowledgeable buyer who watches weights, is familiar with prices, and takes advantage of all of the specials, close-outs, and refunds can save hundreds of dollars a year.

Almost any day you can save 40 percent on day-old baked goods, which could mount up to $25 or $30 a year for a family of four. On baskets of slightly damaged canned goods savings may be 50 percent. Moreover, some bargains may be special treats which ordinarily might not be included in your marketing budget. Weekend specials may be worth picking up at several stores.

When a new packaged food is introduced, coupons for cash refunds are offered in local papers. If it is an item your family likes, send in the coupon. Over a year the cash refunds and the percentage saving on such acquisitions can be worthwhile. Other ways to save are:

Buy in quantity.
Use fresh foods in season.
Use your freezer to take advantage of meat bargains.
Know the different cuts of meat and the grading system.
Buy fish late Saturday afternoon to benefit from price cuts.
Look for meat bargains after 6 P.M.
Buy medium-sized eggs rather than small or large ones as they offer the greatest saving.
Make powdered milk a family habit; in time the children prefer it.
Substitute margarine for butter, chuck for T-bone steak, and fish, bean, or egg dishes for red meat. The price differences in a year for a family of four could be $100.
Try the gourmet trick of growing a few herbs in pots for salads. Try parsley, chives, and celeriac. When you have extra parsley, dry it in a very slow oven and store in a plastic bag or glass jar.
When checking prices, consider both quantity and quality.

Get the habit of figuring in percentage savings on purchases. Set yourself a goal; keep a notebook of your weekly savings and you will be amazed to see how the dollars and cents pile up.

Convenience foods are expensive. If you are on a real economy binge, forgo mixes, grate your own cheese, make your own pancakes, and dry your own onions. Time savers are a joy but they do cost more.

Briefly then, for marketing:

Plan in advance but not necessarily in terms of specific menus.
Maintain a reserve supply of staples.
Know food values.
Read labels, keep informed.
Be familiar with weights and measures.
Check bills and packages to avoid errors.
Know prices, speculate on fluctuations.

STORAGE

Actual marketing is exciting. The tough part is storing a big weekly food supply properly. Sometimes I despair when I see it piled up on the kitchen counter. I yearn for the big old pantry at home, or better still a walk-in freezer. However, when the problem is systematically attacked, it's amazing how much even a small kitchen will absorb. But the truth is few women rate high on food storage.

Surveys show that refrigerators are messy with old leftovers and uncovered dishes as well as items that don't belong there at all. There is a tendency to overcrowd refrigerators and thus reduce their efficiency.

Tackle food storage seriously. First put frozen foods and dairy products away. Milk, cream, butter, cottage cheese, and other dairy products are placed at the top of the refrigerator in spaces provided for them. Wipe off milk bottles and caps before storing. Keep butter in a covered dish or special compartment as protection from odors. Eggs are best stored in plastic or wire racks (or in the place provided on the refrigerator door), big ends up, small ends down. The paper cartons they arrive in will absorb odors and transfer them to the eggs. Ice cream, of course, goes into the freezer.

Fruits are next on the list for disposal. First fill the fruit drawer.

Oranges and grapefruit do not have to be covered if used in a reasonable length of time. Berries mold if covered. Cut fruit should be wrapped in foil before returning to a refrigerator, and cut-up sweetened pineapple, strawberries, and other fruit should be in a covered container. Bananas should not be refrigerated; the skins turn black.

Wash all vegetables and drain several hours before storing. Put all green leafy vegetables in the crisping pan. Carrots, radishes, turnips, and beets should have tops removed and be washed before being stored in plastic bags if crisping pans are full.

Staples and seasonings do not require refrigeration. Dried fruits—apricots prunes, and figs—go on a cupboard shelf. Potatoes, onions, and bananas go into ventilated bins. Vinegar and canned goods are not refrigerated. Bread keeps longer in the refrigerator if there's room for it. A tin box is the alternate storage spot.

Variety meats, such as liver and kidneys, ground meats, chicken, and fish should be unwrapped and stored in the meat compartment and held for not more than twenty-four hours. Roasts, steaks, and chops may be stored uncooked for three or four days. Luncheon meats, frankfurters, and link sausage may also be kept for about a week; this also applies to cured meats, bacon, and ham. If meats are to be held for a longer time, they should be put in the freezer compartment, broken down into meal-sized packages.

Variety meats and fish should not be held more than three or four months even in the freezer. Meat such as beef can be held longer.

Keep brown sugar and confectioners' sugar in the freezer to prevent lumping. Bread, cakes, and pies may be frozen. Crackers and potato chips will stay crisp in humid weather and shelled nuts will keep fresh for a year. Leftovers can be frozen for later use. Frozen fruits, fresh juices, and applesauce served partially thawed are a new taste treat.

This is not a cookbook, but it is impossible to step out of the picture with all of that food on the shelves and in your refrigerator without saying more about it. Your marketing has covered the first two steps in meal planning. You have the food and you have the seven types needed every day for good nutrition. The trick now is to combine foods in interesting menus which taste good, look good, and are easy to prepare.

Taste good. If you have been preparing meals for many years and have been doing it thoughtfully, you already have a long list of foods that taste good together. Such natural combinations are the secret of menu planning. There are endless combinations:

Lamb, mint sauce, new peas, and potatoes
Salmon, with cucumbers in sour cream
Baked beans with cole slaw
Fried chicken, mashed potatoes, and gravy
Lamb chops and mixed green salad
Spareribs and sauerkraut
Pork and apples
Ham and scalloped potatoes

As a first and a last course with fish, something tart, like tomato bouillon and lemon pie are pleasant. Mushroom soup or fruit cup are sympathetic with lamb or beef and any dessert you please. An apple dessert may be delicious with spareribs, and what could be better than a blueberry roly-poly or cherries jubilee with ham or zabaglione with veal scaloppine.

Make notes on combinations you see in magazines or restaurant menus and when visiting. In no time you will develop unusual arrangements of food which will be more mouth watering than the traditional food combinations listed.

Look good. It's true that taste isn't everything and neither are looks, but together they make an unforgettable team. For looks consider both color and texture. Picture a plate of mashed potatoes, boiled halibut, and cauliflower. Ugh, who wants to eat such a white, bland meal? Compare the color and texture appeal of halibut with tomato sauce, baked potatoes, and broccoli. Now visualize pink salmon, orange carrots, and red beets. Leave the salmon on the plate but substitute rice and spinach souffle.

As you collect your combinations note texture, color, and garnish. A dash of paprika or bits of green pepper sprinkled on top of boiled or mashed potatoes can change the appearance of a whole plate. A few shavings of toasted almonds and pitted grapes will give texture to filet of sole. White dumplings make a brown stew exciting. Red tomatoes turn spaghetti into a feast. A slice of hard-cooked egg and a slice of lemon put appeal into black bean soup, and a toasted cheese crust on onion soup puts it in a class far beyond mere nourishment.

Easy to prepare. Unless you are a most unusual and remarkable cook with four or six hands instead of the usual two, don't include more than one fussy or complicated dish in each meal. For instance, nights when you are having a one-dish meal which will look after itself, make a pie too. If you are making an elaborate soup which requires last-minute mixing with an egg, don't have hollandaise sause for asparagus, or broiled chops. If a fussy dish is indicated, select one that requires no last-minute treatment. Reduce last-minute congestion and you will be poised when you sit down and meals can be served on time.

It's also good technique to:

Plan complete oven meals.
Plan complete broiler meals.
Gauge meals by the mouthful, avoid leftovers.
Use leftovers attractively.
Never waste even a crust of bread.
Shred outside leaves of cabbage, celery, and lettuce for soup.
Strive for variety, don't get in a rut.

It is possible to store in a fourteen-cubic-foot refrigerator makings for twenty big meals, but if you are feeding a family of more than four the dream and aspiration of your life should be a larger refrigerator with a frozen-food compartment. There is no other easy way of keeping ample food supplies on hand unless you have an old-fashioned root room, a smokehouse, a flock of chickens, and a garden at your back door.

Handy suggestions

Keep a supply of minced onions in the freezer for hamburgers.

Cook lamb for stew the day before using. When cooked, separate lamb from liquid, refrigerate both. The next day all the fat can be lifted off easily.

Dredge chicken by shaking in a paper bag with flour and seasonings.

Make extra quantities of long-process dishes, freeze part for a second meal.

For easy peeling, douse tomatoes and peaches in boiling water for a minute and the skins will slide off.

Transfer frozen orange juice to refrigerator the night before it is needed. In the morning it can be mixed with water more easily.

Add minced onions and cottage cheese to mashed potatoes for a flavor treat.

Vary menus with a variety of breads: whole wheat, French, Italian, rye, protein, raisin, and pumpernickel. Then there are rolls and biscuits of all kinds, cooked, uncooked, and ready to serve.

Split the stems of asparagus up to but not through the tip for quicker cooking.

Halve artichokes, trim off tips of leaves, and remove choke for quicker cooking. Serve one-half to each person.

Roll bananas in melted chocolate chips, let harden, wrap in foil, and freeze.

Remove crusts from slices of bread, cut each slice into four parts. Delicately brown in a warm oven until crisp as croutons. Roll in a 50-50 mixture of peanut butter and olive oil. Finish with a coat of prepared bread crumbs and herbs. Serve with asparagus.

How about shopping for cookbooks until you have a dozen on a special shelf? They make wonderful bedtime reading.

17 How to Clean a Kitchen

Let's face it, kitchen cleaning isn't fun. On the other hand to stand back and look at a kitchen all neat and clean is a rewarding experience and seemingly one that many women seldom enjoy. A report on a survey of 173,000 dwellings suggests that housewives, not children, do the most damage to a home!

Kitchen neglect is the chief problem. Range burners are clogged and cracked. Cooking units and drip pans are soiled and rusted. Floors are filmed with ground-in dirt. Windowsills are scarred with wet jars and bottles. Refrigerators are damaged due to neglect. Plumbing fixtures are past repair, because of the use of abrasives, and drains are never cleaned. In addition, walls and cabinets are scarred with grease spots and cabinet interiors are cluttered with seldom-used utensils and dirt.

This is only part of the general indictment, but it is enough to make any woman who enjoys her home think twice about her kitchen standards. Some publicists like to suggest that with the latest equipment and cleaners a kitchen will clean itself. But it isn't so. No tornado, white knight, or magic fluid out of a bottle has ever cleaned a kitchen; the real job still takes two hands self-operated. As in the care of the rest of the house there are daily, weekly, and seasonal tasks. In the kitchen the daily stint well done reduces weekly and seasonal chores.

The daily operation is based on cleaning up after meals. There may be several contingencies as well as philosophies involved in this simple problem. The contingencies concern the size of the family, how well you keep things washed up as you cook, and whether or not you have an automatic dishwasher.

With a very large family there is no escape from a thorough kitchen cleanup after each meal. But if you have a small family there is a growing tendency to wash dishes once a day. Pots should be washed immediately after using. But neatly stacked dishes on the counter are no problem, and if you are one of the lucky ones who has a dishwasher, they are completely out of sight and mind.

DAILY KITCHEN ROUTINE

The kitchen should be made orderly and all foods put away immediately after each meal. During meal preparation utensils can be rinsed and tucked into the dishwasher or washed and set aside to drain dry. After using shortenings and seasonings return them to the shelf at once. Such orderly procedure may sound like an invasion of personal freedom but the opposite is true. Once the habit is acquired neatness is involuntary and saves not minutes but hours each month.

Develop the habit of working on a utility tray or on newspapers spread on counters. After each messy job the tray can be cleaned or the newspapers rolled up and discarded. Wipe up spills and spots on counters and range as they occur. Crushed newspaper is excellent for wiping grease from a range top and oven. When frying anything that might spatter grease put an aluminum-foil cuff around the top of the skillet and newspapers on the floor. Vinyl melts at 350 degrees and hot grease will damage it.

Follow this simple procedure daily:

Keep all packaged food stored neatly.
Keep all perishable food properly refrigerated.
Wash all dishes and pots and pans.
Wipe off counters, range, and refrigerator.
Put all waste food through the food disposer or remove it from the kitchen along with cans and bottles.
Scrub sink, clean drain.
Sweep floor after each meal or a minimum of once daily.

WEEKLY KITCHEN ROUTINE

To the fastidious housekeeper weekly cleaning means wiping down the whole kitchen—walls, cabinets, woodwork, doors, light fixtures, and floors. Actually the thoroughness of the weekly performance may depend on the daily care and your personal inclination. In any case, once a week:

Defrost refrigerator, wipe off shelves, clean trays and all bins.

The only exception is if you have a frost-free model.

Scald garbage can and air unless you have a waste disposer.

Scrub range top, wipe out the oven and broiler as well as the drip pan under the burners.

Scrub and use liquid or self-polishing wax on the floor. Use a spray that cleans as it waxes.

Wipe off cabinet fronts.

Wash and air cake and bread boxes.

Polish silver if you feel like it.

Wash and wax windowsills.

Wipe around door knobs and light switches.

Check corners for cobwebs.

SEASONAL KITCHEN ROUTINE

Empty cupboards, doing one at a time. Sort out contents. Discard empty bottles and jars. Wash inside and outside of cupboards and put in fresh plastic-coated shelf papers. If you own the house, it is worthwhile to have a layer of thin linoleum as shelf protection. If metal shelves are not covered, they will rust eventually.

Clean and wash windows, shades or blinds, and curtains. Curtains may need more frequent washing; the steam from the sink makes them limp. Many women use only Venetian blinds, slat shades, or plastic-coated blinds at kitchen windows in order to reduce care and give maximum visibility. Wash light fixtures. Empty broom and storage closets, clean, and refill.

HOW TO CARE FOR KITCHEN EQUIPMENT

One of the greatest advances in refrigerators is the frost-free type which requires no defrosting. However, don't assume that such refrigerators do not have to be cleaned and kept in an orderly way if odors are to be avoided. Bits of food left too long, decaying fruit and vegetables, spilled food which is not wiped up develop gases and odors, so that even though the weekly defrosting is not needed an occasional review of the contents of the refrigerator is needed. Bins must be washed and shelves wiped off. At least four times a year the ventilating panel at the bottom of the refrigerator should be removed and the inside cleaned.

If your refrigerator is not frost-free, don't put off defrosting too long. Frost keeps a refrigerator from functioning normally. It raises the temperature of the box; it does not lower it. When frost is one-fourth of an inch thick it's time to defrost. Defrosting usually is needed once a week; in winter once in two weeks may be enough.

There is some variation in the handling of refrigerators so by all means keep and follow the manufacturer's directions. If your refrigerator has a frozen-food compartment with a separate door, only the main part of the refrigerator should be defrosted. For defrosting of the standard automatic refrigerator:

Empty meat tray and remove lid. Replace under evaporator.
Turn cold control over to defrost or disconnect refrigerator.
Remove all frozen food, pile together, and insulate by covering with newspapers.
Remove all ice trays and all food from refrigerator.

METHOD 1

Let door of refrigerator stand open. In about forty-five minutes or an hour ice will have softened enough to slide off evaporator. Do not jab with a knife or sharp instrument.

METHOD 2

Fill ice trays with hot, not boiling, water and replace in evaporator. The frost will melt in ten or fifteen minutes. Since the hot water heats up the evaporator there is a tendency for frost to form more rapidly when this method is used.

After frost is removed by Method 1 or Method 2, wash inside of refrigerator with baking soda or borax and water (one teaspoon of soda or one tablespoon of borax to one quart of water) and rinse. Wipe shelves, sides, bottom, and evaporator; dry thoroughly. A plastic sponge helps. Finish with a dry cloth.

Clean oil, grease, or spilled food from rubber gasket which seals the door. Avoid touching gasket with hands. Oil causes it to deteriorate.

Set cold control for normal operation.

Return all food to box. Wash and refill hydrators, reload frozen food and ice-cube trays.

Gas and electric ranges. Have you ever heard a landlord, real-estate agent, or kitchen-equipment repairman discuss the average housekeeper's standard of cleanliness? Their denunciations are devastating. They contend that women let ranges go year in and year out and never wash them inside or out. A gas burner can almost fill up with coffee grounds and other grime, but as long as there is a flicker of flame it doesn't get washed. Repairmen say that the inside of ovens are often cased with an inch of carbon that can be removed by merely scraping.

Why all this negligence? Perhaps because a range will work even if it is dirty, whereas a refrigerator will just give up if the frost gets too thick. Constant upkeep is the easiest way to handle a range. Give it a weekly once-over when you defrost the refrigerator and rate as a good housekeeper with your repairman. Wipe off spilled and spattered food when it occurs; don't let it harden on the range.

The exterior of most cabinet ranges as well as most oven doors of built-in ranges are of porcelain enamel. Wash with a warm damp cloth or sponge. A detergent may be used, but avoid using gritty cleaners or steel wool, which will scratch the surface. Stains may be removed with laundry bleach.

Before using a range, season by wiping any chrome parts with a little salad oil (pure, unsalted oil). Spread evenly over the surface then wipe off excess with a dry cloth or soft paper towel. Polish occasionally with a silicone-base polish.

To make cleaning easier most newer ranges can be easily taken apart. Each surface heating unit of an electric range has four parts which can be removed for cleaning. The heating unit itself is self-cleaning; if spills are not wiped off, they will burn off. The chrome rings around most surface units should be wiped off after each use to keep spilled food from burning on them. Once a week, the chrome ring, the rack inside, and the reflector should be removed and burned-on particles scoured off. While these parts are out wipe off the drip shelf beneath the unit.

If your range has a griddle allow it to cool completely before washing. Never use an abrasive cleanser, rinse well, and dry.

Ovens are the hardest to clean but those with removable Teflon walls simplify the problem and, of course, the ovens which are self-cleaning under extreme heat are the final answer.

The broiler-grill should be washed after each use to keep grease from burning on it. Drain all fat into can, wipe with paper before immersing it in water. An aluminum-foil lining in the pan reduces the problem.

Clean oven when it is cool. Remove oven shelves and other removable parts. Lift bake unit to clean oven bottom. Broiler unit may also be released to clean top of oven. Do not disturb the oven thermostat or other oven parts. If a spray cleaner is used protect thermostat bulb and windings with aluminum foil. Other cleaners are wiped on and allowed to remain for thirty minutes before washing out with steel wool, detergent, and a rinse. Instructions for use of special oven cleaners should be followed carefully as they are very powerful and may burn holes in anything they touch. Rubber gloves should be used always.

Ammonia is the base of most cleaners; it is less dangerous to use and acts in much the same way. Use one cup of water and one-half cup of ammonia, put in a cold oven for thirty minutes, then wash out soil and grime. Undiluted ammonia can also be sprinkled on newspapers, and left in a closed, cold oven overnight. To clean, open the door, let out all fumes, then scour and rinse out. It's a mean job.

The removable Teflon walls are easier to clean if cleaning is done frequently. Look forward to a self-cleaning oven.

Gas ranges are cleaned in much the same way. Surface units should be kept clean, grids free, and the drip pan free of spills. Oven cleaning is similar.

If you have a range with a hood without a vent or a range with an exhaust filter system, under normal usage the charcoal grease filter should be replaced once a year. Use a vacuum-cleaner nozzle to clean an exhaust fan over a range.

Don't slam range doors or put heavy weights on them. For best performance be sure that the range sits level.

HOW TO WASH DISHES

This is a job from which there is no escape. If dishes have to be done, in my opinion the sooner the job is finished the better. Do it before you stop to do anything else. Even on party nights I believe in doing dishes before going to bed. It offers a wonderful opportunity for hashing over the evening, and a clean kitchen for breakfast is a joy.

I still feel resentful about one dishwashing episode in my life. It was during my stay in the home-economics practice cottage at college. We entertained our escorts for the Oval Club College dance for dinner at the practice cottage. In my exuberance about getting dishes washed I herded the boys out to the kitchen after dinner to help with the cleanup before going on to the dance. I got any number of demerits for having guests help with the dishes! Since I have negative conditioning on the subject of guests' helping with the dishes I'll make no ruling on the subject. If your guests help, it is your own responsibility and you will receive any demerits being passed out.

. . . even on party nights, wash the dishes before going to bed

If you want to be impressed with the never-endingness of dishwashing, look at these figures compiled by a manufacturer of dishwashers:

When married one year you have washed 18,000 dirty dishes; it took 10 days.
When married five years you have washed 135,000 dirty dishes; it took 75 days.

When married ten years you have washed 300,000 dirty dishes; it took 175 days.
When married 25 years you have washed 850,000 dirty dishes; it took 450 days.
When married 50 years you have washed 1,500,000 dirty dishes; it took 835 days.

Hand method of washing dishes. Equipment required: two-bowl sink with two counters and a dish drainer or one-bowl sink with two counters and a dish drainer and perhaps a dishpan, a variety of sponges, scouring pads, and plastic mops. Experiment until you find what suits you best.

General directions. Work from left to right unless you are left-handed; if you are, work in reverse.

Scrape, rinse, and stack all dishes in orderly fashion before washing.

Learn to use both hands as you work.

Detergents are especially desirable for china and glass in hard-water areas.

After washing rinse with very hot water, a minimum of 150 degrees Fahrenheit from tap or boiling from the tea kettle.

Wash pots, pans, and bowls used in preparation of meal as you finish using them.

Wash glasses first, then silverware, next plates and cups. Cooking utensils come last if they were not washed when they were emptied.

If you are doing the dishes alone, wipe glasses and silverware before washing the rest. Stack dishes in rack, and air dry before putting away.

Do not let wood, plastic, or bone-handled knives soak in water.

For fine dishes put a folded dishcloth in the bottom of sink or pan before washing. Also put a cloth under the rack to avoid nicks.

Give special attention to coffee pots and coffee cups. See that they are scrupulously clean without trace of detergent remaining if you have any sentiments about good coffee.

Special care of china and pottery. Don't let foodstuffs dry on dishes. Scrape off with a finger or a rubber or plastic scraper, and rinse. Use cold water on egg dishes before dipping into hot water. Egg can be loosened by rubbing with salt. Acids such as lemon and vinegar injure the glaze; rinse off at once. Tea and coffee may leave a stain in cups. Lipstick is another offender. A drop or two of laundry bleach or a cleaner that is also a solvent will remove it.

Dishes which are embossed (a raised pattern on the surface) may have to be cleaned with a brush to keep the shadow of dust out of the crevices. If you are not a fussy housekeeper, it is advisable to select dishes with a smooth surface.

Use water softener in hard-water territory to prevent a film on dishes.

In putting plates away don't put too many in one pile or you may find the bottom ones broken when you lift them up. Put circles of thick paper or felt between very fine plates. Use wire plate racks to stand plates on crowded shelves; they are more economical of space and convenient for frequently used dishes. Put plastic caps over the stack of plates seldom used.

Never put china to warm in the oven when the heat is on. Heat oven and turn off heat before warming plates. Cold dishes put in oven may crack or develop a mesh of fine cracks in surface glaze.

Glassware. There are supposed to be unbreakable tumblers on the market, but in most households there are more casualties with glasses than any other tableware. The only preventive I know is to buy dozen or two-dozen lots of sturdy inexpensive tumblers or footed tumblers and then take the consequences. Life is too short to go around gnashing your teeth every time a glass breaks. Don't be careless, but smile when they break. This attitude may have developed from the fact that in my youth I was quite a glass breaker and there were frequent consequences! In my own household glasses may be broken with impunity.

Don't nest glasses; they stick. To separate, stand bottom one in warm water and put cold water in top one.

Never pour hot liquid into a glass without standing a silver spoon in the glass to take up the heat.

Rinse out milk, lemonade, and alcoholic beverages promptly.

Use a brush to clean cut, pressed, or engraved patterns in glass.

Don't use strong soap or a boiling rinse on gold-decorated glasses—the gold may wash away.

A dash of ammonia in water will clear the brown deposits from a vinegar cruet; let stand an hour before rinsing.

A dash of vinegar and baking soda will clear brown deposit from the refrigerator water bottle. In bad cases add some small shot or a spoonful of uncooked rice and shake hard.

Silverware. The more silverware is used the less polishing it requires. The surface on plated silver wears off but sterling is silver all the way through. It will not wear out, and the more it is used the handsomer it becomes and the less it will tarnish. But do not use silver, plated or sterling, in the kitchen for measuring or stirring. Through careless treatment it may become shabby, with bent tines on the forks and scarred surface.

Do not pry anything open with a silver knife or fork.

Do not dig or scrape a pan with a silver spoon.

Do not let silver stand overnight with food on it. Rinse after use and stand in cold water if it is not to be washed immediately. Wash in hot sudsy water. Rinse and dry at once. Do not store silver salt shakers with salt in them. Salt pits silver. Do not let rubber touch silver. Eggs, gas, and smoke are also enemies of silver.

Store seldom-used silver in treated tarnish-proof flannel or flannel-lined silver chests. Decorative pieces like candlesticks, which do not come in contact with food, may be lacquered for long-term protection. Specify whether you want a bright or mellow, antique look. Store flatware in a drawer or box lined with tarnish-treated cloth. Lay a cloth over each layer of silver.

Do not use aluminum plate method of cleaning on sterling or good plated ware. It gives a white finish and removes all shadow from pattern. Use a silver polish made by an established manufacturer. Never use an unknown polish made locally regardless of sales talk. Too many women have ruined their silver with such polishes. Never apply polish in circles. Use straight long strokes. The fine lines which develop from wear and constant stroking in one direction in time give a beautiful patina or velvety surface finish.

MACHINE METHOD OF WASHING DISHES

I have decided that dishwashers are a greater aid to a hostess than any other gadget in the house. Once a woman gets the hang of using one it's almost impossible for even an inquisitive guest to discover when the dishes are being done. Don't say that isn't terrific. But that isn't all; according to expert calculators, in one year a dishwasher will save 365 hours or the equivalent of 42 eight-hour days.

There are almost no tricks in using a dishwasher. Do the job several times following the manufacturer's booklet precisely; then just do it and the washer will do the rest. The methods will vary somewhat with each washer. For all washers:

Scrape the dishes carefully. Loosen egg dried on plates with salt. Wipe grease off with a paper towel or newspaper, use a stiff brush or a scouring pad on sticky food.

Load, putting plates, glasses, and silver in compartments planned for them. Alternate big and little plates; dinner plates, salad plates, dessert plates, so that the water sprays them all. Put the silver in the basket, handle down and blades, tines and spoon bowls up so that the water reaches soiled parts.

Load with cups, saucers, bread-and-butter plates, creamer and sugar bowl, and other small objects. Glasses are placed upside down.

Add the detergent recommended by the manufacturer. Close the door or lid. Turn the control. Automatically the dishes are washed and twice rinsed.

If the water is not a steam-making 150 degrees, the dishes will not dry evenly. If the water is hot, the silver, glass, and china will issue from the washer with a fine luster. You do have to put things away, unless they are left in the dishwasher until the next meal.

Do not wash the following in the dishwasher:

Fine china with overglaze decoration, antique china
China or glassware with platinum, silver, or gold bands
Hollow-handled, ivory, plastic, and pearl-handled flatware
Woodenware and pewter
Non-heat-resistant plastic containers
Rubber utensils, iron skillets, or knives with iron content. The high-water temperature removes the protective grease content.

Care of dishwashers. Since dishwashers are in frequent contact with detergents and hot water very little care is required. Clean out the drain occasionally. If drain is sluggish, fill dishwasher with required level of water. Add two cups of vinegar and run five minutes. Follow with two rinses. This will remove sediment left by minerals in water. An unusual noise may result from a poorly loaded basket. If dishes do not dry promptly, the temperature of the water is too low. It should be 140 to 150 degrees Fahrenheit.

Putting dishes away may not sound like an art or an achievement, but it is both and can help or hinder a cook. My sister feels so deeply about keeping dishes and kitchen shelves in exact orderly array that at one time she pasted labels on the edge of every shelf to indicate its contents so that maids in for the day had no excuse for not putting cups and saucers where they should be. Of course, exact placement can be carried too far, but reasonable order helps make the job easier and reduces wild last-minute searches.

CARE OF POTS AND PANS

If you enjoy cooking you will inevitably have attractive utensils. If they are cared for, not banged around and burned, they offer years of use and will often seem preferable to new ones.

Specialists in corrosive problems urge casual cleaning of cast iron. Vigorous scrubbing removes protective grease which has penetrated the pores and prevents rusting and sticking. If food burns in a pot, set it in a pan of cold water and remove the contents. This treatment is not recommended for a hot enamel pot, which could craze if set in cold water.

If food is stuck to an enamel or stainless-steel pot, soak overnight in cold water with a teaspoon of salt. Remove soil with a mild abrasive. If this fails, put two quarts of water in pan with a spoonful of washing soda or cream of tartar and bring to a boil.

Brownish stains on stainless steel indicate that too high heat has been used; mild scouring powder will remove it.

Never use in the oven covered pots and pans not designed for high heat; handles and top knobs may be plastic or wood and will be damaged by the heat.

Aluminum needs only soap and water and a little preventive care to keep it bright. When food is stuck to the pot, rub with fine steel wool, cleanser pads, or mild scouring powder. Discoloration caused by alkaline foods can be removed by cooking foods like tomatoes or rhubarb, or by boiling a weak vinegar solution. Rinse thoroughly and dry to prevent pitting.

Never let foods stand or soak in aluminum; it discolors and pits the finish. Never use soda, lye, ashes, ammonia, or strong alkalis on aluminum, and do not boil eggs in aluminum pots; it injures and darkens the surface.

If a cast-aluminum frying pan is given a thorough scouring, restore surface film by rubbing with olive oil, heat briefly, cool, wipe with a paper towel and store.

Steel and glass utensils are not affected by foods. Use bleach on enamel. Never use a scouring powder on chromium; polish with a soft cloth.

Copper may be cleaned with a solution of vinegar and salt but it is easier to use one of the many good copper polishes on the market.

Never soak woodenware or knives with wooden handles.

After stains and burns are removed pots and pans can also be put in the dishwasher.

SPECIAL PROBLEMS

Tea and coffee stains in china and pottery cups can be prevented if they are rinsed at once or left standing with water in them. Remove with a little household bleach or baking soda. Use baking soda, not bleach, on plastics.

In hard-water regions, china washed in a dishwasher may develop a cloudy look. If the film is caused by iron in the water, first wash dishes in usual manner with detergent, then wash them again with one-fourth teaspoon oxalic acid crystals in the water. Follow with another wash using detergent. Never use detergent with the acid.

Lime film from hard water is removed with vinegar. After first washing cycle, stop the machine, open the door, and add one pint of vinegar. Close the door, restart the machine, and allow to complete its cycle.

A film in the bottom of a double boiler or tea kettle due to minerals can be removed by adding two tablespoons of vinegar to the water and boiling for a few minutes.

Two teaspoons of cream of tartar to a quart of water will brighten aluminum.

To polish tines of silver forks thrust them down in a jar of silver polish and let stand for several minutes.

Wash and dry pewter by hand. Pewter left standing in water will tarnish. Use a silver or pewter polish on it. Never warm pewter serving dishes in the oven or let stand on top of range. It is a soft metal with no heat resistance.

DRAINS

There is a saying that civilization is keyed to plumbing, for without plumbing large cities could not be. Still the plumbing in the average house gets quite uncivilized treatment and the kitchen drain receives the least consideration.

The chief problems are excessive use of soaps and greases. One gauge of a good housekeeper is her handling of grease. If a trace of the fat in the frying pan or broiler gets into the sink drain, standards are slipping. Fats should be drained off into a disposable receptacle, and the pan wiped out with absorbent paper before it reaches the sink. After each meal remove bits of food from the drain and scour. If you have a waste disposer, follow the manufacturer's instructions to the letter.

Once a month a reliable drain cleaner should be used in all drains. Follow carefully the directions on the package. If the drain is clogged and drastic measures are needed, first try a so-called plumber's helper. This is a rubber suction pump on a stick. The rubber cup is placed over the drain and the stick is worked up and down. This may dislodge the block enough to let the water, standing in the sink, drain off. Follow with drain cleaner for a thorough washing out.

If the plumber's helper fails, dip out the water in the bowl and remove the strainer if possible. Put drain cleaner into drain. Let the cold water tap drip and leave standing several hours or overnight. If water boils up in sink it can be stopped by pouring in a half cup of cold water.

Caution: All drain cleaners are caustic. They will burn skin, clothing, and eyes. Do not bring in contact with metals. Measure with enamel or glass. Do not let drain cleaner come in contact with floors or work counters. Protect all linoleum, vinyl, chromium, and stainless steel near the sink before using plumber's helper on drains in which caustic has been placed. Splashing may result in damage.

If you can cope with really drastic action get a pail and put it under the trap under the sink. Unscrew the plug with a pair of heavy pliers or a monkey wrench. With a steel brush clean out the inside of the trap. Don't do this unless you are an adventurous soul or until you have watched a plumber do it. Then you know what you are letting yourself in for—and frankly it's a man's job.

18 How to Avoid Accidents

We all have a quaintly complacent attitude toward household accidents. It's a cross between "It couldn't happen to us" and "Accidents will happen."

The fact is no one is immune to accidents and the two most dangerous places in the whole country aside from the automobile are the kitchen and the bathroom. Accidents in the home are rated the number-two killer. Although home accidents are not the leading cause of death among children under fifteen, they are the major cause of nonfatal injuries.

In 1967 the U.S. Health Service estimated that among the home injuries to be expected would be the following:

100,000 hurt while mowing lawns
125,000 hurt in home workshops
125,000 serious burns
40,000 major cuts from walking through glass doors
100,000 maimed hands and fingers from washer-wringers

This is only a partial list. The American home accounts for over a million casualties annually, many of which could be prevented. The National Safety Council reports that one out of every six home accidents is the result of carelessness or disorder. It is time to start a family safety campaign to anticipate trouble and learn how to avoid accidents, or at least make them less lethal. It should be possible to stay home and still stay alive.

Falls account for about 19,500 deaths and about 2,600,000 injuries each year. The National Safety Council offers these tips: When you feel yourself falling, relax instead of stiffening up; it may make the difference between a blow to the ego and real injury. When falling backward try to turn your body so that you will land on a well-padded part; dropping backward in a straight sitting position can be hard on the spine; when falling forward, reach out with your arms, spread your fingers to distribute the area of contact and let your arms fold in toward your body as you roll to one side.

Many falls could be avoided if certain aspects of security were built into the home and grounds. Check these points: Are the steps and stairways well lighted; have they sturdy handrails? A star goes to carpeted stairs or those with sanded paint to reduce slipperiness.

How is the rug situation? Area and throw rugs should be anchored with a foam-rubber nonskid liner. Furniture in traffic lanes is a hazard and rocking chairs with ankle-high horns can cause bad falls. Is there a tool room or closet that is a booby trap where things fall off shelves and go bang when the door is opened? Is the swimming pool fenced in and are old wells blocked up? Have the terrace and entrance walk a nonskid surface when wet? Have all floor-to-ceiling windows been marked with masking tape so they can be seen? In some states it's the law.

Has the bathtub a grab bar? Incidentally don't mistake the soap dish or wash-cloth holder for a grab bar. Like tile they are held only with mastic, not with bolts, and a hard pull will dislodge them. Are bath tubs and showers equipped with nonskid mats? If there are young children, are there side rails on their beds and gates at top and bottom of stairways? Are low-hanging pipes or ducts over basement doors brightly painted so that six footers can duck and avoid them? Have all electric outlets been covered so that children will not be tempted to stick their fingers into them? Are you careful to see that wax is thoroughly rubbed into wood and vinyl floors?

More serious accidents may involve gas, electricity, fire, and water. Do all the adults in your household know where the main controls are for these basic utilities? Finding the control point is not a difficult matter if you have plenty of time, but when you are in a panic it may elude you and you may even delay an emergency repairman a few minutes. If there is a basement start your search there; otherwise head for the utility room.

For electricity the fuse box holds the answer. Each fuse should be clearly labeled and the master switch separately marked.

For gas you will find the cutoff where the pipe enters the house.

For water look near the water tank and trace the intake pipe. Paint the critical valves red for easy spotting.

Do you know where the safety switch for your furnace is located? Is your oil tank fitted with an antisiphoning device and automatic shut-offs? Your serviceman can tell you about them.

Keep firearms under lock and key. If they are merely hidden in a drawer or on a high closet shelf, children will find them. When children are eight or ten years old they should be given basic instructions on the use and handling of firearms as a protection against accidents.

Keep electricity and water widely separated in the bathroom. Don't ever touch an electric appliance when your hands are wet.

Be conscious of the fact that accidents don't happen; they are caused usually by carelessness, often from fatigue.

FIRES

Every minute of every day there is a new fire starting somewhere in the United States and a total of one thousand home fires every twenty-four hours. Children under five and people over sixty-five are the most frequent casualties. The annual total loss is almost $300 million. Most fires are the result of carelessness and lack of elementary precautions. Three out of four are caused by:

Careless use of matches and cigarettes
Sloppy housekeeping
Faulty heating equipment
Mishandling of gasoline and flammable fluids
Defective wiring and electrical equipment

Post the telephone number of the fire department so that the whole family knows where it is.

Matches and cigarettes. Matches mean death in the hands of children and careless users. It's a little silly to say it again, but don't leave matches where the kids can get them. Every year hundreds of children are burned to death because their parents left them alone a few minutes. Last year there were seventeen cases in which children were burned to death playing with matches when their parents were in the very next room.

One of the problems is the availability of matches. It is estimated that 850 million matches were used last year, over half of them for lighting cigarettes. The gesture is so natural that there is no consciousness of danger associated with it. Nevertheless, careless smoking and disposal of matches is one of the leading causes of home fires.

Smoking in bed, falling asleep watching TV with a cigarette in hand, leaving a burning cigarette or cigar on the edge of an ash tray, emptying a pipe or ash tray with live ashes into a waste basket are repeatedly the cause of home disasters.

Because of the extreme flammability of some synthetic fabrics there is agitation for expanding and strengthening the Flammable Fabrics Act.

Sloppy housekeeping. Grease-crusted broilers, ovens, and surface units of ranges cause thousands of fires every year. Accumulation of old newspapers, magazines, boxes and cartons, and a thousand odds and ends of trash which pile up in garages, attics, and closets are a perfect breeding place for fires. Even cobwebs are dangerous and should be cleaned out of attics at least every twelve months. Fire chiefs have a saying that a clean house seldom burns.

Outdoor rubbish, leaves, high grass, waste piles near the house are potential dangers. A spark from a chimney, a match from a passer-by can start a quickly spreading fire.

Heating equipment. Fireplaces, stoves, furnaces, chimneys, flues, pipes, and portable heaters are the source of fires. Never overheat them. If the ceiling or walls near them feel hot to the hand, it is a warning. Nothing flammable should be left within eighteen inches of a heat source.

Soot should be cleaned out of chimneys and flues periodically, cracks caulked, and rusted flashing at the roof line of chimneys replaced. Ashes from the fireplace should never be put into a cardboard carton. There still may be live coals twelve hours after the fire burns down. Fires have been caused by leaving mittens and socks to dry on a floor grate.

Is your oil burner approved by the Underwriters' Laboratories and is the oil tank fitted with an antisiphoning device and automatic shutoff? Are the basement and door of an attached garage metal sheathed?

Flammable fluids. A lighted match, a burning cigarette, a spark of any kind can cause an explosion and fire. Gasoline and other solvents used for dry cleaning, gasoline used in the lawn mower, benzine or naphtha used for spot remover can be dangerous and should not be stored or used in the kitchen with a pilot flame, in the basement with a furnace, in an attached garage, or in any closed space. These produce heavier-than-air vapors, which settle to the ground and follow air currents. If the fumes come in contact with a spark, they flash back to the source, even if it is several rooms away. A spark from stroking a cat's fur, from snapping on a light, from a fire burning in the fireplace, or from the friction of rubbing fabric can cause a fire.

If home dry-cleaning fluids are needed use nonflammable kinds. Check furniture polish, window cleaning fluids, and other household cleaners, and insist upon products labeled nonflammable. Oily cloths or mops from cleaning or painting should be stored outdoors or in a tightly closed metal can, for such treated cloths may build up enough heat to cause spontaneous combustion.

Defective electric equipment. Substandard appliances, old, defective wiring, frayed electric cords, overloaded circuits, cords running under rugs, and cords with broken or spliced wires are common causes of home fires.

If you have an old house, but have been adding more appliances year after year, you should have the wiring checked. Overloaded wiring can catch fire inside a wall or under a floor. Even a nail driven into a wall to hang a picture, if it contacts an electric wire, can cause a fire. Amateur wiring, including garden and Christmas lighting, are always suspect.

"Act of God fires," so labeled by insurance companies, are caused by lightning. The risk is greater than you think. It is estimated that some eighteen hundred thunderstorms are in progress over the earth's surface at any given time, and lightning strikes the earth's surface one hundred times a second. In the United States there are six hundred deaths and fifteen hundred injuries annually attributed to lightning.

During a thunderstorm do not use the telephone and stay away from radios, television sets, lamps, ranges, and refrigerators. Do not use plug-in electrical equipment such as hair dryers, electric tooth brushes, razors, or knives.

People struck by lightning carry no charge and can be handled safely. They will suffer severe electric shock or burns.

FIRE DRILLS

In case fire breaks out everyone in the family should know what to do. What happens in the first five minutes may save lives.

First call the fire department. Remember to give your address.

In the country if you have a cistern, pond, or swimming pool, keep access to it clear, and tell the fire fighters about it at once.

Don't underestimate fires which have just started. Keep your head and act quickly. If draperies catch fire from a burning candle, don't try to save them; tear them down and stamp on them, smother the flames. Small rugs, pillows, blankets, heavy wool coats are useful for this. Use the same procedure on a carpet which has caught fire from a spark from the fireplace.

If the source of the fire is in an appliance or wiring do not throw water on it. You could get a serious electric shock. Water is also hazardous in grease fires in the kitchen! It may spread the fire throughout the room. If the grease in the broiler catches on fire, cut off the air supply by throwing a small rug over it. Cover the first rug with a larger one. Another way to put out the fire is to throw a bag of flour, salt, or baking soda on the flames.

Fires that start at night may be serious before you are conscious of them. If your bedroom door is hot, don't open it, or the blast of heat on the other side could kill you. Open it gradually and close it after you. If there is smoke, tie a wet towel over your mouth and nose if possible and crawl along the floor. Don't jump except to avoid actual burning. Climb down, using knotted sheets if necessary.

Smoke inhalation is often more lethal than burns, especially in fires in upholstery or bedding. Smoldering textiles give off carbon monoxide, carbon dioxide, and hydrogen sulphide gases, which quickly produce unconsciousness and may cause death.

Many houses have fire detector systems, fire extinguishers, and sprinkler systems, but too often years go by and they are neither used nor checked, and when the emergency comes, are found defective. A reel of garden hose, placed near an outdoor faucet, is one of the most practical forms of extinguisher except for electrical, grease, or oil fires.

WATER FOR EMERGENCIES

If you are notified that your water supply will be turned off for any period of time, you will need to collect at least a half gallon of water a day for drinking purposes and for food preparation. For each child under three allow an additional two gallons for laundry and bathing. Store in plastic and glass bottles; use the bathtub for a reservoir.

POISONS WITHIN REACH

No one ever feeds a child poison! Nevertheless about a half-million children swallow poison every year. Toddlers are the most common victims. They are curious, everything looks interesting, and their mouths are their greatest sensation centers. Experts agree that 90 percent of all poisoning cases could be prevented if reasonable precautions were taken.

About half of all the poison cases involve medications; the other half are due to household or garden chemicals. There are more than 250,000 toxic products designed to make life easier; many of them are kept in the average house: bleach, ammonia, lye, insecticides, pesticides, detergents and other household cleaners, kerosene, gasoline, turpentine, furniture polish, lighter fluid, ink, crayons, insect poisons, bath oil, perfume, disinfectants like iodine, laxatives, vitamins, and all drugs. Oral contraceptives are the most recent addition to the list. Ordinary aspirin is probably the most common hazard although tranquilizers are also a growing menace to children.

Almost anything can be poisonous if taken in large enough doses. Andrew T. Weil of the Harvard Medical School has reported the case of an eight-year-old boy who died within twenty-four hours after eating nutmeg, the aromatic kitchen spice. It is a narcotic and the lad ate two whole nuts. Too much vitamin A or D can be poisonous. Many garden plants are poisonous if taken internally. These include yew berries, laurel leaves, poinsettias, jack-in-the-pulpits, foxgloves, horse chestnuts, and many more.

In cases of poisoning, speed is essential. If you know the antidote, use immediately and call a doctor, a hospital, pharmacist, the local Poison Control Center, or police rescue squad. While waiting keep the patient warm. Do not force liquids on unconscious persons and do not induce vomiting if the patient is having convulsions. Keep the container from which the poison was taken; try to estimate how much was consumed.

BURGLARS AND ROBBERS

Legally speaking burglaries take place when no one is home; housebreaking becomes robbery if someone is there and the penalties become more severe. Both types of crimes are on the increase in cities, suburbs, and even semi-rural areas. If criminals are determined, even a twenty-four-hour watchman won't keep them out, but you can arrange deterrents.

Thieves fall into three main categories, teen-agers who have been drinking and are out for kicks, dope users looking for anything they can turn into cash, and professional criminals, who may pose as service or delivery men.

Locks, lights, and alarms are the first line of defense. They may discourage housebreaking or give you time enough to notify the police.

Doors, windows, and locks. Dead bolts offer the most security, as snaplocks which lock merely when the door is closed can be opened in a few minutes with a thin strip of celluloid or flexible metal. To prevent this all entrance doors, front, rear, and side, should be equipped with dead bolts which are square at the end rather than beveled and are harder to force open. They can be added to any door. Doors with glass can be cut so that locks can be reached from the outside. Heavy, tempered glass cannot be cut and is harder to break.

Chain locks add extra security. They are designed primarily to safeguard occupants when they open doors to unknown callers. Some chain locks can be locked with a key. An intercom and a door peephole offer additional protection and are required by law in some cities.

Windows that can be reached from the outside should be kept locked and ladders or other equipment that would aid climbers should be kept out of sight. Even then there are the neighbor's ladder or the one the burglar himself supplied. If you live on the seventeenth floor of an apartment, don't decide your windows are inaccessible. Balconies and adjoining buildings or apartments may offer means of access. There are devices which will secure a window so that even if the pane is broken and the window unlatched it will not open beyond a certain point. Such locks may be a hazard in case of fire.

Lights and alarms. Flood lights controlled by a master switch may frighten intruders. Do not turn on lights indoors as they might warn the intruder that you know he is there. It is wiser to call the police quietly.

If you are away for the evening, two lights left on inside the house are greater protection than an outside light left on.

Police think well of burglar alarms. They rate highest the silent kind connected with police headquarters or a private agency. Even the seal of a protection agency in a window is a deterrent.

Local alarms that create a big noise, bells, or sirens are effective. Some work by radar, others by sonics. Such wiring is expensive and burglars have a way of picking the unprotected spots.

Barking dogs are useful, especially police dogs and Dobermans with professional training. Household pets are too often diverted with a dog biscuit or a bone.

Unoccupied houses. Before you go off on a trip check all doors and windows, including the basement, garage, and attic. Install a timing device which turns lights on and off. Notify local police of your absence. Stop delivery of milk, newspapers, mail. Arrange to have the grass cut regularly if you will be away for some time. Ask a neighbor or friend to keep an eye on the house and give the police his name. Don't mention your plans or schedule in any public place, a bar, the checkout counter of the supermarket, or to trades or service men.

Apartment houses. Summertime means vacation season and country weekends and it is the busiest season for the burglary division of the New York police. Many of the precautions taken by home owners are applicable for apartments. In addition to a light that goes on and off, a radio may be set to play at night.

Valuables should be stored during vacations in a safety deposit vault and extra locks put on closets.

Women known to be alone are often an invitation to burglars. They should never open the door to admit anyone until they know who it is. All service men should identify themselves and it is better not to let delivery boys inside the door. Once in they should not be left alone.

Increasingly, large city apartments are getting better protection in terms of guards at all doors, better lighting in public areas, closed-circuit television, supervision of elevators and halls. Tenants too need to cooperate. If you do not use your door peephole before you open your door, if you fail to report suspicious loiterers in or near the building, you are undercutting the efforts being made to protect you.

Inventories. Keep a list of all television sets, radios, stereos, watches, clocks, typewriters, and cameras, with serial numbers and other identifying marks. When stolen goods are recovered, unfortunately few people are able to supply positive identification.

19 How to Cope with Pests

When with superior attitude you condemn all insects to instant death you might as well know what you are up against. Insects are among the oldest species of life. They were the first living creatures to fly. Fossils of cockroaches probably twenty million years old have been found. At the present time the number of insects on earth is beyond computer calculation and is made up of more than one million known species, more than all other animal and plant species added together.

It has been estimated that the insect population found on one square mile equals the total human population of the entire world. Fortunately only a limited number of insect species favor living under the same roof with man.

Some people have the idea that if a house is spotless there will be no pests. In my opinion this is not entirely true. My experience, especially in the country, is that the war on pests must be year-round and relentless. Like the flowers and birds, certain pests time their arrival with the seasons; then they disappear until the next year at the same time.

Natural precautions are:

Store all food in tight containers or in the refrigerator.
Keep all refuse covered; dispose of it as quickly as possible.
Keep attic and basement clear of refuse.
Vacuum the cracks in floors, baseboards, and closets; don't let lint or cobwebs collect anywhere.

If you live in an apartment report to the superintendent or agent if you have the problem of pests. Regular visits of the exterminator can rid an apartment or house of both insects and rodents.

In the country don't use an open garbage dump. Bury or burn all refuse or use a metal container designed for food disposal. Locate and exterminate nests and travel routes of insects.

Great advances have been made in pest control. Unfortunately, pests seem to develop immunity to each new development. But new methods continue to appear. Sound is being increasingly used; rats are sent scampering by a high-frequency whine too shrill for human ears. Dogs are fed an anti-flea food which makes their blood unappetizing, and no doubt other out-of-this-world ideas are just around the corner.

Insecticides in common usage include Sevin, chlordane, lindane, pyrethrin, diazinon, or DDT; they are lethal to practically all insects and are used in a variety of forms for the control of pests in both house and garden. It may give you confidence to note that Ceylon's death rate was cut almost in half in seven years simply through the use of DDT in a battle against insects.

There are three basic methods of using insecticides:

Space or area sprays kill insects on contact.

Residual sprays are used as a deposit on window and door screens, woodwork, and even furniture, and may be effective for several weeks.

Powders can be sprinkled on surfaces and blown into crevices around baseboards.

All insecticides are toxic to humans and should be used with care; read the label carefully before using. If space or area sprays are used in a child's room, they must be confined to a mist in the air. Do not direct the spray at any object in the room, whether furniture or toys, for no residual deposit should be left on anything a child may touch or handle. Remove birds and fish bowls from room before spraying. Don't feed pet birds greens that have been sprayed. Insecticides should be kept out of the kitchen and away from children. If you have pets do not use powders and dusts (except flea powder). Liquid insecticides should never be sprayed near electrical outlets or exposed connections as short circuits may result. If the insecticide comes in contact with the skin, the contaminated area should be washed immediately with soap and water.

ANTS

There are eleven different species of ants that come indoors in the area of New Jersey where I live. Some wander around aimlessly; certain very small red ants appear only when the temperature is over

85 degrees. Ants range in size from microscopic to half an inch long. There are red and black varieties; some like sweets, others are attracted by meat, and some channel through wood and are a real problem in old houses.

Ants usually live in large colonies or nests. These should be destroyed. Jab a hole in the nest with a stick, pour in an ounce or two of nonflammable liquid spot remover and close the hole. The heavy vapor will drift through all of the tunnels. If the nest cannot be located, apply a 2 percent solution of chlordane with a brush to baseboards, refrigerator, sinks, tables, cabinets, wherever they appear.

For more complete information write for a leaflet "Ants in Home and Garden, How to Control Them" (No. a 1.77.23), price 10 cents (no stamps), Superintendent of Documents, Washington, D.C. 20402.

BEDBUGS

Bedbugs may be brought in on clothing or in old luggage or they may move in from the next apartment, but wherever they come from they cannot be tolerated. Evidence may be a crushed bug, a bloody streak, or a disagreeable odor. Clean entire room thoroughly. Then with a 5 percent residual solution spray both sides of mattress, the bedframe, around the baseboard, the cracks in the floor, all the furniture, behind the pictures and the interiors of all cupboards and closets. Close the room tightly and leave unopened for twenty-four hours. Inspect carefully. If there are any left, repeat the operation or, better still, call the exterminator.

CARPET BEETLES

These wool-loving beetles are running neck and neck with clothes moths as "fabric enemy number one." They do not restrict their activities to carpets; they prefer a balanced diet of all types of fabrics. They do steer clear of fairly new wool carpets, the majority of which are treated with chemicals which upset their stomachs. The easiest way to avoid them is to vacuum rugs thoroughly on top and underneath, behind, under, and around all furniture, including dark unused corners.

The carpet beetle, also called the buffalo moth, is a quarter-inch beetle. See "Moths" for complete treatment.

COCKROACHES

Cockroaches and water bugs antedate man's arrival on earth and are the largest and oldest order. The ravaging locusts of the Bible as well as katydids, crickets, and grasshoppers are their first cousins. They are tough. In the South and in apartments in big cities constant vigilance is necessary. They may be brought in on groceries, in the laundry, or come visiting along the water pipes from another apartment.

If you see a cockroach, act at once. Discard immediately all boxes and containers from food stores. Fill all cracks in walls, floors, and baseboards around plumbing fixtures and pipes with elastic caulking compound. Never leave food exposed on counters and clean crumbs and food particles from stoves, cabinets, floor, and sink drain. If the children eat snacks in their rooms, the crumbs, if left, may attract these insects.

Cockroaches have become somewhat immune to DDT, chlordane, dieldren and lindane. Insecticides containing organic phosphates such as malathion are considered more effective. Pyrethrins are also used. If a spray is used it must contact the body. If powder is used it should be blown into cracks and crevices and along baseboards, which are often their point of entry.

One young couple, spraying, squirting, and painting everything in sight, stayed up nights trying to locate the point of entry of cockroaches in their old house with no result. In desperation they rigged up a flash camera with an ultra-sensitive shutter trip which would go off at night after all was quiet. It worked; when the flash went off it showed the little so-and-so's rushing pell mell out of the electric clock on the wall. The slight warmth given off by the motor kept them cozy even in winter.

If cockroaches appear to have the upper hand and you haven't a trick flash camera at your command, call an exterminator. Select a name from the yellow pages of the phone book or write for advice to the National Pest Control Association.

On the day the exterminators come arrange a four- or five-hour jaunt or an overnight visit for children and pets.

FLEAS AND DOG LICE

Fleas and dog lice are problems, especially where cats and dogs are allowed the run of the house. Dust dogs and the places where they sleep with a pet powder containing 10 percent DDT. Don't use on cats as they will lick it off. Burn old bedding and spray new bedding with DDT. Spray rooms to height of four feet. Wash pets, including cats, with an insecticidal shampoo.

HOUSEFLIES

More than eighty thousand species of flies have been described and there are many varieties not yet recorded. Fortunately only a few kinds are serious household pests. Houseflies, fruit and vinegar flies, and bluebottle flies are the most frequent visitors. Houseflies can find enough food to live on almost anywhere because they need so little to survive. One thousand adult flies weigh less than an ounce.

With the new insecticides reasonable care inside and outside the house will keep them under control, even though one adult fly can lay as many as two thousand eggs in a twenty-four-hour period. Spray first with DDT. If it is not effective try one of the mixed sprays which contain methoxychlor methoxphenyl, trichlorethane, and other poisons. One is sure to be effective.

Spray garbage cans regularly. Use a residual spray on door and window screens around porches and terraces. Close doors and windows and fill a room with a good mist from an efficient sprayer. Leave room and keep closed for twenty minutes.

Flies around barns and outbuildings should also be controlled with residual sprays and insect powder on animals.

MOSQUITOES

To rid house of these annoying insects use method outlined for flies. Also see that there are no stagnant pools of water or buckets and tin cans holding water where insects are likely to breed. Use tight-fitting sixteen-mesh wire screens on doors and windows. Use DDT residual spray on all screens and pyrethrin sprays to gun down flying insects.

MOTHS

Moths live on a diet of wool, part wool fabrics, and fur. They favor soiled garments. All garments should be cleaned, aired, and pressed before storing, with special attention given to pockets, trouser cuffs, seams, and linings. Don't forget part-wool clothing, hats, mittens, mufflers.

Prepare closet or chest for storage by cleaning thoroughly with a vacuum before treating garments. If closet is suspect, fumigate with paradichlorobenzene crystals. Use a pound of crystals to an average closet. Either use the de-moth attachment of your vacuum cleaner, following directions given, or put crystals in a cheesecloth bag and hang high in the closet. Close door, stuff cracks, and leave for three or four days. Clothes may be left hanging in the closet during this time but don't crowd them. Air should be able to pass freely around them.

To mothproof clothes spray thoroughly until the fabric feels damp. Store in chest or moth-free closets. If closet storage is used, spray to a full mist once a week.

Wool upholstery, rugs, and draperies also require mothproofing. A cold-storage warehouse is insurance against moths, but if any other storage space is used, take utmost precautions. Have carpet professionally cleaned, mothproofed, and wrapped.

Furs are the real focus of moths, as this little verse suggests:

> The lowest kind of vermin
> And the one I most abhor
> Is the bug that ate my wife's mink
> When it was only half paid for.

Cold storage is best for furs. Furs used during the summer season should be aired and shaken frequently and kept in a chest or drawer well covered with a residual spray.

SILVERFISH

Silverfish are a great problem to libraries. They favor dark, damp, warm places and the starch used in book bindings. They do, however, feed on other starchy cotton and rayon fabrics. In an old house peeling wallpaper may be caused by insects eating the paste. Spray shelves, closets, walls, baseboard, and along wallpaper seams with a 5 percent residual spray. Sprinkle a 10 percent DDT powder on bookshelves.

SPIDERS

As long as spiders stay outdoors and build fascinating dew-spangled webs on my grapevine in the fall I rather like them, but they are undesirable around the house. Preventive measures include a clean house with walls and ceiling clear of webs, and doors and windows well screened to keep out the insects spiders prey upon. If spiders are seen around windows, ceiling, or baseboard use a DDT pyrethrin spray. Don't overlook the tracks of double-hung windows, cornices, and the backs of picture frames. Use the open nozzle of the vacuum cleaner to suck up the webs.

TERMITES

Termites, one of the worst of insect enemies, could be called the undercover agents of the insect world. Their objective is the house itself and they can undermine it while the occupants remain unaware of their presence.

There are both dry and damp wood termites which live and propagate in basements. They form channels on concrete but their goals are the floor joists, sub-floor, and other portions of the house.

There are three common signs of termite infestation. One is swarms of what appear to be flying ants, another is a shelter tube that looks like gray macaroni on the basement wall, and the third is a wooden beam or post that is as soft as butter when jabbed with a pocket knife.

Getting rid of termites is a difficult job. It begins with the use of wood preservatives. If you want to do the work yourself write to the Small Homes Council, University of Illinois, Urbana, Illinois 61803, for their seven-page booklet, "Termite Control," index number Fa.5.

EARWIGS

An earwig is a brownish insect about three-quarters of an inch long with a pair of pincers on its tail. They do not bite you or your pet but can become a nuisance if they decide to come indoors.

Usually earwigs prefer damp locations outdoors and it's best to keep them there. But if you see any indoors apply Sevin, chlordane, diazinon, or DDT in a barrier band extending about ten feet out from the foundation. Concentrate especially on porches and crawl spaces. Use a sprinkling can or garden spray to make the application.

WASPS, HORNETS, YELLOW JACKETS

Wasps are primarily a fall problem in the country. They have a tremendous urge to come indoors and usually manage to one way or another. Hornets and yellow jackets are less persistent about living under the same roof as humans. All three are useful as they destroy other insects. However, they sting humans too. The result is painful and to people with allergies dangerous to life.

Before cold weather comes find their nests and destroy them. Hornets and wasps make large globe-shaped gray nests in shrubbery and under eaves of houses. Yellow jackets nest in holes in the ground.

Tackle them on a cold night after dark as they are day workers. Use chlordane or DDT for control purposes. Spray high nests. Use dust in the holes in the ground and throw a shovelful of damp earth over entrance after the treatment. Don't try to remove hornets' nests until you are sure insects are dead. To be completely safe enclose nest in a cheesecloth bag before removing it.

Wasps, big black wood ants, and other insects sometimes gain entry in firewood. There is less danger if the fireplace wood is not brought into a heated room until it is needed; never pile it against the house.

If wood seems to be infested keep a push-button aerosol can handy for outdoor application—never direct it into the fireplace.

For more details an eight-page leaflet, "Wasps, How to Control Them," No. 365 of the United States Department of Agriculture (5 cents) may be obtained from the Superintendent of Documents, Washington, D.C. 20250.

MICE AND RATS

Mice can be kept under control with wooden traps. Use bacon or cheese pressed firmly into the tripper. After each mouse is caught, boil the trap or lightly singe it with a match to destroy the mouse odor. Incidentally, the newest traps are impregnated with the odor of burnt bacon and require no bait or processing.

When a house is left vacant in the winter place poison grain around freely to keep winter ravages under control. To confine the spread of seed put them in small aluminum-foil pie pans.

Call on a professional exterminator or consult your county agent if you have rats.

GROUND HOGS AND SKUNKS

If you live in the country some wild life around can afford entertainment and in the completely rustic setting of a summer camp may even be encouraged. But if you have a vegetable or flower garden, wildlife must go.

Ground hogs and skunks often make their homes under porches. They are not dangerous and at first it may seem amusing to have them, but that attitude won't last. From the ground hogs we nurtured for several years I learned that it was safe to eat nasturtium and phlox leaves, hollyhocks, and tulip leaves and many other floral delicacies; but I also learned that ground hogs multiply very rapidly and are intolerable.

After trying traps, poison bait, and physical destruction of their nest, my conclusion is that shooting is the only sure method of getting rid of these rodents.

SQUIRRELS

Squirrels can be very destructive. They frequent attics, and red squirrels have been known to gnaw almost through a beam. If they get into the rest of the house they will chew up anything available. In houses closed for the winter seal all openings in the eaves, the chimney tops, and other points of access. Sprinkle moth crystals liberally through the attic.

If you want more information about any of the pests listed or about other animals, insects, or birds who like living close to you, write the National Pest Control Association, Inc., 250 West Jersey Street, Elizabeth, New Jersey 07202. Also send for "Our Struggle Against Pests," Office of Information, U.S.A.S., Washington, D.C. 20250. Ask for PA-772.

4 *About the Laundry*

20 Fabric Facts

The key to washday success begins in the store at the time the garment or article is purchased. The fabric world is experiencing a revolution. Every few months a new fabric or new finish which aims at easing care (but often complicates it) is introduced. Changes are coming so rapidly that eventually, instead of marveling at wash-and-wear clothes, we will very likely accept without a murmur wear-and-discard clothes.

In the meantime, whether you are buying a carpet, sheets, or a snow suit, read the label before you make the purchase. If there is a term you don't understand, ask the salesman about it. By accident you may be dealing with a rarity these days, a salesman who knows about the product. The label or hang tag should list the fiber or fibers used, state the finish, and give other pertinent information related to the care of the fabric or garment. A statement of fiber content is required by law, but manufacturers do not have to give methods of washing or dry cleaning. However, the better fabric manufacturers volunteer this information.

Not so long ago fabrics were made of cotton, linen, silk, or wool. There were many weaves, weights, qualities, but today there are by one expert's count 242 different man-made fibers or modifications of these fibers on the market representing 16 generic types. The generic names sound more like something from the moon than a fabric you would find in today's homes. The fibers now in use carry such names as:

Acetate	Olefin
Acrylic	Polyester
Azlon	Rayon
Modacrylic	Saran
Nylon	Spandex
Nytril	Vinyon

In addition to the terms listed above, each manufacturer names the fibers he makes. Thus nylon may be referred to as Caprolan by

Allied Chemical, as Cumloft by Chemstrand, and Antron by Du Pont. Rayon may be referred to by any one of a hundred names, including Bemberg, Avisco, and Coloray.

Mills in turn may mix the fibers of two manufacturers to create blends for special texture and color effects. Thus, if Caprolan and Antron are woven together, then dyed, the Caprolan areas will be darker than the Antron areas, because, although they are both nylons, their chemical formula is slightly different and the Caprolan is more responsive to dyes. The new sheets of 50 percent Fortrel (a polyester) and 50 percent combed cotton stay fresh, crisp, and smooth night and day, washing after washing, and never need ironing.

Identifying fibers and finishes used for fabrics has become so complicated that even textile experts can no longer identify them by touch. Reading the label is the only guide.

While checking fibers note whether the fabric is woven or non-woven. A woven fabric is made on a loom with shuttles that interlace yarns. Today, time is money, so increasingly knitted, tufted, and felted fabric are being used as they can be produced faster on less-expensive equipment and can be sold for less.

There are also many more fabrics with special backings. A fabric too light for use as upholstery can be given body by laminating it to a heavier backing. Smooth backings can make a rough texture wearable, and a scrim, plastic, or urethane backing gives stability to tufted or knitted fabrics and carpets. Wherever two layers, a front and a back, are put together as one it is known as a laminated or bonded fabric. It is done to give body, stability, weight, and acceptable texture or extra warmth to light-weight, less-expensive fabrics which otherwise could not be used. It is important to understand the care of bonded fabrics. Dry cleaning may weaken the adhesive holding the lining to the outer fabric or one or the other color may bleed and ruin the whole garment.

CARPETS AND RUGS

Carpet fabrics also have gone through a revolution. The standard carpet weaves are gradually disappearing from the market. Axminsters, chenilles, and velvets will be collectors' items in another generation. Speedy tufting will have replaced the slow, expensive, cumbersome looms. One tufting machine in a day can turn out fifteen rolls of carpeting to one roll produced by a standard loom in the same length of time, a fact which has a salutary effect on the price of the finished product.

Almost three-fourths of all carpets have a synthetic pile. After tufting, carpets are given a patent back consisting of some kind of plastic to anchor the tufts; in better grades a layer of scrim or burlap is bonded to the back to stabilize and give body to the fabric.

FINISHES

The finish on a fabric is as much a factor in its care and handling as the fiber. The finish may affect both washing and ironing temperatures, and have other advantages as well.

There are processes designed to resist soil, mothproof wools, increase or decrease luster, prevent shrinkage, reduce flammability, add body, or make fabrics softer. There are antistatic finishes often used on nylon carpets, color-fast processes, water-repellent, mildew-resistant, and germicidal finishes, and finally permanent-press finishes.

Permanent press, also called *durable press,* is an advance beyond drip dry and wash-and-wear. If washing instructions are followed on a garment with a high-quality finish, the results are very successful. The finish is applied to the flat fabric, but it is usually not heat set until after the fabric has been made up and the seams pressed. The curing at this point gives the fabric "a memory" not only of a smooth surface, but of pleats, seams, curves, and hems. Garments so treated can be shortened and taken in, but if they are lengthened or let out the original creases and stitches will always show.

To launder permanent press use a cool rinse before the spin cycle in the washer and a cool drying cycle. Tumbled drying gives the best results. Sometimes garments may need touching up with an iron because the zipper and other details may not have been processed. Use a warm, wash-and-wear, or permanent-press setting on the iron.

Do not let any garment get too soiled, wash frequently. Prompt removal of stains is doubly important for oil or grease. If such stains are left on nothing will remove them, and this includes the stains on the neckband of men's shirts. Pretreat oil stains before laundering with a cleaning solvent. If the stain persists, apply a detergent paste and let it stand overnight before washing. Gravy, blood, ice cream, salad oil, and car grease should be soaked in cold water and detergent just before washing.

POINTERS ON CARE OF DECORATIVE FABRICS

Sun is hard on draperies and curtains; winter sun and reflection from the snow are more harmful than summer sun. Lining and even interlining are desirable for fragile fabrics such as taffeta. Nylon is especially sun-sensitive.

Even so-called fast colors change, and impurities in the air may cause fading as much as direct rays of the sun. Vacuum or shake fabrics often. Dust carries impurities that deteriorate fabrics. Colors also change as a result of oxidation if they are stored for long periods.

Length of draperies and curtains may vary from day to day because of the humidity in the air. No fabric is completely stable, but some of the synthetics respond more to humidity than the natural fibers. Be tolerant of this problem. It is reasonable to expect a 3 percent change in a 108-inch-long drapery—that is, about three inches.

Wear is an inevitable factor even though there are fabrics in use and on display in some museums which are hundreds of years old. Wear will vary with use. Covering on a favorite chair will not last as long as that on an unused chair in the corner. Also some weaves are stronger than others.

Fabrics like to rest. In museums when old fabrics are used for draperies and slip covers, every few months they are changed, cleaned, mended, and rested before being rehung.

Synthetic fibers such as nylon, Dacron, Fortisan and fiberglass are making an invaluable contribution, but too much is expected of them. Like all fabrics, those woven of hardy fibers must also be cleaned and cared for.

Finishes do help fabrics resist spotting and improve the texture, but they do not do away with the necessity of proper care. Spills should have immediate attention. There is little advantage in using any of the stain-resistant finishings on dark fabrics, draperies, and bedspreads, and dining-room chairs will soil no matter what is used. But these processes are particularly useful for white and light-colored slip covers and upholstery.

Sanforized fabrics have been processed to reduce shrinkage.

Vat-dyed fabrics have faster colors than piece-dyed fabrics, which are processed after they are woven.

21 How to Plan a Laundry

Laundries not so long ago were always a mess. There was no way to escape slopping water, steam from the washboiler, and piles of soiled or wet clothes. The new laundry equipment has made as big a change in washday procedures as the new fibers have in the care of clothes and household fabrics.

Before planning a home laundry decide whether or not you need one. Check these points:

Will the laundry be sent to a commercial laundry?
Will you take it to a wash-it-yourself laundry?
Will you do it at home?
Will hired help do the wash?
Will some be sent out and some done at home?

Don't feel sorry for yourself if the laundry is going to be done at home. You are lucky! Your sheets will last longer. Your linens will be something to be proud of. Things won't get lost. Towels will be fluffy and the wash will smell good. Moreover, with a little planning and careful maneuvering the week's wash can be done without great time or energy. With automatic equipment laundry that once might have taken eighteen hours can now be done in a flash.

The first step in mastering home washing is to decide on the right location for a laundry, then organize the space along modern, efficient, labor-saving lines. The problem may be to remodel an existing laundry or to plan a new one. In either case drastic steps may be necessary.

LOCATION

The laundry is no longer a stepchild shunted off to a dark corner of the basement, the garage, or back porch. New laundry equipment and revised washing methods have eliminated washday odors along with slopping water and general disturbance.

In new and remodeled houses laundries have come out of the basement to the first and sometimes even the second floor. The neat way in which washing is done with an automatic washer and dryer has brought about this small revolution. With the flick of a switch clothes are soaked, washed, rinsed, bleached, blued, wrung, and dried.

With an automatic washer and dryer the operation is so simple that washday can no longer be called Blue Monday. In many households a load is washed every day or whenever it accumulates. As one woman explained, "I run through a load of wash every morning while my husband is shaving. There's nothing to it. I spend exactly eight minutes twice a day in my laundry." Time is not the only advantage of washing more frequently; hot water is used to better advantage, and fewer sheets, towels, and children's play clothes are needed, saving both drawer and shelf space.

When the wash is handled in this casual manner the value of getting the laundry out of the basement is clear. It has been logical to locate the laundry in the service or kitchen wing of the house, but now many architects and builders have faced the fact that over four-fifths of the laundry comes from the bedroom wing of the house—clothes, sheets, and bath towels. As a result space is being found in that section of the house for a laundry. Sometimes it is in one of the bathrooms. In other houses it is behind sliding doors or a bamboo curtain opening from the bedroom hall. Ideally the laundry is a small utility room backing one of the bathrooms in the bedroom wing so that one plumbing line can serve both spaces. In a one-story house it may have an outside door which also offers direct access to the bedroom wing.

A laundry in the bedroom wing may present a problem in venting the dryer. A laundry in the kitchen may mean carrying clothes back and forth through the living areas. Review the pros and cons and work out the arrangement that will please you.

Before you go shopping for laundry appliances check your plumbing and wiring needs, as local codes vary. The washer should have separate hot and cold water faucets, shutoff valves to relieve pressure on the hose when the washer is not being used, as well as a means of drainage close by.

Unless your dryer is a no-vent model, it should have an outside vent, not through a chimney or under a porch because of fire hazard.

Many elaborate laundries are shown in magazines. They include an ironing area, a sewing machine, and all sorts of other equipment.

However, in ninety-nine houses out of a hundred there is no space for such elaboration. Moreover, for ironing and sewing it isn't necessary to have a waterproofed room close to plumbing lines. The family room serves well enough—with TV for entertainment.

Washers come in a range of sizes from small portable ones with a pound or two capacity to standard ten- to sixteen-pound models. In general, washers and dryers placed side by side take about five feet of wall space, a single washer or dryer requires twenty-six to thirty-one inches, and combination washer-dryers thirty-four inches. If space is limited, consider washer-dryer combinations that stack on top of each other like children's blocks. Allow three feet of working space in front of the appliance if they stand side by side and four feet if they are on opposite walls. A space about six feet by four-and-a-half feet will accommodate an ironing board and laundry cart. In a two-story house an in-the-wall ironing board on the second floor is a convenience for wardrobe touch-up. Laundry chutes are also staging a comeback.

If space and cost are no problem, the laundry may include:

Sorting bins for storing soiled clothes.

A sorting counter, three to five feet long, to keep clothes off the floor and to serve as a base for folding clean, dried clothes and for stain removal.

Clothes hangers and a place to hang garments that do not need ironing when they come from the dryer.

A sink for pretreating badly soiled areas and spots and a storage closet for detergents, starch, bluing, and stain-removal equipment.

A sewing area with scissors, needles, and thread for prewash attention of buttons and tears.

A cart or basket for transporting the laundry around the house.

APPLIANCE DATA

Today's washer and dryers are probably the most highly automated of all household appliances. The newest ones are programmed like a computer. By merely punching an assortment of buttons you can get the exact combination of water, temperature, agitation, spin speeds, washing time, drying heat, and time required. Given the right instructions the washer and dryer can handle the laciest lingerie, your best dresses, heavy bedspreads, and grimy work clothes. But, like a computer, it must be fed the right instructions in proper sequence, and that is up to you. Washers and dryers with transistorized (programmed) circuitry are usually said to have solid state controls. These are terms that will be used more and more for household equipment. Learn not to duck or close your ears when you hear them.

. . . how big a washer do you need?

Most women feel underprivileged if they do not have an automatic washer and dryer. They look on them as a necessity not a luxury, and they become adept at operating them. Actually automatic washers do not do a better job of getting clothes clean than the nonautomatic ones, and they do require quantities of hot water. Because there are more working parts, breakdowns are more frequent. Their virtue lies in the magnificent saving of time and energy and the neatness of the whole operation. With an automatic washer and dryer, machines take over the whole washday job. They need no watching, laundry tubs are not necessary, and clotheslines are a thing of the past. Nevertheless, it is handy to have one tub for odds and ends of hand washing. Keep outdoor clotheslines also for airing clothes and an occasional sun bleaching for household linens.

Clothes dryers. The latest addition to the laundry is the clothes dryer. The most popular type of dryer automatically tumbles clothes in a chamber of hot air. Both gas and electric models are available and, as a rule, hold a full washerload of clothes.

Dryers cost less than automatic washers but are fairly expensive to operate. They require careful installation. Regardless of claims to the contrary, it is desirable to connect the dryer with an exhaust to carry the heat and steam outdoors.

But don't be misled by this gloomy picture. Women who have dryers find them a joy, especially through winter months. A women in Oklahoma says her dryer actually saves her more time than the washer. A woman in Minneapolis says that now a helper who comes in by the day can handle both washing and ironing in one day.

A woman living in the suburbs of Chicago says that the fluff drying of her tumble-type dryer is so easy on the clothes that over 50 percent of the laundry does not have to be ironed as there are no hard creases. It makes fluffy new towels of hardened old towels. I have yet to meet a woman who doesn't think the advantages of the new equipment outweigh the increase in operating expenses.

Washer-dryer combinations. In addition to separate automatic washers and dryers there are so-called "combination" or "duomatic" washer-dryers which add a drying cycle to the usual washing cycle but which can be used as a washer alone. The claim is that an average family's laundry can be washed and dried in fifty-eight minutes, but this allows for just two sheets.

For a small family of two or three a combination is a fine solution, but for a large family with children and mountains of deeply soiled play clothes and sheets a separate washer and dryer will pay for themselves in the long run.

When shopping for laundry equipment the price quoted is not the whole story. Ask also about installation costs; these may run quite high, depending on your community and the wiring now available in your house. Automatic laundry equipment requires heavy-duty wiring. If you already have an electric range there will no trouble, but there will be a considerable charge if a heavy-duty cable has to be brought in from the street.

CARE OF WASHERS AND DRYERS

Laundry equipment has a high priority rating with homemakers, yet both washers and dryers are temperamental and short-lived appliances. From the beginning it is important to fully understand their handling and care. Don't think that just because you have used a washer for years you know how to deal with your new automatic washer.

Nothing is gained by being a know-it-all. Ask for a thorough demonstration. Have the washer and dryer installed by a qualified service agency. For satisfactory performance the washer should be on a separate circuit. Read both the instruction book and the guarantee carefully. Keep the instruction book tied to a hook in the laundry and file the guarantee among your archives.

Servicemen report that the chief causes of washer and dryer difficulties could easily be avoided with a little care.

Number one troublemakers are pins and needles left in clothing, which work their way into the pump and cause motor trouble. Any metal of any kind in pockets or pinned to garments should be removed before they are put in the washer.

Number two trouble in older washers is the result of small things such as women's handkerchiefs or children's socks floating over the top of the washer basket and into the machinery. This can be avoided by putting all small items, handkerchiefs, socks, bras, diapers, into nylon net bags before washing.

In other words, carelessness is behind most washer and dryer breakdowns. Much difficulty can be avoided if you follow the instructions given for your machine. The following rules apply to all washers and dryers:

Do not overload; weigh wash loads until you know correct load weights.

Don't have any other appliance plugged onto the same circuit as the washer.

Use only the detergents, bleaches, and water softeners recommended. Use a measure, don't guess the quantities.

Press buttons in the order given in the instructions. Once the cycle has started don't try to change it unless you stop the machine completely and start over.

If the washer gives trouble signals, such as excessive vibration or unusual noise, stop it at once. Check the distribution of the load in the tub.

Keep filters clean. Clogged filters can be a major source of trouble. Give washers a periodic checkup as a preventive measure. Keep bolts and screws tight. Keep the manufacturer's booklet handy for reference. On a wringer-type washer, rinse rollers after use with clear water; keep free of contact with grease or oil and release pressure after use.

If clothes are not clean ask yourself these questions:

Are you using water to proper level?
Is water the correct temperature for the fabric being washed?
Is the load too small or too large?
Are you using the correct amount of the recommended detergent?
Did you pretreat bad soil and stains?
Did you separate white and colored clothes?

Hot-water heaters. One of the principal requirements of an automatic washer is a good supply of water. The cold-water process will serve well for colored clothes but other household laundry done without plenty of hot water may prove disappointing.

Each washing operation requires eighteen to twenty-four gallons of water. The average family has four to five loads a week so that a review of your water supply should parallel the purchase of an automatic washer.

Automatic hot-water tanks are available with electric, gas, and oil fuels.

PUBLIC LAUNDRIES

There are several advantages to using a public laundry. You may not be able to program the process as precisely as you can your own washer, but you do not have to worry about breakdowns and hot water. Soft water is supplied in hard-water areas. If you have a big washing, by choosing an unpopular hour in the early morning or at noon you can do five or six washer loads at one time. Thus in the space

. . . keep a radio close at hand

of one hour, washing, drying, and folding can all be accomplished without fuss. Moreover, there is an attendant to answer all questions.

There is no better place to learn to use a washer and become indoctrinated with laundry processes. There is usually a pleasant air of camaraderie and, by asking a question here and there, it is possible to learn first hand about many new laundry products and ways of using them.

IRONS

There is a wide choice of styles and types available, offering almost every known convenience except the actual manipulation. There are steam irons and nonsteam irons; the newest ones have a special temperature gauge for special finishes as well as different fibers.

In making a selection it may be worthwhile to consider whether you prefer an iron that stands on end or whether it is more convenient to rest it on a plate. If you iron many ruffles and gathers, a flexible nose on the iron may be handy.

If you have been commissioned to keep the creases in your husband's trousers or do much home sewing, a steam iron or a combination model is indispensable. Steam irons are ideal for pressing wool and steaming velvet and all quick pressing jobs.

In new irons look for nonstick. Teflon coatings, gauges that indicate when more water is needed, and temperature dials, which can be set for the many new fabrics on the market today.

22 How to Wash Clothes

If you are just learning to cope with a laundry, do not take lessons from your mother or grandmother. Methods of doing the washing have changed tremendously in the last twenty-five years. Only the principle of washing remains the same. First there must be thorough wetting, an agent to loosen the soil, then the soil must be floated away. Water is still the best wetting agent, and it may be used hot or cold. A detergent, not soap, softens the soil and agitated water floats the soil away. Adjustments in the water temperatures and detergents vary with the finishes and fibers in the articles being washed.

LAUNDRY ADDITIVES

Synthetic detergents have almost completely replaced soaps in the laundry; they are not affected by hard or cold water and have more cleaning power. Like soaps, there are detergents for heavy duty and for fine fabrics. All-purpose detergents are built up with added chemicals to soften water, to increase soil removal, and to bleach. Fine-fabric detergents do not clean as deeply but they are kinder to texture and delicate colors.

Detergents come in powdered or liquid form and in premeasured packs. It is important to find the type that works best in your washer and with the local water. If you move to a new area a different detergent than the one you have been using may do a better job, or you may need to use more or less of your regular brand. Always remember that the amount of detergent needed increases in direct ratio to the hardness of the water.

All-purpose detergents

(A) NORMAL SUDSING

Granular: Tide, Fab, Rinso Blue, Cheer, Oxydol, Silver Dust, Super Suds, Premium Duz

Liquid: Wisk

Pre-measured: Tide, Redi Packs

(B) CONTROLLED SUDSING

Granular: Dash, Ad, All, Cold Power, Cold Water Surf
Liquid: Cold Water All
Pre-measured: Salvo, Vim, Quick Solv

(C) MILD

Granular: Dreft, Vel, Trend
Liquid: Liquid Lux, Ivory Liquid

Read package labels and be familiar with the quantity and type of detergent recommended for your washer. In general always measure detergents carefully. The amount needed will increase with the size of the load and the amount of soil. Oily soil always requires extra detergent.

Fabric Softeners are a chemical additive. Their job is to turn out a soft, fluffy wash. They are most effective on synthetic fabrics and help cut down static electricity. They are used in the final rinse water and for best results there should be a few minutes' agitation after adding. Some washers have special bleach and fabric softener dispensers. They are filled and the dials set before the washing cycle begins and the additives are automatically made to the rinse water at the proper time.

Bleaches help keep fabrics white and remove simple stains. It is best to use small quantities regularly rather than an occasional strong bleach which could weaken fabrics.

There are two types of bleach; in one oxygen is the active ingredient and in the other chlorine. Both come in liquid or powdered form. The oxygen-containing bleaches are mild, safe on all fabrics, and are a staple in the stain-removal cabinet. Hydrogen peroxide and Care are liquid, and Snowy and Dexol are powdered types which contain sodium perborate.

Chlorine bleaches are stronger and should be used only on cottons, linens, and most white synthetics, but never on silk, wool, or rayon or fabrics that are not colorfast. They too come in liquid and powdered form.

Bleaches are strong chemical substances and should be used with care. Read and follow the directions for use carefully. Do not use bleaches containing chlorine and household ammonia in the same wash. Never add the powder after the clothes are in the wash. Dissolve it in a quart of water first. If a cake of bleach is used, put it in first with a little water before the clothes are added. Chlorine bleaches and detergents work in harmony. Washers automatically rinse well; but in hand laundry care should be taken to remove all bleach.

Difficulties with bleach are usually the result of using too much, not diluting or mixing properly before clothes are added, or carelessness in handling bleach such as spilling it on dry clothes.

Bluings. Washing is a matter of checks and balances. Detergents encourage the action of the water, the bleach backs up the detergent, and any trace of yellowing left is checkmated with bluing. Bluing makes no contribution to the cleansing action; it is purely camouflage.

Bluing is available in liquid, flake, or beaded form. Formerly bluing was a part of the rinsing operation, now it is usually added at the beginning of the cycle and less is needed.

Always read the label and follow instructions exactly.

Starches. Generally speaking, less starch is used now than formerly. Starches are divided into lump, powdered, cubed, liquid, or pregelatinized, plastic, or spray types. The spray types are properly a part of the ironing operation.

Starch stiffens and gives a glaze to cotton fabrics. It is used on cotton dresses and blouses and on men's shirts. Use it with a light hand, but heavier starch is recommended if a dryer is used. Tint starch used on dark cottons; use bluing for black and blue garments, strong tea for brown.

Liquid plastic starch is preferable for nylons, rayons, and silks, and is used on some table linens. It retards staining and is removed completely in each washing.

WASHING TECHNIQUES

Even with a completely programmed new washer and dryer the first step in the actual laundry operation is yours. Sorting and pretreating requires judgment and thus far no machine can supply that.

Divide the articles into the following piles:

1. White and colorfast pastels, such as bed linens, towels, handkerchiefs, cotton undergarments, aprons, and shirts. Chlorine bleach may be used.
2. Washable colored garments, including cottons, linens, rayons,

white nylons, Orlon, and Dacron and cotton blends. This pile will include colorfast dresses, blouses, sport shirts, colored table linens, pajamas, colored sheets and pillow slips, bath towels, and cotton and linen slacks.

3. Garments with heavy soil, ground-in dust and dirt, such as men's work clothes, children's wear, garden clothes, and denims. These garments may need a short warm soak wash, followed by a long hot wash.

. . . empty pockets

4. Wool and wool blends such as blankets, socks, shirts, slacks, and skirts. Even when woolens have been treated for shrinkage, they should be carefully handled, and the same mild temperature should be used for all steps.
5. Delicate fabrics which formerly were always washed by hand may be machine washed, using a cold-water process. Typical items are nylon hosiery in a mesh bag, sweaters, lacy lingerie, blouses, and washable dresses.

Each of the five groups calls for a slightly different handling. If only one load is put through a day, at the end of the week each of the five piles could be handled.

In sorting be sure to empty pockets. A nail, a pin, or needle left in a pocket may overflow the basket, work its way into the motor, and wreck the machine. An indelible pencil or ball-point pen may ruin a loadful of clothes. Chewing gum makes a bad smear and a watch left in a pocket quite definitely will never be the same again. If pockets have sand and dirt in them, use a brush to dislodge particles. Fancy buttons are bad performers; remove them.

Spot-clean stains; washing may set them. Mend fragile garments with beginning tears that washing might make worse. Close zippers; they will behave better. Scrub badly soiled neckbands and knees of overalls with detergent and a brush to loosen the soil before putting in the machine.

THE WASHING PROCESS

As you sort, divide the articles into loads. Most washers take from six to sixteen pounds; overloading strains the motor and produces a dingy washing. It doesn't take long to develop the knack of estimating weight. When washing large articles like sheets and table cloths, it is best to wash only two or three at a time, filling up the rest of the load with smaller articles. A list of articles and their average dry weight appears on page 215.

Loading. At this point follow the letter of the law laid down by the manufacturer of the washer you are using. Learn the directions like a catechism. Be able to recite them backward and forward. It is the manufacturer who should have the last word and the machine is the boss. Overloading will turn out a poor wash. If the basket is overloaded or if the load is not evenly distributed, the motor will grind heavily or it will vibrate. Many washers will automatically stop if this happens. Whether it stops itself or you stop it, reduce and redistribute the load before restarting.

Washing. Once an automatic machine starts on its cycle the entire process through rinsing, bluing, and wringing is taken care of. With a standard washer the clothes may be run through a rinse in the machine or they may be transferred to a set tub for rinsing and then be put through a wringer or the spinner basket of the washer.

Number	*Item*	*Weight in Pounds*
1	double sheet	2
1	twin sheet	1
3	pillow cases	1
2 to 3	bath towels	1
4 to 5	hand towels	1
16	face cloths	1
2	luncheon cloths	1
16	luncheon napkins	1
2	men's shirts	1
4	undershirts	1
4	men's shorts	1
1	pair overalls	2 to 3
18	socks	1
4	boy's shirts	1
2	boy's blue jeans	3
2 or 3	women's dresses	1
3 or 4	girl's dresses	1
4	women's slips	1
3	night gowns	1
6 to 8	diapers	1

In a nonautomatic machine do not try to use the same water too long. To wash clean, clean water must be used.

Washing time will vary with the washer, the fabric, and the degree of soil. Fragile things may require two to three minutes, heavily soiled garments 10 to 15 minutes, with the average for sheets and shirts five to eight minutes.

Rinsing. Extracting additives and water is as important as washing. Lack of rinsing may be the cause of a gray look as much as hard water and inadequate washing. Several rinsings in clear water are needed. The first rinse may be warm; the following rinses for cottons, linens, silks, and synthetics may be cool. For woolens lukewarm water should be used throughout the entire washing process.

Wringing. With an automatic washer this step is skipped entirely; however, as any woman knows, wringing is simply the extraction of water. To do it the hard way, clutch a roll of fabric with the two hands and twist in opposite directions. The easy way is to use an automatic washer, which does the job without interference from human hands.

On a nonautomatic washer a roller wringer presses out the water or a spinner basket throws it out by centrifugal force. The spinner must be loaded carefully but it does a good job. A roller type of wringer, whether it is run by hand or electrically, requires coaxing and fussing over. Careless wringing will snap off buttons, tear clothes, and cause hard, unnecessary creases, and may even crush a finger or two.

These six rules should be observed with a roller wringer:

1. Fold the clothes before feeding into wringer so that the bulk is evenly distributed over the roller.
2. Do not try to put clothes with large buttons or buckles through the wringer; it will damage the rollers. Fold small buttons or zippers under a layer of fabric and feed in flat.
3. Feed small articles like handkerchiefs through in group lots or fold them inside other clothes before wringing.
4. Release pressure on rollers when putting through heavy material to avoid hard-to-iron creases.
5. Let the machine wring at its own pace. Do not try to speed up an electric wringer or let your finger get close to it.
6. When through, release the pressure of the rollers and wipe the rubber clean with fresh water. Soap will damage the rubber.

Drying. Women who have automatic dryers wonder how they ever managed without them. They make washday independent of weather, there are never wet clothes hanging around, and there is no delay in ironing. Even a big laundry can be washed and ironed in one day. So time is saved with a dryer, to say nothing of the two hundred or so stretches and bends required to hang an average wash and the fifty-six pounds or so of wet clothes which have to be heaved around.

When a dryer is used follow instructions exactly; do not overdry. There will be fewer wrinkles and textures will be softer and fluffier if there is some moisture in the fabric. If clothes are removed while still damp, iron at once without sprinkling.

If you are a fiend for fresh air and hang the wash outdoors to dry, handle the clothes properly; it will make the job of ironing easier. The signs of an old hand are:

Sheets evenly folded and hung from hem ends
Shirts shaken out and neatly hung by their tails
Towels hung double with a fluff shake before anchoring to line

Dresses hung by hems from side seams or straight of cloth to prevent sagging. Better dresses hung on hangers
Jackets adjusted to coat hangers or hung on hems
Skirts and slacks hung by the waistband or a hanger
Slips and nightgowns with the hem over the line
Colored things hung in the shade

SPECIAL WASHING METHODS

Electric blankets. Electric blankets are seldom wool and should be washed, as dry cleaning can harm the wiring. Keep the hang tag on the package and follow the instructions. Spot clean stains. Sponge soiled binding with detergent. Wash only one blanket at a time. Use 100-degree water and one-third cup of mild detergent. Set the controls for a minute and a half and set for gentle agitation. Follow with a fast spin and two thorough rinses. Add a fabric softener to the last rinse.

If it is to be machine dried, use a high heat setting for fifteen or twenty minutes. Put three or four bath towels in with the blanket to serve as buffers. When dry remove, raise nap with a stiff brush, and press binding with a steam iron set at "synthetic" setting.

If it is dried outdoors, place carefully over two lines in the shade.

Wool blankets. Soil left on hardens and attracts moths and is more difficult to remove.

To wash, first shake blanket to remove loose dust. Examine for soiled spots. Brush spots and binding with soft sudsy brush. Mend binding or holes before washing.

Use lukewarm water and wash one blanket at a time. The water should be soft. Run machine three minutes only. A longer run may felt the wool and make the blanket stiff. Rinse several times in fresh lukewarm water; run the machine two minutes and no more for each rinse. For hand methods, just douse up and down, agitating the suds. Handle the blanket carefully when it is wet or it may tear. Press dry between towels or use terry towel or clean sponge to blot up excess water. Straighten the edges, but don't tug or pull them. Shake frequently, but gently. To hang, follow instructions for electric blankets. Turn when half dry. Fluff up nap by stroking the surface with a nylon brush when dry. Press binding, using a dampened cloth; do not press blanket.

Washable bedspreads. Follow the directions for electric blankets. Use cool water for colored spreads, hot water for white ones. If line dried, fold carefully, pull hems straight. White spreads will benefit from the sun.

Slip covers. If the fabric is washable and color fast, washing presents no problem. Wash before they are heavily soiled. If slip covers are spot soiled on arms and back they can be freshened right on the chair. Use rich, dry detergent suds. Apply with a soft cloth, work in the lather, rinse with a clean damp cloth. Work in circles rotating from the spot to avoid a ring.

Before washing remove all lint, dust, and cigarette ashes from the seams. Use a brush or vacuum cleaner. Next pretreat spots with dry suds, rubbing it lightly with a soft brush following the grain of the fabric and the seams.

To machine wash do a sofa slipcover alone, but two chair slipcovers may be washed together. Close zippers and other fasteners. If they are extremely soiled, two wash cycles may be necessary.

If you have no washer, after pretreatment soak covers in the bathtub briefly. Change to clean water, add detergent, and plunge briskly up and down in the suds. If you have a rubber suction plumber's helper, use it to simulate washer action; it pulls the suds through the fabric.

Partially dry in dryer or over two clotheslines. Stretch the seams, welts, zippers, and hems while arranging on the line.

Ironing is usually not necessary if the slipcovers are put back on the furniture while still damp. Smooth the surface with your hands, pull seams into place, pin pleated flounces in place. When all is in order, direct an electric fan on them for final drying. Touch up with an iron afterward if you think it necessary. Use a warm-to-hot setting for natural fibers and a cool-to-warm setting for synthetics.

HOW TO WASH CURTAINS

Concern for curtains should begin with their selection. Since curtains act as sieves, they catch and hold dust and dirt that blows through open windows and they absorb dust and soil from indoor air. Frequent dusting helps, but laundering must be frequent also. Heavy soil rots fibers and also requires harsher cleaning methods to remove.

To make curtains last longer, make them shorter or longer than the windowsill. If they rest on the sill both friction and soil will shorten their lives. If several windows take the same-size curtains, rotate them. Curtains in sunny windows wear out faster. Tailored curtains may be made with identical hems top and bottom so that they can be reversed to distribute the exposure to sun.

Cotton curtains. White cotton marquisettes, scrims, and lawns may be washed like any other cottons in your washer. Dark colors should be washed alone in warm, not hot, water. Cottons with special finishes such as permanent press must be handled like synthetics and washed in warm water.

If curtains are machine dried, avoid crisp drying; remove while slightly damp to prevent baking in wrinkles.

Glass-fiber curtains are the easiest of all curtains to care for. They should be washed not dry cleaned. They are not affected by sun exposure and do not absorb soil. Friction is their only enemy. Hand wash, squeeze suds through the curtains, rinse thoroughly to remove grime. Shake free of water, hang while wet, do not iron.

Synthetics, blends and fabrics with finishes. Today Celanese, Dacrons, Orlon and other synthetics are more often used than natural fibers. Many curtains are treated with durable finishes which make them easy to wash and dry. They shed surface soil, do not need scrubbing and should not be wrung out but drip dried. In general machine washing is safe; however, it is best to read the label and follow the directions of the manufacturer.

Four to six pairs of curtains make an average load in a washer. Delicate curtains should be put in open mesh bags to prevent tangling and twisting. Unless badly soiled, hand washing in a bathtub or laundry tub is adequate. Pat or press out water and allow to drip dry. Handled this way such curtains require minimum ironing.

Do not use a chlorine bleach on synthetics or fabrics with finishes. They contain resins which interact with chlorine; when pressed the fabric may discolor or fall apart. Perborate or oxygen-type bleaches are safe.

If curtains are machine dried, use low heat and remove while still damp. Work ruffles and hems with the fingers. Clever manipulation can do much to eliminate ironing.

TABLE LINENS, CLOTHS, NAPKINS, PLACE MATS

Remove all stains before processing. Most tablecloths can be machine washed, but should be included only in the slightly soiled loads.

Dark linens tend to pick up lint and should never be included with turkish towels. Large linen cloths should not be washed with cottons.

Delicate fabrics. Both cotton and nylon lace cloths which appear quite delicate may be machine washed. Less sturdy laces should be put in a mesh bag.

Very fragile heirloom laces may be basted to a backing of clean muslin, then gently squeezed through suds and rinse water.

PILLOWS AND MATTRESS TICKING

Protection from perspiration, stains, dust, and soil is the most important step in the care of pillows and mattresses. Change pillow slips frequently; use an underslip which ties in place and is washed only occasionally, or use a plastic cover that gives total protection.

To wash pillows soak in cool or lukewarm water; if very soiled add one-fourth cup washing suds to the water. Put in washer or douse and squeeze in suds. Rinse in several clear waters. Pin to line, reversing ends several times during the drying, fluffing and plumping each time.

To transfer feathers to a new ticking, baste the open seam of the old case to the new one and gently shake the feathers into the new case. But first wash feathers in old case by hand or machine. Completely dry before transferring them to new case. Never try to handle feathers without a cover.

Feather pillows should be refluffed and sterilized every five to ten years. Most laundries and dry cleaners offer this service.

Keep mattresses dust free with the vacuum cleaner. They should be covered with a quilted pad held in place with elastic corner bands, but if there is bed wetting or extreme perspiration use a plastic cover.

If something is spilled on a mattress or if an old one needs cleaning, use the same method that you would for upholstery. Avoid using excess water. Whip soap or detergent into a thick lather. Apply with a stiff brush, doing a small area at a time. Follow with a clean damp sponge or cloth to take up suds. Repeat. Dry thoroughly before turning. Speed drying with an electric fan or wash mattress outdoors on a hot sunny day.

GLOVES

Many leather gloves are washable; the label in the gloves is your guide. However, washing is not successful after dry cleaning. Wash by hand in soft lukewarm water and castile soap. Soiled finger tips can be handled more easily if gloves are worn while washing. Turn inside out and scrub seams with a brush. Rinse lightly, press out excess moisture with a paper towel. Blow into gloves to reshape them and dry slowly, never near heat, on a bath towel. When almost dry put on and work the leather with fingers.

White cotton and nylon gloves. Machine or hand wash. If they are to be hand washed and are badly soiled, a soft brush used on soiled areas will help make gloves spotless. Wash on both inside and outside. Black, navy, brown, or other dark-colored gloves should be washed separately, even when they are marked color fast by manufacturer.

TO WASH SWEATERS

Fibers used to knit sweaters include wool, cashmere, angora, rabbit hair, cotton and synthetic fibers such as Orlon, nylon and Acrilan. Unless the label says otherwise they can all be washed.

Wool, cashmere, and angora are subject to extreme shrinkage unless they have been "finished" or are carefully handled. Use the following procedure to wash wool sweaters:

Lay sweater on paper and draw outline of sweater. Wash in cold water with special cold-water soap, Woolite, for example, using the same temperature for both washing and rinsing, and washing according to the manufacturer's directions. If the articles are very soiled also add a few drops of ammonia to the Woolite solution. Squeeze suds through sweater, avoid rubbing or twisting, handle sweater so that at no time does it support a weight of water. Rinse. Lay between two bath towels and roll to absorb excess moisture.

Lay sweater on paper, shaping it to the outline drawn previously. Dry slowly out of the sun and away from a hot radiator. To restore the nap and remove balls of fuzz brush the sweater while still damp with a clean nylon brush. When dry, press on the wrong side.

23 How to Iron

It's easy to get the impression that nothing needs ironing. What with drip-dry, wash-and-wear, and permanent press, as well as relaxed standards, the whole operation of ironing seems headed for a museum that features quaint folkways of past generations.

Nevertheless, there are usually a few things that look better after a touch of the iron. Ironing isn't for looks only; it delays soiling by smoothing down small surface fibers and, as my bacteriology professor used to say there is no better way of sterilizing fabrics.

Whether you have decided to iron or not to iron, you would be classified as a fussbudget if you ironed the following items:

bath towels and wash cloths
bath mats and cotton rugs
knitted T or polo shirts
bed pads
hosiery
flannel garments
corduroy children's clothes
chenille and tufted bedspreads
glass-fiber curtains
diapers

Increasingly the following things are being included in the no-iron category:

seersucker blouses, shirts, and dresses
sheets and pillow cases
drip-dry shirts, dresses, and blouses

EQUIPMENT

If you have decided that certain things must be ironed, time and energy will be saved if you set the stage carefully before you start.

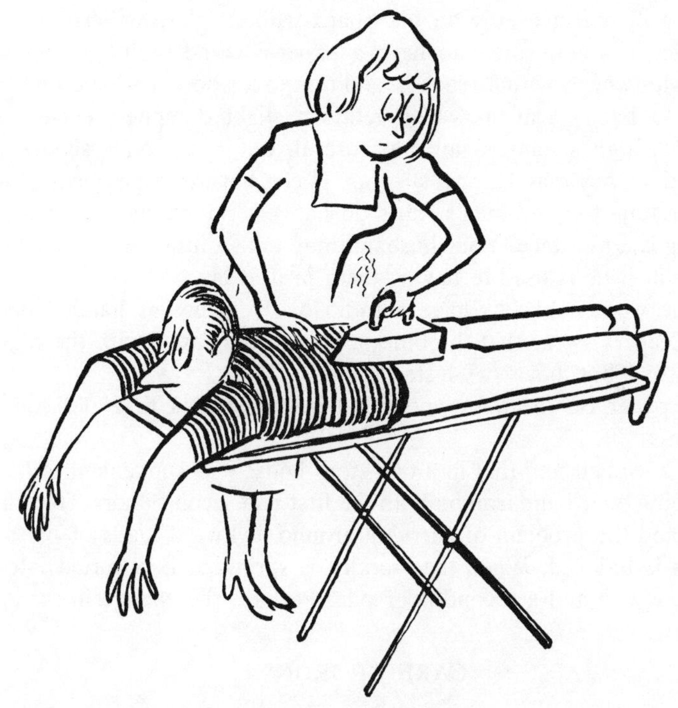

. . . never iron polo shirts

Basic equipment includes:

iron
pressing cloth
standard ironing board
sleeve board
wet sponge for spot dampening
stool or chair
rack for drying
suitable light
clothes hangers

Easy-to-use irons have a nonstick Teflon coating. Silicon-treated ironing-board covers are excellent.

It is important that the light, either natural or artificial, be placed so that it will reflect evenly on the board without glare or shadows. If possible, it is convenient to have a paper-covered shelf, counter, or table with wheels within reach in addition to a wood or plastic rack on which to hang garments which retain a slight dampness even after ironing. Clothes hangers are also useful, but metal ones should be avoided as they may leave rust spots. If you have enough closet space it saves time to store men's shirts on hangers rather than in drawers. Folding is a nuisance. Your husband may take a little conditioning on this point if he is used to having them in drawers.

Some women like to have a radio or TV close at hand. Young housekeepers swear that the time not only goes faster with the radio, TV, or hi-fi but they work faster.

Put paper on the floor under the ironing board to avoid soiling garments.

Some women find that in a two-story house it is convenient to have an ironing board and iron on both the first and second floors. Steps are saved and the problem of carrying around awkward loads of pressed clothes is reduced. When the laundry is sprinkled it is sorted into a first-floor pile and a second-floor pile. Perhaps the change in scenery helps.

CARE OF IRONS

With care an electric iron may last years. Periodic changes are desirable in order to benefit from new developments and just because it's nice to have new shiny equipment. Interest in new things is a sign of youth and proof of a flexible mind.

Never leave the iron connected when the telephone rings or there is someone at the door. You may forget it and irons left too long have a bad reputation for starting fires.

Do not wrap the cord around the iron when it is hot and never bend the cord sharply. If the casing on the cord becomes worn and shabby, replace it with a new one.

Have the convenience outlet for the iron in a good location, preferably above the level of the ironing board. Work will go more smoothly if you are demanding about such things. Men never would put up with inconveniences that women endure. Have the gumption to assemble efficient equipment for each job. While you are in the mood check up on the ironing board, the pad, and its cover. Are they all in good condition?

Do not scuff the bottom of the iron on buttons or buckles. Starch will stick and scorch on the iron. Never scratch it off with a knife or razor, if the bottom of the iron is marred it may catch fragile fabrics. If the condition isn't bad and the iron is hot, shake salt on a newspaper. Rub the iron over the salt and this will bring back the high polish. A cold iron can be scoured with fine steel wool or fine scouring powder. A smooth starch is less apt to stick than lumpy starch. Adding a pinch of salt to starch water before putting in the starch mixture helps prevent lumps and by raising the boiling point of the starch may aid cooking. Another preventive against sticking starch is a little beeswax or paraffin. Put the paraffin between brown paper and rub the iron over the paper to avoid picking up too much. Better still try spray-on starch and avoid these problems.

Steam irons. Follow the instructions that come with your iron. Even though tap water can be used, distilled or demineralized water is better, especially in hard-water areas.

If the iron becomes clogged with a mineral deposit, fill the water tank with a solution of water and water softener or water and vinegar. Heat, then empty it completely. Repeat with clear water.

Use the setting recommended by the manufacturer. Too cold a setting will not produce steam and may cause water spots. Steam created at too high a temperature is too dry for best results.

Empty all water from tank while iron is still hot. Water left in iron may cause rust or mineral deposit, or it may seep out and discolor the sole plate.

Conditioning the clothes for storage or ironing begins when they are taken from the dryer or off the line. The first two processes are the same—sorting and folding.

PREPARATION FOR IRONING

Sorting involves putting all like things together: bath towels, wash cloths, handkerchiefs, shirts, sheets, and pillow cases. As you do this, separate the things to be ironed from those to be stored.

Folding is equally important. If sheets, pillow cases, and towels are all folded neatly hem to hem and if they are smoothed as they are folded, wrinkles will be fewer. If shirts and shorts and other garments are snapped into shape and garments to be stored in drawers without ironing are precisely folded, the results are surprising.

Preparation for ironing may include dampening and starching, as well as careful sorting. Remove pongee, rayon, and silk from the dryer or line while still damp. Roll to hold moisture as sprinkling may cause water spots on these fabrics.

Cottons, linens, and blends come out crisper if ironed damp. They too may be removed from line or dryer while still damp; however, sprinkling or a steam iron won't spot them.

Dampening methods vary. Linens must be evenly dampened all over. Sprinkle, roll in a clean cloth, wrap in paper, and put in a warm oven with the heat turned off. Steam forms inside the roll and produces an even dampening. Only a few minutes are needed.

The plastic bag method is good for a miscellany. Any large bag will do; however, most laundry departments have special laundry-dampening bags. Put the pieces in the bag, separating white and colored items into different bags. When bag is full, sprinkle in a cup of cold water. Press out all air, close tight, and store in the refrigerator. Overnight the dampness will be evenly distributed.

Fabrics should not be dampened more than a few hours ahead in hot weather because of mildew. Things that are damp but can't be ironed at once may be stored in the refrigerator if space permits. Mildew will not develop at low temperatures. Moreover, when things are ironed fresh from the refrigerator, more steam is generated, which gives a finer finish.

IRONING—TEMPERATURE AND DAMPNESS CHART

Fabric	*Dampness*	*Temperature*
Pure silk	slight	low
Rayons	slight	low
Spun rayons and silk	dry	low or medium
Blended fabrics	read labels	low or medium
Permanent press	very damp	low or medium
Cotton—lightweight	damp	medium high
Cotton curtains	slightly damp	medium high
Cotton—heavy sheets	slightly damp	high
Linens	quite damp	high
Woolens	damp cloth	high
Cotton suitings	damp cloth	high
Gabardines	damp cloth	high
Men's ties, scarfs, etc.	damp cloth	high
Velvets, pile fabrics	damp cloth	high, steam

To dampen tablecloths, sprinkle one third, fold it over as you would a letter, then fold the top third over it. Roll. Sprinkle every third napkin or handkerchief and roll together. If linens dry out during ironing, redampen with a steam iron or rub an ice cube over the dry areas.

SPECIAL IRONING TECHNIQUES

Learn the order of ironing garments and the whole operation works out easily. To iron blouses, shirts, and dresses first iron the collar inside and out. Then do the neckband, yoke, cuffs, and sleeves. Do the back, then the front. The skirt of a dress is done last.

Iron button bands, plackets, hems, collars, and cuffs on the wrong side first. Finish on the right side.

Learn to fold slacks and boys' pants correctly to give sharp tailored creases. Iron dark cottons, rayons, and wool on the wrong side to avoid shine marks from the iron. If you know a garment fades, protect the ironing board before ironing it. Never iron the following: elasticized garments, because the heat disintegrates the rubber content; corduroy and chenilles, because it flattens them; shower curtains of pliofilm, pyroxolen, rayon and rubber to avoid burning them; articles with a waxy waterproofed finish such as raincoats; turkish towels and wash cloths as it makes them less absorbent and mats the pile.

Linens should be ironed with a hot iron until dry. For a glossy finish press first on the wrong side and repeat on the right.

Large tablecloths should have only one crease, down the center. To store roll on a tube or hang over a rod.

Table mats, doilies, and runners should have no creases and should be rolled or stored flat.

Press circular open-work cloths from the center out, working with the grain of the fabric and swinging the iron back and forth in an arc. This helps preserve the shape.

To press lace, initials, and embroidery place article face down on a soft cloth and press the back to raise the design on the right side.

Veiling can be freshened by pressing on wax paper.

To press ruffles, smooth the hem first, then gently point the iron into the gathers as the left hand straightens them.

Crisp napkins are pleasant to handle and damask napkins need ironing to bring out the luster. First iron them on the wrong side, then on the right side. If there is a monogram or embroidery, bring it up by pressing it on a pad, right side down. Dark napkins should be pressed with a cloth to prevent iron shine.

Fold breakfast, luncheon, and tea napkins in squares, always using the same routine. Lay the napkin on the board right side down, with the monogram or decorated corner in the bottom left-hand corner. Iron. Fold the top half of the napkin over the bottom half, matching up the hems and corners carefully. This move will expose half of the right side for ironing. Now fold the right half over the left half. Iron and turn over for final polishing. When placed on the table the napkin may be folded loosely to form a rectangle or a triangle.

Large dinner napkins are usually folded in thirds, first lengthwise, then crosswise. The final fold is not pressed.

Seldom-used linens should be stored clean, dry, and unironed. Wrap in blue or black tissue paper to prevent yellowing.

24 How to Remove Spots and Stains

It was easier to cope with spots and stains back in the days when I was textile tester for the Bon Marché department store in Seattle, because then most fabrics were silk, cotton, wool, or linen. They were easy to handle because they always acted according to the laws of nature.

In this era of test-tube fibers you never know what is going to happen when you apply a chemical. Nylon, Dacron, or glass fiber, alone or in combination, can strangely affect the behavior of a fabric.

If there is a spot or stain on synthetic fabric which you can't identify or if the spot is on a valuable article, rush it off to a first-class cleaner.

Tell him everything you know about the fabric and the stain. Cleaners are also having their troubles with new fabrics and intelligent cooperation brings better results.

In all households, accidents will happen. Things are spilled on tablecloths, rugs, sofas, chairs, and clothes. Quick action is the principal ingredient in the removal of the spot. Blot up at once and remove any remaining stain as soon as possible. The fresher the spot, the more easily it will come out. Don't wait until washday.

Before beginning work on a stain, review these questions:

1. What is the article made of—wool, silk, cotton, linen, a synthetic, or a mixture? Has it a special finish?
2. Is it a washable material? If so, the chances are good for removal. Fabrics which require dry cleaning are more difficult.
3. What caused the spot?
4. Has the fabric a smooth, hard surface or a rough one? Smooth surfaces are harder to work with, as the cleaning agent may leave a ring.
5. Is the color delicate? Pastels are often fugitive.
6. Is the fabric clean? If a spot is removed from a soiled fabric, the

clean spot will show. The remedy may be to clean the whole thing.

About 90 percent of the spots on washable fabrics can be removed by sponging with cold water while they are still fresh. Don't use soap or a detergent on a spot unless you know it has grease in it. Don't use hot water on a spot until you have used cold. Hot water will set an animal stain such as meat, eggs, or blood that contains albumin. Don't use a hot iron on the article until you know that the substance which caused the spot has been removed. Sugar solution, for instance, may not show on wool, but when pressed it stiffens into a dark stain. Cod-liver oil will do the same thing. If you sponge the spot with water without results, let it dry before trying any kind of cleaning fluid. When a fabric is a blend of fibers treat one that contains wool like wool and one with cotton like cotton. Cotton and linen synthetics will hold up under hot-water first aid, but the wool synthetics may need cool temperatures and may respond to solvents rather than water. Before using a stain remover, test the action on a concealed portion of the material.

The techniques of stain removal are simple. First, blot up excess liquid quickly with facial tissue, cloth, or paper towels; scrape off solids, using a dull knife or spatula. After solids and excess liquid are removed turn the stain face down on a blotter or absorbent surface. Work on the back to avoid drawing stain through the fabric. Of course this is not possible on upholstery or carpets. Start treatment at outer edges of the stain, work toward the center. On small spots use a medicine dropper or glass rod to apply chemicals; flooding the spot may enlarge it. Blot between each application, always using clean area of the blotter. Keep shifting to dry areas on pad underneath stain. Pat, don't rub. Never leave traces of cleaning agent in the material, as it could damage the fabric. This applies especially to the bleaches, acids and alkalis.

In addition to water, spot-removal agents include absorbent powders, bleaches, acids and alkalis, and grease solvents. There is a wide choice of each type and many of the agents are available around the house. In addition to these, keep on hand commercial spot removers for quick application to uncomplicated spots. Many of the agents recommended are poisonous. These should never be stored in the kitchen or left on a counter. Keep them on a high shelf in the laundry out of children's reach.

STAIN-REMOVAL AGENTS

Absorbent powders for grease; especially useful for application on wallpaper, upholstery, and carpets. May be applied dry or as a paste mixed with water or cleaning fluid. Use Fuller's earth, French chalk, cornmeal, cornstarch, talcum powder, or flour.

Bleaches. Hydrogen peroxide is a mild, all-purpose bleach. Chlorine bleach is used only on cottons and linens.

Solvents. Turpentine, denatured alcohol, commercial dry cleaners. Use out doors or in well-ventilated room, never near a flame. Read label.

Washing agents. Water and detergents.

Acids. White vinegar, citrus acid.

Alkalis. Baking soda, Epsom salts.

In a basket with your stain-removal agents keep:

A glass measuring cup
Several glass or enamel bowls for solution (do not use metals —aluminum, steel or copper)
Clean white cloths torn into twelve-inch squares
White blotting paper, white facial tissue, paper towels
Medicine dropper
Glass stirring rods
Dull knife or spatula
Art-gum eraser (a substitute is fresh white bread)

HOW TO REMOVE COMMON SPOTS

Adhesive tape. Sponge with carbon tetrachloride, benzine, or kerosene. If kerosene is used wash in suds to remove oily sediment.

Alcoholic beverages. Both alcoholic and soft drinks may leave tannin stains which do not show until after laundering, and then the brown stain cannot be removed without a bleach. While the stain is still fresh, sponge with water, blot. Repeat. Then sponge with a solution of liquid detergent, one teaspoon to a cup of water. If stain remains, apply one tablespoon white vinegar in three tablespoons water. Rinse with diluted ammonia solution.

Blood. If possible, before the stain dries, wash in cold water; hot water sets the stain. Salt added to the water may help; use two tablespoons of salt to one cup of water. Soak old stains on washable materials in a solution of two tablespoons of ammonia or two cups of salt to a gallon of water, but test the fabric first for discoloration. If stain still shows, sponge with hydrogen peroxide, a mild bleach which can be used with any fabric; but test on a seam for color fastness.

On blankets and carpets remove fresh bloodstains with a paste of dry starch and cold water. Apply thickly, let it dry, and brush away. Repeat if necessary.

Candle wax. Apply ice to harden. Blotting it while soft will spread the wax and grind it into the fabric. Crack off or scrape away as much as possible with a knife. If wax is white, place blotting paper on both sides and press with hot iron. Shift the blotter around as it fills with wax. When blotter comes away clean, sponge the spot with cleaning fluid. If spot still shows and material is washable, bleach. If wax is colored, after removing excess pat the stain gently with diluted denatured alcohol. Use one part of alcohol to two parts of water.

Catsup. Wipe off surplus, sponge with cold water. Work in glycerin and let stand. Press to blot up excess, apply white vinegar, rinse in cold water.

Chewing gum. Apply ice to harden the gum. Then snap or scrape gum from the fabric. This method is applicable to rugs, upholstery, blankets, and even gum in your child's hair.

Egg white and carbon tetrachloride will soften gum so that it can be removed. But usually the ice treatment is satisfactory. Macy's says that they remove two tons of gum a year from rugs and fixtures in the store by this method.

Chocolate or cocoa. Since fat, milk, sugar, starch, and coloring matter are present, several treatments may be necessary. First scrape off all excess matter. Then, if material is washable, put through regular laundry. If stain remains apply hydrogen peroxide and wash again.

If fabric is not washable, sponge with cool water after scraping off excess. Dry and apply cleaning fluid.

Cigarette stain. Launder in hot suds.

Cod-liver oil. Fresh stains are easily removed with glycerin or cleaning fluid. Rinse in water and wash in warm suds. If it is not removed, ironing will produce brown spots.

Coffee, tea, and wine. Remove before drying if possible. Mop up excess. If it is a big spot and the material is washable, stretch part with spot over the top of a bowl. Hold in place with a rubber band and from about twenty-four inches above pour hot water through stain. If a trace of stain remains after this treatment touch with hydrogen peroxide and rinse thoroughly.

Deodorants. Most deodorants of the cream, stick, or spray variety can be removed by laundering in warm suds. A deodorant with an oily base can be removed by sponging with carbon tetrachloride, followed by warm suds. It is most important to remove deodorant and perspiration stains *before* pressing a garment.

Egg. Avoid anything that will harden albumin. Sponge with cold water then carbon tetrachloride before laundering. Be sure spot is removed before pressing with a hot iron.

Fruit. Cherries, plums, peaches, and pears contain tannin. Remove spot if possible before it has dried, then rub lightly with glycerin. After two or three hours add a few drops of vinegar, rinse after two minutes, then launder. See coffee and tea method for other fruits.

Grass stains. When fresh, grass stains come out with soap or detergent. Lingering traces disappear with a bleach. If the fabric is not washable, sponge with benzine or alcohol. Test color reaction in an inconspicuous spot. Do not use alcohol on rayon unless you dilute it—one part alcohol with two parts water.

Gravy. See Greases.

Greases and oils. Salad dressing, machine grease, gravy. Remove spots when fresh if possible. Mop up excess. If the material is washable, use warm soapy water. Do not use hot water, especially if there is egg in the salad dressing. Use the same caution with gravy, as heat will set the albumin which is in meat. Soapless shampoos are also excellent for removing grease, fat, and oil.

Nonwashable materials may be sponged with carbon tetrachloride. If the spot is deeply embedded, loosen by rubbing on a little glycerin before treating with solvent. If the material is not fragile, sponge gently with warm water and soap after application of solvent. For tarlike or heavy greases, rub spots with lard, then wash in hot suds.

On fragile fabrics use an absorbent such as cornstarch or French chalk. This method is useful for grease stains on wallpaper, rugs, and upholstery. Apply as a paste, dry and brush off.

Hair dyes. Wash in suds with vinegar added. Bleach with hydrogen peroxide and relaunder.

Hair rinses. Sponge with vinegar and rinse thoroughly. Then apply a thick solution of soap or detergent suds and rinse again. Follow by laundering in clean suds with a little ammonia added. If necessary, use bleach on white or colorfast fabrics, and relaunder.

Hair sprays and lacquers. Most sprays and lacquers can be completely removed with hot suds. Sponging with alcohol will remove stains made by a spray with a shellac base. But first pretest to make sure that alcohol doesn't harm the dye or fabric—especially if it is an acetate fabric.

Hand lotions. Most types, including those with silicone bases, can be removed with hot suds.

Ice cream. Such stains should first be sponged with cold water, to remove any egg or sugar desposit. Dry. If washable wash. Chocolate or coffee ice-cream stains may require a bleach. If fabric is not washable, sponge with carbon tetrachloride or denatured alcohol.

Ink. The many ink formulas complicate stain removal. On washable fabrics rinse in cold water before ink dries, then wash in detergent solution. On nonwashable fabrics apply absorbent powder, such as French chalk, while ink is still wet. Shake off. When dry make a paste of the powder and apply. Use ink eradicator according to directions if ink is dry; follow with clear water. Ink in ballpoint pens has an oily base. Place fabric on blotter, apply tetrachloride with glass rod; change pad frequently. Use same method on India ink. On old stains use hydrogen peroxide.

Iodine. Soap or detergent and water will remove fresh stains from washable fabrics. If the area is large sponge with diluted white vinegar before washing. Nonwashable fabrics should be sponged with alcohol while stain is fresh. Alternate with steam from a boiling tea kettle.

Lipstick. On washable fabrics rub with fatty substance such as glycerin, cold cream, or shortening. This dilutes the dye. Let stand five or ten minutes, then wash with detergent solution. If stain resists, remove article from solution, add washing soda to solution, and dip again. Lingering stains on white cotton or linen can be bleached.

On nonwashable fabrics sponge with cleaning fluid. Liquid lipstick is almost impossible to remove from many fabrics—it should be entrusted to a professional spotter.

Liquid shoe polish. Fresh stains can usually be removed by laundering in warm suds. If necessary, follow up by sponging any residue on white or colorfast fabrics with a weak solution of bleach, and relaunder.

Liquid make-up. Most types can be removed by laundering in a thick solution of hot suds. If necessary, follow with bleach on white or colorfast fabrics.

Medicine. If the composition is unknown, experiment a little. Blot at once; treat while damp if possible. First, using a glass rod or dropper, apply a liquid detergent in a solution of one teaspoon to one cup of water. Blot with white cloth. If some of the stain transfers to cloth, repeat. If it does not, try an acid solution, using one teaspoon of oxalic acid or white vinegar in four teaspoons of water. Rinse.

Mildew. Fresh spots may come out in regular wash. Drying on the grass in the sun after moistening with lemon juice and salt was Grandmother's method and it still works on white cottons and linens. Soaking all night in sour milk or buttermilk is also a mild method excellent for fine white linens.

More drastic methods for bad spots involve sponging with white vinegar before washing or soaking in a solution of one tablespoon of household bleach to each quart of water. After fifteen minutes rinse thoroughly. Do not use bleach on silk or wool; it will dissolve these fabrics.

Mud. Let mud dry, then brush. Sponge with clear water. If stain persists, sponge with alcohol. Dilute alcohol used on rayons.

Mustard and curry. These are difficult to remove. Large stains should be handled professionally. Small stains on washable fabrics may be massaged with glycerin before washing, then bleached.

Nail polish. Nail polish may damage synthetic fibers or blends. Removers or thinners may also leave holes. Apply chemically pure amyl acetate, available at drugstores, directly on stain with eyedropper. Sponge with cloth pad.

Oil. See Greases.

Paint, varnish, or shellac. If container is available read directions and use thinner recommended or turpentine. Sponge from edge toward center. When clear, sponge with dry-cleaning solvent. The type with a nitrocellulose base may be removed with any acetate, followed by carbon tetrachloride. The type with a resin base is soluble in acetone, followed by carbon tetrachloride. *Caution:* Test the fabric first to make sure that acetone can be used safely.

Water-emulsion paints. If paint is still wet, it can generally be removed from washable garments by using lots of suds. Once it is dry, there is no practical solvent for either latex-base or casein-base cold-water paints.

Plastic paints. Send to a professional cleaner for expert use of such strong solvents as trichlorethylene or perchloroethylene.

Spray paints. Use a dry-cleaning solvent, such as carbon tetrachloride, then launder with suds.

Pancake make-up. Sponge with carbon tetrachloride followed by warm suds.

Perfume and cologne. Launder as soon as possible in hot suds, followed by bleaching with sodium perborate if the stain remains on bleachable fabric. Then relaunder. The longer perfume "ages," the more damage its alcohol content may do to a fabric.

Perfume solid. This should wash out with warm suds. If it has an oily base, sponge with carbon tetrachloride, then relaunder.

Permanent-wave lotion. Wash in hot suds immediately because chemicals may harm dyes.

Perspiration. Sponge with diluted vinegar, launder at once. If fabric is exposed to ammonia fumes while damp, color may be restored. On washable fabrics yellow stain may be bleached. Such stains can also be removed by soaking in a little benzine and Epsom salts. Pat the stained area until it is saturated, then press out the dampness between paper towels. Repeat if necessary.

Rust. On white washable materials the old-fashioned methods are still the best. Lemon juice is the old standby, but do not let it dry on the fabric or a lemon stain may replace the iron stain. To prevent drying spread the fabric over a pan of boiling water; then apply lemon juice with a medicine dropper or glass rod. Rinse thoroughly in warm water. Diluted 5 percent oxalic acid may be used instead of lemon juice on cottons and linens. Oxalic acid is poisonous; handle with care and keep out of children's reach. After application rinse thoroughly. To last rinse add a dash of household ammonia to neutralize any remaining acid.

Rust seldom is found on silks or fabrics to be dry cleaned. If rust appears on wool or silk turn it over to a dry cleaner.

Salad dressings. If spilled on colored material, apply weak ammonia water or baking soda to the spot immediately to prevent any vinegar or lemon-juice content from injuring dyes. Sponge delicate washable materials with lukewarm suds (not hot if egg or cream was used in dressing). Apply a grease solvent such as carbon tetrachloride or benzine after the stain has been sponged with water and dried.

Scorch. A light scorch on cotton will disappear in the wash. Deeper scorches may be bleached by dampening fabric and laying on grass in the sun. A deep scorch weakens the fibers. If the bad stain disappears a hole may be left. A scorch on nonwashable materials may be sponged with hydrogen peroxide.

Shoe polish. If fresh it will wash out. The base is a grease so it will dissolve with an application of carbon tetrachloride. If ground into the fabric it can be loosened with glycerin or vaseline. On wools sponge with denatured alcohol. If a stain remains when grease is removed, bleach washable fabrics with hydrogen peroxide. Rinse.

Soft drinks. See Alcoholic beverages.

Spinach. Green spinach stains should be moistened, rubbed well with suds, and bleached in the sun. Then launder the piece as usual.

Suntan lotions. Sponge with carbon tetrachloride, followed by a suds solution with vinegar added. Tannic-acid stains may be bleached out of white cottons or linens. Then launder with clean suds.

Tea. See Coffee.

Tomato soup, juice. Sponge with cold water. Massage with glycerin. Sponge with soap or detergent solution. If stain remains on white washable fabrics, bleach with hydrogen peroxide. Rinse.

Urine stains. These frequently occur on rugs and carpets when there are young pets. The acid content can seriously affect fibers and may change the color. Work quickly; first blot up excess and repeatedly sponge with cold water and blot. Apply a mixture of one tablespoon ammonia to one-half cup of water. Rinse. Sponge with soapless (liquid) detergent, one teaspoon to a cup of water. Rinse.

Varnish. See Paint.

Water spots. On handwoven, nonwashable fabrics water may leave a ring. If the fabric is clean, the spots may disappear if they are gently rubbed around the edge. If this does not bring results steam over a teakettle. Dry slowly, rubbing from outside toward center.

Wine. See Coffee.

For a complete directory of stain removal send for Farmer's Bulletin No. 1474, "Stain Removal from Fabrics." U.S. Department of Agriculture, U.S. Government Printing Office, Washington, D.C. 20025. Price five cents. Directions for removing 103 stains are included.

5 *About Management*

25 Household Management

After scrubbing the house from cellar to garret it is time to put on a white collar, sit down at a desk, and be an executive. Desk work is soothing, stabilizing, even habit forming. It gives dignity to a job.

Desk work for a housewife consists of organizing future projects, developing plans, and arranging the financial affairs of the family. Of course, management requires planning. Planning is the result of thinking, and thought, as Emerson said, is the hardest kind of work. But thought is a creative activity and offers an opportunity for increasing family satisfactions.

What do you do when you plan and manage? Let's picture it. There is a question as to whether Billy should have a bicycle or whether the girls should have new coats. The account book and checkbook may be studied and the facts lined up for discussion with your husband and the children.

Again, you may be thinking of redecorating the living room. You take from the file the living-room folder. In the folder are the floor plan of the room drawn to scale, and an inventory with prices and the sources of present furnishings with color samples. Now you are ready to do an accurate job of redecorating the room and estimating the cost.

Or imagine that you are a devoted gardener. It is February and time to put in your order for spring plants and seeds. At your desk you have seed catalogues and a plot plan of the garden. Whenever you have an empty hour, have a delicious time dreaming about the garden you will have next summer. The by-product of your dreams will be your plant order.

Management then is the fascinating business of setting the stage for your family's special kind of living with the accents right where you want them. It is equally involved with the spending of time and money.

Someday someone may produce a household computer into which you can pour your problems; then you can punch a button and get decisive advice on plans as well as workable schedules; but until that time comes family councils offer the only help. After each session someone, meaning you, must list decisions and put them into operation. In business today this is known as a PERT-type process. PERT, otherwise known as Project Evaluation and Review Technique, is revolutionizing many operations requiring careful scheduling. Diagrams are drawn of projects, assigning responsibilities and giving dates for review and completion. The chart changes daily and often reveals new problems, which require rescheduling. Few of us are actually going to cast PERT charts, but the idea can be applied to the operation of the home. Even a little PERT thinking would improve the management of many homes.

Roughly the managerial process consists of planning, controlling, and evaluation. Planning means mapping out a course of action to reach goals; this is done before the action starts. Controlling the plan is watching its development, and evaluation consists in looking back over what has been accomplished and judging the results in light of family goals.

A MANAGEMENT CENTER

If you want to garden, you must have a place to dig and plant. You can't get very far with a reading program without books to read. And if you really want to make an honest effort at household management, set up a household office. If you have had business training such a center should give you real pleasure. Even without office experience you will soon discover that bills, records, addresses, appointments should be kept in an orderly way.

It is possible to do household planning out of your head as you wash dishes or change the baby's diaper, and some of it inevitably is done that way. I have an unfortunate habit of having some of my best ideas in the gray hours of the morning. But, obviously, to plan or manage with any accuracy books and reference material are necessary, and for efficiency everything should be assembled in one place.

A household desk does not have to be a big, imposing affair. It can be tucked into almost any corner. The fact that it exists is an indication that the owner is running her household efficiently.

A well-known motion-picture star converted a closet in her beautiful Hollywood home into an office. It opens from the library. There is just space for a chair when the door is open. There, at arm's reach, is everything—files, accounts, reference books, address and date books, telephone, and typewriter.

In a remodeled house in Connecticut, the former pantry, opening from the kitchen, houses a big flat-topped mahogany George Washington desk and a file. Ruffled curtains froth at the window and the ivy-green walls are studded with photographs of the family.

In a house just built, also in Connecticut, there is a desk in the kitchen. It is opposite the L-shaped work area, under a window which is completely surrounded by bookshelves housing a collection of cookbooks, both new and old.

A woman in Maryland discovered that the book-lined library was really her husband's province and there was no place there for her housekeeping necessities and thoughts. She picked up her things and moved them to a storeroom in the attic. She had closets with shelves put on one side to accommodate piles and piles of old reference magazines. With the help of her father-in-law she converted an old sideboard into a generous workmanlike desk. In contrast to the dignity of the rest of the house, she painted the walls shocking pink with white trim and used cherry-red cushions on white-painted chairs. There is a white rug on the black-painted floor, which is spattered in cherry, pink, and gray. Now it's a retreat, an office, and a workroom that's fun to have and to use.

In an attractive house in Denver the guestroom is also an office. There is a desk as well as a built-in wall closet which hides files, drawers, and reference material. The typewriter and phone have their place on a big coffee table in front of the sofa bed. Janet, a former secretary, says that the typewriter on the coffee table reminds her less of the office.

The family desk in a beautiful Fifth Avenue apartment in New York is in the living room in front of a window overlooking Central Park. The window and sides of the desk are banked with plants which have the effect of a room divider. Even though it is in the living room, the desk corner has a feeling of seclusion.

The important thing is to have a desk, it doesn't matter where, at which to plan and in which essential records may be kept. Of course, if a file can be incorporated with the desk that is an advantage. Desk drawers do well enough for paper and pencils but they seem to be designed to foil anyone trying to find anything else in them.

BASIC DESK SUPPLIES

calendar
pencil sharpener
pencils and pens
paper clips
paper and envelopes
postage stamps
post cards
matches
wastebasket
elastic bands
Scotch tape
paper scissors and letter opener
files
incoming and outgoing baskets
a mirror
a ruler
erasers and ink eradicator
carbon paper
blotters

NICE-TO-HAVE DESK ACCESSORIES

typewriter
small radio
telephone
address book

HOUSEHOLD RECORDS

For efficiency all household and family records should be kept in one place accessible to both husband and wife. There are an increasing number of records, formal and informal, which must be kept. The formal records are a must. The informal records are optional but once organized they are the source of a great deal of pleasure which will carry on through a lifetime. Some items of the following list might well be kept in the safe-deposit box, but kept they must be.

FORMAL RECORDS

checkbook
securities—stocks and bonds
savings bank books
insurance policies
hospitalization receipts
social security cards
pension papers
state and federal income tax reports and data
inventories of goods in storage
receipts of important purchases such as fur coats, diamond rings, and carpets
guarantees on merchandise
mortgage, deeds, and leases
military discharge papers
naturalization papers
automobile titles and bill of sale
birth certificates
wedding certificate
divorce papers
a medical record for each member of the family
passports
diplomas
wills
time-payment papers
receipted bills
club membership cards
other tax records

INFORMAL RECORDS

budget and account books
household inventory
address books
guest book
personal records and family tree
diary
personal correspondence

Looking after such items is more or less routine. The important thing is to do it conscientiously and not haphazardly. To have one thing tucked away in a sugar bowl, another behind a loose brick in the hearth, something else sewed into a mattress, and others just kicking around in a top bureau drawer is the way of madness. Eventually such maneuvers may result in headlines in the newspapers. Every day such curious goings-on come to light and are reported. Good housewifery demands competent filing and storage of valuables.

Keep receipts of all major purchases. Have a separate file on the automobile, on the house, on furniture, taxes, furs, insurance premiums, on stock and bond purchases and jewelry.

Canceled checks or receipted bills for department stores, gas and electricity, or telephone may be discarded after a year if there is no error evident.

Receipts or canceled checks to doctors, dentists, churches, theaters, clubs, or charities should be kept for income tax reference. Any other material relating to property evaluation should be preserved for the same reason. Such receipts should include all major repairs on the house and property.

INVENTORY

The necessity and value of a household inventory comes only through sad experience. You say, "Oh, I'll never have a fire," or "I've never even known anyone who was burglarized." Then one or the other happens. If you have no inventory and perhaps no insurance, there may be difficulty in even arranging a tax deduction to cover your loss.

I speak from experience. It was only after my apartment was robbed that I started an inventory. But, having started, I find it entertaining business.

Keep an inventory like an account book. Room by room itemize each rug, lamp, and piece of furniture, list the price, where purchased, and date of purchase. In a packet at the back of the book keep important bills. If you have an elaborate household, a professional evaluator may be consulted. He will also appraise the present value of each item. His charge will be about $5 per $1,000.

A separate inventory of clothing should be made.

Inventories are invaluable in cases of real emergency, but they are also helpful as a control on the upkeep and repair of the house. They are useful if you sublet furnished, if you move, or if you are settling an estate. Incidentally, most of the big fire-insurance companies have special booklets made up for household inventories, which are free on request.

If you are a collector, records are most important. Whether you collect pictures, sculpture, or accessories, photograph or sketch each individual item and mount it. The book will be a pleasure to have, and in that future day when your estate is being settled it may be a great help in evaluating items.

Reference file. In relation to the inventory it may be wise to start a file which includes the catalogues and booklets giving directions for the care and use of household equipment. Such a reference library might cover the refrigerator, range, kitchen cabinets, washer, ironer, rug, and paint or paper on walls.

Usually such bulletins are strewn around the house, some in the kitchen, others in the basement or stuck in between books on the bookshelves. Eventually they are lost. Then something goes wrong and a repairman is called who sends an unnecessarily high repair bill, whereas it is possible the guarantee might still be in effect or the repair could have been done at home with the data and the booklet to refer to. You know the old story of the man who complained of a high repair bill. A duplicate bill was sent, which itemized the first bill; it read:

To tighten one bolt	$1.00
To know what bolt to tighten	$49.00
Total	$50.00

INSURANCE

Of course you have personal insurance of some kind. You may even have a policy for the children's education. But is your house properly protected? Ask your insurance broker for possible coverage.

On the apartment in town we carry burglary insurance, as thievery is old stuff in New York City. In the country there is fire insurance on the house; the mortgage holder requires it. We are also insured against loss from hurricanes and floods. There is a dam on the property above the house, and if it gave way in an unusual rush of water we might all merrily sail away. There are also servants' and workmen's liability. This is required in the state of New Jersey and since there are always workmen on the place, a very good thing it is. The burglary policy in the city includes the country house, though the risk in the country is slight.

Other policies which might be considered are against:

furnace explosion
loss of research files
aircraft and motor vehicle damage to property
vandalism or malicious mischief

WILLS

Perhaps you think that you haven't enough property to make a will and you aren't going to die anyway. You aren't the only one who feels that way. It's a very common notion, but if the unforeseen does occur, it's very unfair to the family not to have a will, for an intestate settlement may mean a loss to them.

Both husband and wife should have one. Details vary in different states; investigate local requirements. The most perfect will on record is the twenty-three-word will of Calvin Coolidge. It reads: "Not unmindful of my son, John, I give all my estate, both real and personal, to my wife, Grace Coolidge, in fee simple." The last phrase is a legal one which conveys absolute possession by law.

Don't overlook the need for a safe-deposit box at the bank. For important papers, such as stocks, bonds and deeds to property, don't begrudge the small annual payment which insures safety. It's wise to keep a listing of everything in the box.

MANAGEMENT TIPS

Don't be a Sally Spotless. Make it a rule to do nothing better than it needs to be done unless it gives you deep personal pleasure. Learn to estimate how long each job will take and you will save time.

Family goals should not be static; they will change just as resources change and the years pass.

The latest tools, equipment, and time savers are not extravagances if they are true time savers and work simplifiers.

Avoid overambitious goals, the desire for perfection, too crowded plans and too costly projects; these lead to frustration.

Control your wants. Be sure that your goals serve your family and are within your resources. Don't permit any advertising, publicity, neighbors, or even your children to push you into a purely status-seeking project.

Allow some time every day for pure enjoyment, to look at the sky or water, or clean your plants, look at pictures, admire your baby's feet, listen to music, take a walk, or read a book.

Make your plans flexible enough so that they can be adjusted to meet unexpected interruptions, delays, and demands.

Learn to delegate jobs and show proper appreciation when they are well done.

26 Money Matters

I have a widespread reputation for not being able to add two and two. Nevertheless, since taking a household-management course in my senior year at college, I have kept an account of my expenditures, made yearly summaries, and pursued sound financial practices. Scotswoman Effie I. Raitt, founder and late head of the home economics department of the University of Washington, succeeded in reaching me on this subject. Until taking her course I was as improvident as a grasshopper.

All through college I was flush the first of the month when my check came from home and in dire straits by the time the thirtieth rolled around. On holidays, in order to get home, a trip of a hundred miles, as a rule I had to pawn my books at the college bookshop. My sister, who received the same allowance, always had enough for a trip home and sometimes could even make me a loan. Is there any wonder I recommend record keeping? It can save you from yourself!

Money, as everyone knows, has a sly way of slipping through fingers, with nothing to show for it. If you are ever to have money enough to do the big things you dream of, a feeling for money is necessary. Only through accumulation, only by having enough at one time, can really big projects be launched. To save for ambitious dreams and quality purchases it is necessary to be very strong minded and resist even twenty-five-cent gadgets.

Men formerly controlled the purse strings of the family and doled out the household money to their wives. But now that almost all women have earned and handled their own money (and often contribute to the family finances after marriage) this has changed. Today husbands and wives usually talk over all major purchases, and this is good; the handling of money should be a joint affair as the welfare of a family is tied up with its financial standing. However, it is the wives who actually make the bulk of the family purchases, do the banking and pay the bills, and they are often more conversant with family finances than their husbands. Where husbands and wives don't co-operate on finances, money problems are the number-one source of quarrels.

Every young bridegroom should be given this advice:

1. Tell your wife what you earn and exactly what your job is and what you do.
2. After the bills are paid, the savings account covered, share the remainder equally.
3. Ask yourself whether your wife is spending on herself the equivalent of your expenditures on tobacco and at bars.
4. Never forget that for the sake of harmony a woman will nurse a grievance.
5. Silence does not mean contentment.

Family finances must have short-, intermediate-, and long-term goals. The short-term program covers current expenditures, the operating cost of the household. The intermediate goals cover major purchases for the house, and vacations. The long-term goals involve building an estate.

The only way to tackle these goals is to examine your finances minutely and know to the last cent how much money comes in and where it goes. This leads directly to accounts and budgets, two very unpopular subjects. Women by the million turn the pages of a magazine without reading when they see these words in a title. But face them we must.

A budget is an estimate of expenditures in different classifications made in advance. Accounts, on the other hand, involve listing expenditures after they are made in order to show where the money has disappeared. The sincere auditor points out that keeping accounts is the same as locking the barn after the horse is stolen.

I have never been able to make a workable budget. My system is a combination account-budget-survey system, plus very ambitious goals. The first step involves a survey. This consists of an analysis of the income and outgo.

Well over 50 percent of the average income is spent in relatively large sums. Begin the analysis by putting down on paper your yearly income. Under it compile this list of known or fixed expenditures:

State income tax	$
Federal income tax	$
Insurance premiums	$
Rent or payment on mortgage	$
Hospitalization	$
School tuitions	$
Installation payments	$
Church	$
Clubs	$
Total	$
Grand total	$

. . . every household must have an accountant

Now subtract this sum from yearly income. Remaining is the amount which can be manipulated for better or worse. Divide by 12 both the total of fixed expenditures and the sum remaining from the yearly income after the fixed expenditures are subtracted. This will show how much must be put aside each month for incontrovertibles and also how much is available for food, clothing, operating, recreation, savings, and incidentals.

If you have never really analyzed expenditures in order to come to grips with the problem it may be necessary to keep detailed accounts for several months. Start the accounts in a loose-leaf notebook.

Under "Food" list every purchase:

meat	dairy
vegetables	fish
bakery	restaurant
candy	snacks

Under "Operating" list:

gas and electric bills	telephone
water rates	garbage disposal
household help	cleaning bills
cleaning materials	gardener
laundry	floor finisher
window cleaner	laundry

Under "Clothing" keep separate accounts for each member of the family.

Under "Automobile" include:

payments	oil
garage rent if any	upkeep and repair
gasoline	

Under "Recreation, Education, and Welfare":

gifts	charity
movies	theater
concerts	dances
doctor bills	

After keeping a detailed account for about three months it's time to simplify the system and have a family council. You are living within your income, just breaking even, or you are spending more than you are taking in. In the latter two cases something must be done. Only the federal government can overspend and still remain solvent. Every family should build up a reserve for emergencies.

The thing to do is to build up a family attitude and enlist complete cooperation. This is the way to avoid quarrels over money, always a degrading experience. When still young, children should learn that "things" are not important, it's the point of view that counts. They should learn that it isn't where you live that labels you, it is how you live; it isn't expensive paid-for recreation that will give you the greatest pleasure, but the things that are free like sunshine, trees, and just plain breathing deeply. As Thoreau said, "Money is not required to buy one necessity of the soul."

I've always found that you can save money if you want to badly enough. The leaks in most budgets today are great and many. We eat extravagantly, we dress extravagantly, we consider expensive recreation a necessity. We don't bother to count the cost of the car.

Talk to a group of people on this subject and they will produce dozens of ways of saving. One woman let her cleaning woman go; another bought an automatic washer-dryer and does her own laundry. Many women do their own shampoos and sets. A mother with three daughters saves hundreds of dollars by making all their clothing, and a woman with two sons has set up a barber shop and now cuts their hair as well as her husband's.

But there is also the woman who writes:

> We can't save by not having a laundress for six dollars a week! This is a luxury I never enjoyed. I don't enjoy cleaning up garbage but I always have, and my boys are learning to do it too. No nasty niceness allowed. We can't afford it.
>
> I can't save on beauty parlors. In my whole life I've never spent over $25 on hair-dos. I can't save on baby sitters by my husband and I going alternate nights to a movie or concert because we don't go to movies or concerts. We don't even go on Sunday drives or take vacation trips.
>
> Now, if anyone can tell me how to save any money, I'd be grateful. Please understand we are not complaining. We are happy and don't feel cheated. To those of us who have never known a more luxurious life it's just a matter of pinching each penny one more time before letting go.

Regardless of whether a family is just breaking even or whether there is a surplus for saving, a survey of your financial situation is desirable. Begin by keeping accounts. Develop your own system but keep accounts; it will add not only to the entertainment value of the money you spend but it will also give you a feeling of controlling your cash destiny. Don't keep accounts on a penny-pinching basis and don't waste time chasing a dime at the end of the month to make the accounts balance, but know where the money goes. Include a summary sheet in your account system. Transfer total monthly expenditures to such a chart for better comparisons. On the summary page also chart the fixed expenditures and star the months when payments must be made. If you have never tried keeping accounts start now. It is surprising the sense of mastery it gives.

PURCHASING AGENT

In addition to making budgets, keeping accounts, and stopping the small leaks, it's necessary to have a spending or, if you prefer, a buying program. There must be plans for vacations, for the children's education, for church contributions, for community activities.

As we acquire more things, more wants, and more money, household spending becomes more complicated. Now the housing dollar competes with the automobile dollar and the vacation dollar robs the new television account. One automobile isn't enough; the family wants two. Children and parents alike have developed the psychology that they must have everything at once when they are young, without waiting.

All these wants and family demands are dumped into the lap of the homemaker, who is chief arbitrator and purchasing agent. Even though decisions on major items should be joint decisions, it is the purchasing agent who must make balanced recommendations that cover the total problem.

Merely deciding to make the purchase is only half the problem. The next is to make the selection and make it at a price that is right. Women do 85 percent of the purchasing. This clearly involves being an expert in many fields or doing a pretty poor job. From what I know from behind the scenes women do just a fifty-fifty job as purchasing agents. With a little work, a little effort, with a boycott here and there, they could revolutionize the consumer market.

Certainly household buying isn't easy. It requires being informed about all the new foods, packaging, and prices. It means having a smattering of knowledge about all of the many new fabrics, fibers, and blends. It means being aware of fashion trends for boys, men, teen-agers, and children as well as what Paris dictates. It requires delicately balancing the cost of a new party dress for teen-age Sally against the psychological need for it.

The family purchasing agent must keep up with the rapid change and development in major appliances and small appliances, and decide when it is time to replace the old one.

Whether she is happy about it or not or whether she feels confident of her ability, every homemaker is in a measure a home decorator. Rugs, sofas, chairs, draperies must be replaced every ten years or so throughout a lifetime. Face it, study, keep files, be aware of styles, prices, trends, and this area of purchasing can be a great pleasure. Moreover, your measure of success will determine the mental picture of home the children will always carry with them.

The planning must go beyond the family. If the household is to be a happy one, financial plans must include social life, parties, and friendly times together. Events in a family don't just happen; they have to be made to happen.

In fact, it doesn't take much study to discover that Mother is the standard setter, the creator of the home atmosphere. If she sets physical standards of neatness and cleanliness, if she promotes punctuality and gracious personal relations, these too will become family characteristics.

It may be difficult for very young homemakers to realize that they are responsible for the character of their own households. But the sooner they adopt an adult role and recognize that they must be leaders, the sooner the family will become a going enterprise. If a homemaker will guide and direct, if she promotes planned action, the family will develop strength, attain varied satisfactions, and be a proud and stable unit.

BUYING ON CREDIT

If you would believe what you hear today, only a fool pays cash. You know the phrases, "no down payment," "easy terms," "just charge it." It all sounds so simple. You are offered check credit, installment credit, charge-account credit. All stores offer easy credit. With a Diner's Club card, an American Express card, a Bell Telephone credit card, an airlines charge plate, a Hilton Carte Blanche and a Sheraton credit card you can travel around the world, stay in any hotel, eat in any restaurant, call up your best friends every evening, and spend not a cent of actual money. But the bills will have to be paid eventually, and any normal person knows that following a charging binge the day of reckoning comes. Charge accounts are not advisable for young families just getting started. Pay cash and avoid monthly crises.

Once you start a charge account you are launched on an association more permanent than marriage. Your name goes into the files of the National Credit Association. They keep an active file on all the financial affairs of your life which will continue until you die. As a sideline the Credit Association operates a private detective service. Through it an employer or anyone else can get a fairly complete picture of your reliability, stability, and financial worth. If you move from one town to another your file will be transferred. Good credit can play an important part in your life, help you get a loan when you need it, clear the decks for a better job, and give you a feeling of belonging, but you are ready for charge accounts only when you have the money to pay cash.

Pay bills promptly. Don't overbuy. Don't buy articles and return them. If you find yourself in a difficult spot, don't wait for the credit manager of the store to come to you; go to him, explain the problem, and arrange some kind of weekly or monthly payment on account. Do this and you won't have to worry about your credit.

The purchasing power of this country is based on installment credit. Automobiles, major appliances, furniture, clothing, vacations, swimming pools, and boats are bought on credit. When installment payments don't swallow up every pay check, when they are kept within reason, our economists say there is no harm in it. But time payments can very easily get out of hand.

If you are loaded up with monthly payments and lose your job or have sickness in the family, you may lose everything you have. Remember, most bankruptcies are family bankruptcies, not business bankruptcies.

Moreover, if you buy on time you never get a bargain. The interest you pay always makes the price you pay a high one. For instance, you want to buy a sofa on the installment plan. You are told that the interest will be only 1½ percent a month computed on the unpaid balance. That sounds reasonable enough, but 1½ percent amounts to 18 percent a year in any language; 2 percent monthly is 24 percent yearly and 2½ percent monthly is 30 percent yearly.

Installment charges are usually quoted in an obscure way which makes them seem less.

The next time you are tempted to buy on time or take a personal loan for something you can do without, remember these three practical suggestions made by a bank:

1. Ask the cash price of the article right at the start. Also add up the total of all payments you will be required to make, including the down payment, if you buy on time. The difference is the extra cost for buying on credit.
2. With the facts clearly in mind decide whether you still want to make the purchase. If the answer is yes, shop for the best financial plan. Financing costs vary.
3. Deal only with responsible merchants and lending institutions. Read all of the fine print in the contract and be sure that all parts of it are clearly understood.

Even though care may protect you from gross overpayment, it is wiser and cheaper to start a savings account and save up for major purchases. If a time purchase is necessary, make the largest possible down payment, to cut interest costs.

It is also important to learn how to forecast bargains. When to buy is often as important as what to buy. Wise buying of food can save hundreds of dollars a year and like savings can be made in other areas.

Instead of buying a new car when it is introduced, buy at the end of the season when the current year's models are being closed out. What difference does it make if your car model is a year old? This same method of buying applies to many other items. The time varies somewhat in different parts of the country, but the chances are that if you key your buying to the calendar below you may save 15 to 30 percent over untimed purchases. When buying at seasonal sales watch especially for close-outs rather than for special purchases. On special purchases prices may be lower but quality may also be lower. Nothing is a bargain if you don't need it and don't like it.

January—storewide clearances: resort wear, furs, sheets, pillow cases, towels, silver

February—furniture, rugs and carpets, home furnishings

March—housewares, luggage, silver, china, garden supplies
April—men's and boy's clothing, garden supplies, spring-cleaning supplies
May—radios, television, handbags, draperies, slipcovers
June—draperies, slip covers, camp clothes, sportswear, refrigerators, air conditioners, rug cleaning
July—storewide clearances after July 4; clothes, shoes, furniture, appliances, rugs
August—furs, back-to-school specials, garden furniture and equipment, summer clothing, Christmas cards, sheets and bedding
September—back-to-school specials, home furnishings, curtains and draperies, china, glass, housewares
October—Columbus Day specials, furs
November—Veterans Day, Election Day, and Thanksgiving specials, winter coats, pre-Christmas specials, table linens, blankets
December—storewide sales after Christmas, winter clothing specials, toys, gifts

SAVINGS

No family is a going concern until it has a personal savings program entirely independent of social security and whatever pension or insurance plan the head of the family has where he works. Don't let such group-savings programs lull you into neglecting this important area. Even a small amount kept in a savings bank, compounded semiannually, expands beautifully over a thirty- or forty-year period. Develop the habit of saving regularly early in life.

Insurance. In addition to life coverage, you will usually need automobile and fire insurance.

Savings accounts. Savings accounts will help you accumulate funds for major purchases, vacations, stock purchases.

Savings bonds. Government savings bonds in modest denominations provide a simple and sound way to expand savings.

Mutual funds. A conservative way of getting into the stock market is to buy mutual funds. But even with this type of purchase, where you are not selecting the stock yourself, it is important to select the right conservative company.

Dollar averaging. This is another sound method of buying stocks for the small investor. It is based on investing the same amount each period, usually by the month. Read the financial section of the newspaper. Begin a long-term, conservative program. You will never regret it.

To stimulate thought in this area, subscribe to *Changing Times,* The Kiplinger Magazine ($6 a year), 1729 H Street, N.W., Washington, D.C.

27 Personal Records and Family Lore

If you are thirty or thereabouts, you will understand what I'm about to say, but if you are twenty I'm not so sure. At least when I was that age I felt more competent than my parents and I was quite confident that, given the opportunity, I could get along beautifully without them.

This attitude of youngsters toward their elders is normal. The self-assertion of the teenager is an indication of developing adulthood. The critical attitude is the natural method of breaking parental control and may persist until the time the child establishes a home of his own. Then gradually the normal person, the adult, will swing around to a keen appreciation of family. By the time the ripe fifties are reached, interest in one's antecedents may even lead to hours spent in tracing the family tree!

However, if each young family realized that its point of view might change with the years, much interesting material might be preserved and more family self-understanding could be gained. No one can escape the influence of his forebears, and every one has an equal number: two parents, four grandparents, eight great-grandparents, and so on. Children are a composite of past generations. Your child may have Uncle Charlie's nose and Grandmother Gregg's mouth. He may also have other family characteristics which, if recognized, might aid in guiding his development. For our heredity carries the treasures and secrets of our family, both the strengths and weaknesses.

It is said that 90 percent of what we believe has nothing to do with thought process, but comes from four sources: family inheritance, individual temperament, national culture, and our economic level. Thus most of us inherit our politics, our religion, our food preferences, and our social customs.

The young tend to ignore the inevitability of family factors, but with age comes a realization of the importance of the stabilizing influence of having roots in the past. Often this knowledge comes too late. Older members of the family may have died without leaving records, and only with real effort can the story of the past be uncovered. The keeping of family records should start on the wedding day with a marriage certificate. One couple went a step farther and had a recording made of their marriage ceremony, which can be run off once a year on their anniversary. Bit by bit, additions can be assembled

. . . no one can escape the influence of his forebears

about each side of the family. Older members of both families almost always have copies of old family photographs and will be pleased to pass them on.

I recall with pleasure hours spent in poring over family albums when I was a child. Page by page, I knew the stories about Grandfather and Great-grandfather, beruffled aunts, mustachioed uncles, and queerly dressed cousins. I enjoyed the album pictures just as much as those in my nursery books, and I am now pleased to have them in my library.

Make an album for each baby. It may seem sentimental, but such a record may save you or the child trouble later. As you know, to get a passport or to collect social security a birth certificate is necessary. If official records are lost or defaced by fire, it may be difficult to establish date of birth unless clear home records are kept. One friend has his birth date established in State Department files by a letter from a brother several years his senior. The brother wrote that his first memory went back to the night of his brother's birth on a farm in Nebraska. He wakened in the middle of the night to see, in candlelight, a red devil getting in bed with him. He was desperately frightened and it was not until morning that he learned that his bed companion was not the devil but the village doctor in a long-sleeved red union suit!

The children's albums should be continued until they marry. In one family with two teen-age boys, evenings for two winters have been spent assembling an album for each of the boys to be delivered into their hands when they marry.

In discussing the problem the mother of these boys pointed out that keeping up with relatives is like a three-ring circus. There are three distinct group: the elderly members on both sides of the family, the group in the middle years, and the young nephews and nieces. Eventually there will be a fourth group—the grandchildren. The rule of this family is to visit or write a newsy letter to each of the elder members of the family at least once a year and to work out a reasonable number of contacts with the younger groups so that the boys will have some knowledge of their relatives.

Another family, also interested in putting down roots and aiding in the establishment of a sense of family, has started a labeling campaign, with a duplicate record in a notebook. First they dug out all of their old family relics, the bird inkwell carved by Great Uncle Bogardus, the picture Aunt Bertha painted on velvet, Grandfather's shaving mug, and the paisley shawl Grandmother treasured.

Typewritten labels were made for each object, including as much of the history as could be gathered. Typewritten white muslin labels were sewed on the fabrics. A label on a pitcher reads: "Pitcher given to Mrs. John Jones when she was married in 1905, by her uncle, Sam Hines, who got it when he attended the coronation ceremony of King Edward VII of England in 1901. Given to me in 1936 when the old Hines house was dismantled." On the back of a recently acquired heirloom of the future may be this item: "Gift to Madge Joyce by her husband, Jack Joyce, when he returned from World War II, 1945. Gaudy Staffordshire soup tureen circa 1795 bought in Shannon, Ireland, where Jack spent two weeks before returning to this country."

In somewhat the same vein another family worked out a tradition keyed to dining chairs. Since the early nineteenth century, whenever a daughter was married she was given a set of side chairs, which have now been divided up among the family. The study in style created by these chairs is fascinating. The collection I saw included:

a gilt Sheraton-type parlor chair	1805
a mahogany Duncan Phyfe chair	1830
a round-backed rosewood chair	1850
a high-pointed Gothic Victorian chair	1873
a reproduction of a Tudor oak chair	1921

There is a struggle going on now between two generations. Mother favors eighteenth-century chairs but daughter, who is soon to be married, is holding out for modern ones.

Even items of little value passed on from one generation to the next may grow in value. In one museum exhibit with the theme "My favorite heirloom," one of the most unusual items was a beribboned kitchen broom. It had been loaned by William Shippen Davis and had started on its road to fame in 1883 when William W. Shippen's daughter Kate was married. According to an old Scottish custom, if the bride and groom jumped over a broom together they would live happily ever after. Since then three generations of Shippens—twenty-six couples—have "jumped the broom" and all have lived happily. Each couple has tied to the handle of the broom a ribbon bearing their name and date of marriage.

Gift record. Rather than label more recent acquisitions, it may be easier to start a gift record. Divide the book in two parts. In one division keep a record of gifts received with dates and in the other a list of gifts given. In a large family such a record can be a great help at Christmastime.

If your possessions include any valuable, unique pieces of furniture, pictures, or accessories, take a photograph of each item, and paste it in the record book. Below it give all of the data known about the piece—how acquired, date of acquisition, source, artist or maker if known, value, etc. Such written records can be important in many ways.

Household diaries. With so many other pleasant things to do, diaries and letter writing seem to have gone out of fashion. However, as keeper of the archives in your family don't overlook either old family diaries and letters or the possibility of starting a diary of your own.

If you have any old letters and diaries of interest written by great grandfathers or uncles who fought in World War I or II, or letters reporting on travels or just every day events, collect them, label carefully, and store where they will be safe. As time passes such records become more valuable, not only in their personal interest but as a record of the past. Not a year passes in which there are not some diaries published of ordinary people who long ago wrote of their daily activities, thoughts, and longings.

But even without the prospect of converting a diary into cash, it's fun to develop the notes-to-yourself habit. Again it links you with the thoughtful ones of all ages. Don't drive yourself to it every day unless it seems natural. Perhaps your record could be made once a week, or perhaps only after important family events. I'll promise you that notes written to yourself make fascinating reading ten to twenty years later. It's surprising how the simplest fact seems interesting. The weather, the flowers blooming in the garden, what you had for dinner, and the color of a new dress gain interest and charm with the years. The happenings of the children, their honors or demerits at school, the names of their friends, and the spoon-bread recipe you got from Aunt Clara are items for your book.

Along with her diary one young mother keeps a continuing log on each member of the family. She says:

"I use a regular loose-leaf notebook with alphabetized tabs on colored separators for my family data book. I use it for everything I have to do, instead of various slips of paper which disappear. One page is for groceries under G. There are several pages under M for meals we especially like. Under A I list appointments. Under T are much-used telephone numbers and addresses. The letter H includes all kinds of data on the house.

"In addition to this practical stuff I have a page or pages for each member of the family. There is a page for Lee, one for Bill, and one for Mike. Yes, there is one for me personally, as well as for Charles and the chores I think up for him to do. I refer to it before I go shopping for clothes sizes and everything else I need to know—when the boys went to the dentist last, birthdays, wants and wishes. I've tried a card file but I prefer my system."

Family names. Old diaries are a source of interesting, meaningful names for babies that are too seldom used. Although some babies are still given names with family significance, some parents turn to books and the Bible, while many young parents seem to prefer the names of current movie stars or even names featured in popular songs. The New York Public Library reports that their Local History and Genealogy Department receives over one thousand inquiries a year from expectant parents doing research on names.

Guest books. If you do much overnight entertaining, it's nice to keep a guest book. At a summer place it is convenient. Perhaps you will want to invite some friend up at the same time each year; then the guest book will guide you. Perhaps a friend invited in June may return in September the following year so that both seasons may be enjoyed.

In one home, the family diary and the guest book are combined. A daily diary is kept, either husband or wife making entries in it. When there is a house guest, he is invited to make an entry on the last day of his visit. Even a year later it is pleasant to review the happenings of a happy weekend.

Correspondence. No family is complete without a letter writer. If letter writing doesn't come naturally to either you or your husband, put it down as a talent that is important for one of you to acquire.

Radios, automobiles, televisions, telegrams, telephones, airplanes, all may suggest adequate means of quick communication. There is no denying that they function, but they have by no means eliminated the joys, pleasures, and value of personal correspondence. With families far flung as they are today, letters offer the perfect link.

Make the job easy by having several kinds of paper on hand. Large size for the long, chatty letter, small sheets for thank-you and bread-and-butter notes, and postcards for a speedy message. Also keep stamps and prestamped post-office envelopes on hand in various denominations.

One woman I know carries note sheets and cards in her pocket-book. Whenever she has to wait for an appointment or for her luncheon date in a restaurant or on a train, she dashes off notes to friends in trouble, or who are ill, or who warrant congratulations or a pat on the back. Not a day passes but one or two notes are mailed.

Another friend runs a clipping service for friends. For two young nephews he clips animal photographs; for another Lincoln lore is accumulated; political data of significance goes to another. Carried on now for years, it is an interesting hobby and adds excitement to the postman's ring.

An invalid in Tennessee keeps track of visiting celebrities. She clips newspaper notices and sends them to the visitors without charge. Her grateful service has elicited a file of thank-you notes with famous signatures.

Children should learn to write letters just as they learn to talk and walk. Start them off with crosses for kisses and their printed name. Follow up by supplying them with their own notepaper. From the time they learn to print they should write their own thank-you notes for Christmas and birthday gifts. It is a good habit to acquire, and brings children closer to distant aunts and uncles. When eventually they go on trips and go to college the letter-writing habit may be established and you may get a return on your investment.

28 About Books and Magazines

"I don't mind buildin' them, lady, if I gets paid for it. But I'm curious what you're goin' to do with them." Gramp stood looking with interest at the floor-to-ceiling bookshelves he had just installed.

"This house has stood here since 1885," he continued. "John lived here first. He was the retired railroad man. Next, George lived here. He was a poet. Then came that no 'count Ainis family and none of 'em had any shelves."

"You will see, Gramp," I answered. "Books will fill those shelves in no time and then we will have to build more shelves."

"No schoolteacher 'ud ever have me no more than two days in a row—so I don't know much about books," Gramp went on, and then with a twinkle in his old eye he added, "And no books are gonna help you cut down a tree the way you was going at it t'other day up yonder on the hill."

And how right Gramp was! But books do help in a lot of other ways and no house is complete without a fairly generous supply.

When we were very young my sister Ruth and my brother Lloyd ran a race to see which one could read all the books in the Bellingham Public Library first. They read up and down the shelves like ravenous rats and every few weeks they had to have a fresh library card. I've forgotten the outcome now. It was probably a tie.

Even though it never occurred to me to join the race, my early exposure to reading as a pastime has made me a confirmed believer in books. From the time we were tiny tots all five of us had two shelves each in the family library. There were shelves common to all, such as those housing the encyclopedia. But on our own shelves were the books which were our personal property.

This feeling for books is so deep that when I go into a house and see no bookshelves or books I wonder how the family manages. It is almost as surprising as it would be to find no chairs or beds. As far as I am concerned even the fact that you don't read is no excuse for having no books.

Reading is one of the true pleasures of life. Holbrook Jackson says in *The Reading of Books,* "The art of reading is not a virture or a duty, but a faculty—when we read solely to please ourselves . . . we rob no one, hurt no one, annoy no one, compete with no one, and expect nothing in return but the pleasure of the experience." In this day of dashing about in automobiles, listening to noisy radios and hi-fi and watching television, what a mild innocent pleasure is reading!

If you just won't read, books can do other things for you. Their presence can give you a good reputation, however false. They say to all, "Nice people live here." Books are also a decoration; they animate vast wall spaces and they introduce rich color and pattern. And, as much as I dislike being so utilitarian, they also insulate. Line the north wall of a living room with bookshelves and the books and the heat loss will be reduced. That's all insulation is—just wood pulp of one kind or another. The only difference is book wood pulp has printing on it and it may easily cost $10 to $20 more a yard than standard insulation.

Where to build bookshelves. As André Maurois, French author and critic once said, "Books are my friends and a 'library' is any place you choose to keep books."

In the many years I've been decorating houses I've designed and built hundreds of yards of bookshelves. Most of these shelves were very simple.

I like floor-to-ceiling bookcases. They seem more complete that way and there isn't a top to collect bric-a-brac. Bookcases look well flanking a fireplace or set in the wall behind a sofa. They may surround a window at the end of the room. They may enliven an uninteresting hall, and I've also seen dining rooms turned into dual-purpose rooms with bookshelves added. The bright bindings add warmth to the room and interest to dinner discussions. Until you have experienced it you can't imagine how a reference library, close at hand, will enrich the discussion of the mealtime autocrat.

I usually find that by searching through a house from cellar to garret I can collect enough books to launch a quite impressive library. The collection may be quaint, ranging from the *Rover Boys on the Mississippi* and *Huckleberry Finn* to an old Rand McNally geography. Once they are assembled as a library, however, it is always interesting to me to see how it grows.

Dimensions. If you have a library, an analysis of the book sizes will offer a key to the depth and height of the shelves you need. If your library is still to be assembled, plan shelves eight to nine inches deep with ten, twelve, and fourteen inches between shelves. A base twenty-eight or thirty inches high (table height) may be as deep as twenty inches. When cased in with doors it will hold deep folios, record albums, scrapbooks, magazines, and game equipment. Put the base unit on a four-inch platform like a kitchen cabinet to insure that the door swings over the rug.

It is common practice to make bookshelves adjustable. The least expensive adjustable shelf is made by making continuous holes in the wood siding of the bookcase to hold metal shelf brackets. More expensive are slotted metal straps. Adjustable shelves cost more and I find that once the shelves are in they are practically never moved. Save by planning the shelf spacing ahead of time and make the shelves rigid.

For appearance put the deeper shelves on the bottom and shallower ones at the top. Up to nine-by-twelve-inch books should stand. Taller ones should lie on their sides to prevent warping.

Any of the hardwoods may be used for shelves, but their cost is almost prohibitive. Substitute poplar, chestnut, or well-seasoned pine. These woods are easily handled and make satisfactory shelving. If bookshelves are to be backed with wood, install convenience outlets before putting shelves in place. Cut holes so that the outlets can be mounted on the back of the bookcase. Place one low and the other at the top, in case you want to install lighting at any time. Bookshelves offer a wonderful method of covering small, high, awkward windows. Just pull down the shades and stand the bookcase in front of them. Use a screw or two at the top to keep them stationary.

Even renters may have bookshelves. There are many types of furniture units that can be assembled like blocks to fill whole walls. These are excellent for move-about families. There are also shelf units which hang from tension rods installed between ceiling and floors with no screws to mar the wall, floor, or ceiling. If you install brackets and shelves do it carefully. Be sure that the plaster or wallboard is sturdy and use a leveler to insure that shelves do not slope one way or the other.

Two methods of acquiring shelves used by youngsters setting up housekeeping are worth mentioning. One couple visited a brickyard and, free of charge, were allowed to collect about fifty bricks, which they carried away in baskets in the back of their car. Then they visited a lumber yard and got four sixty-inch planks ten inches wide. As a base they laid two bricks side by side, sixty inches apart. On this firm foundation they laid a plank. On the plank they built up a double row of bricks. Then another plank was added. They continued piling up bricks and planks until all were gone and a bookcase was achieved.

An even easier trick was used by another couple. They bought two stepladders. These were painted daffodil yellow. Four planks were painted the same color. The planks were laid on the open stepladders and books were installed. Ivy was trained to grow up the outside supports. Result, a widely commented-on achievement.

How to arrange books. For purely decorative purposes, it is possible to weave a tapestry of color in bookshelves with book bindings. To do this, sort books for color and size. Then place them on the shelves in color groups. I can already hear the screams from bibliophiles and I agree with them. This arbitrary color and size method should be used only for libraries assembled with no particular thought to subject matter.

As soon as you become a serious book collector inevitably the subject matter will fall into four or five special categories. In such a case it is only sensible to sort first for subject matter and divide for color and size within each classification. Keep dust jackets, the paper covers that come on the books. They add to the value of first editions if you consider a resale.

Never crowd books on a shelf. Sliding them in and out scratches the covers and the slight swelling of books in humid weather puts pressure on them and may split the bindings. Never let books lean against one another in partially filled shelves. To keep in good shape they should stand upright, held by a book end if necessary.

If the shelves covering a wall are adjustable and you do not yet have enough books to fill them, remove several shelves at the center and hang a picture or a group of pictures there. It is also quite permissible to intersperse interesting bits of china and glass between the books. The shelves will seem less spotty if these accessories are arranged in attractive groups rather than stuck around, one here and one there.

Care of books. The enemies of books are several, ranging all the way from humans through dust, dirt, heat, and humidity to insects and mice. Human enemies are probably the most destructive. I remember that I learned back in the fourth grade how to open a new book. Today few people seem to bother to do it correctly. The technique is to lay the book on its back and carefully open a few pages on one side, then on the other, pressing lightly along the bound edge. The object is to condition the back so it will not break. Using books as coasters for dripping drinks is nothing less than a minor crime. Still another misfortune to books which can be laid at the feet of humans is thick wads of paper often used to mark a place.

Certain atmospheric conditions also create problems. Fine libraries are sometimes kept in air-conditioned rooms in order to regulate heat and humidity. Some collectors recommend keeping books in glassed-in shelves to protect them. Sunshine fades and dries books and humidity induces mildew. Winter heat from the furnace dries them out and takes the oil out of leather bindings. In fact only the most perfect air conditioning is suitable for books.

However, there are ways of combating adverse conditions. Keep the direct sun from books by lowering shades. There are drying agents now which, left in a room, will reduce the humidity. Another preventive is to start the furnace several times during moist summers. It is also possible to dry the air by turning on an electric heater. Humidity can be introduced in many ways during the winter.

If mildew actually exists, the room as well as the books will have a musty odor. The easiest way to cope with mildew, which is a fungus growth, is to get a commercial product called Mil-Du-Rid for use on bindings. The paper pages will have to be wiped off individually with a clean dry cloth and the book put in the sun. If you have books with real leather bindings in your library, clean them as you would any leather surface.

Dust and dirt. The vacuum cleaner will take care of weekly once-overs. Several times a year the books should be removed one shelf at a time. Dust the shelf and the books with a clean damp cloth. Both the shelf and the books should be dry before they are reassembled.

Silverfish. These white, wingless, flat insects, one-fourth to one-half inch long, frequently infest books. They feed on the starch in the bindings. Silverfish often get started in a library when the room is closed and dark for several months. Once established they are hard to oust.

Some time ago, I advised a friend to rub her silverfish-infested books with pennyroyal, an herb oil. When she asked for the oil at her local drugstore she was sternly reprimanded and informed that its sale was illegal. Investigation proved that this old insect remedy has other uses and its sale is controlled. You can trap silverfish instead of poisoning them. Flour is the bait. Here is the method: cover the outside of a small jar with adhesive tape to make it rough in order to offer foothold for the insects to climb. Put a little white flour in the bottom of the jar. The silverfish crawl up the jar, leap for the flour and lose their lives because they can't get a foothold on the smooth inside walls of the jar.

A suspicion that you have silverfish can be confirmed by simply looking at several books. Even if you can't see the insects, the bindings will tell the story.

Magazines. Places to store current and old magazines are as necessary as shelves for books. No house is complete without magazines. When I was very young I used the fashion pages as a source for wonderful paper dolls. Later, magazine pictures were convenient sources for illustrations for school themes; the *National Geographic* and *Asia* were indispensable for lubricating geography lessons. The possibilities of *Holiday,* the magazine which ranges the seven seas and the fifty states, are terrific.

When I advanced from geography classes, magazines were a source for classified scrapbook material in architecture and decorating. Magazines also supported my interests and kept me in touch with new developments and ideas when I taught school in the Far West. Literally I was miles from any professional stimulation and I felt it deeply.

Magazines can be a vital force in a person's life, and good management suggests that children should be exposed to them at an early age. But do keep them weeded out. Make a schedule. Keep monthlies two months and weeklies a month at the longest. Then get them out of sight.

Use end tables with a shelf beneath for stacking magazines. Plan a shelf in the bookcase where they can be piled up. Perhaps there is a wall space or a doorback where a magazine rack can be installed. In any case don't let magazines get the upper hand or they will overrun the place. Back issues must be cleared away. Those the children find useful for school should be kept where they can get at them.

Make your magazine subscription list carefully. Give yourself a balanced ration. Let the children have a magazine of their own. For the adults of the family, include a news weekly, a woman's magazine for its homemaking material, a literary magazine, perhaps a garden magazine, and, if you are thinking of building, a house magazine. In addition to these you may want professional, fashion, music, or art magazines. This is a long list. Each family should appraise its collection carefully to see that it is the best possible assortment. Do not be content with an accidental list of magazines made up because you could not say no when a friend asked you to subscribe.

29 About Plants, Pianos, and Records

PLANTS

Plastic plants and permanent flowers are no substitute for the real thing. If the sunlight and your patience do not extend to growing plants, big bouquets of magnolia, rhododendron, laurel, or huckleberry leaves are attractive. For parties it is fun to tuck frankly fake paper flowers among the leaves. However, if you like to fuss over things and have time, plants can become a fascinating hobby. It is important to learn their habits and preferences and cater to them for if plants are not happy they won't flourish. Look on your potted plants as pets; they are dependent on you for water, food and protection against pests. Keep them healthy and they will reward you with a healthy look.

Exposure. Before getting plants consider where they are to be located, as light is the most important factor in their care. Blossoming plants such as geraniums, Jerusalem cherries, and cinerarias should have full sun. Only foliage plants can be raised with little sun. These include ferns, palms, Chinese evergreens, hen and chickens, philodendron, and rubber plants.

Water. More house plants are ruined by overwatering than anything else. The amount of water will vary somewhat with the type of plant, the size of the container, and the humidity in the room. When watering, do it thoroughly, not just a little today and then a little the next day. Give each plant a good soaking, then don't water it again until the soil is dry. Only a few plants should never go dry. If a plant is in a pot standing in another container, blocks or pebbles should be put under the pot for air circulation, and water should not stand in the outer container.

Feeding. Keep plants well nourished during the growing season. When pots are too small a balanced plant food serves as a supplement to too little soil, but do not overfeed. Use water-soluble food and follow instructions exactly.

Cleaning. Big shiny-leafed foliage plants should look glistening and fresh. To keep them that way wipe the leaves off with a damp cloth at least three times a week. Better still use a plant cosmetic; these usually contain emulsified oil and can be sprayed on to create a glossy, well-scrubbed look.

Pests. Inspect plants frequently for signs of red spiders, scales, mealy bugs, and aphids. Counterattack immediately. Consult your florist. There are stomach poisons for the control of biting and chewing insects and contact poisons for those which pierce and suck.

PIANOS

The care and feeding of pianos requires the regular attendance and consideration of a living thing. They are valuable instruments designed to give a kind of pleasure that is possible only when the instrument is well cared for. Abuse more than use causes depreciation of the average piano. Specialists say that the life expectancy of a well-maintained piano is forty years.

The temperature and humidity you find most comfortable for yourself are acceptable for a piano. Drafts and extreme changes of temperature should be avoided. Never place a piano near a radiator, near a window that will be left open, or where the sun will shine on it. However, the rule that stipulates that a piano should never be placed against an outside wall need not be followed in today's well-insulated houses.

Most pianos need tuning at least four times the first year; after that a semiannual tuning will be adequate unless you have a concert artist in the family or the piano is moved.

A piano should be kept reasonably clean inside but that is a job for a professional. Even retrieving a toy or other object that has fallen inside can cause trouble. Formerly housekeeping manuals suggested putting moth balls inside to protect the felt; today this is really useless since the felt in all newer pianos has been mothproofed.

Keep a soft cloth or chamois for use only on the piano keys and case. If the keys are soiled, wipe them with a dampened cloth, with no soap or detergent on it, then dry thoroughly. Piano cases usually have many finishing coats and even furniture polish is not recommended.

If a piano is to be left in an unoccupied house for some time, wrap it with blankets. Incidentally, a television instrument left through winter in an unheated house will require fewer adjustments if it too is wrapped in newspapers and blankets.

RECORDS

Records, like books, pictures, and furniture, are susceptible to damage and deterioration if not given some consideration.

Dust is their worst enemy and in the dust-laden air of most urban areas this is a real concern. Always keep records stored in their wrappers. Do not leave records in your machine or stacked up beside it. Return them to their albums as soon as you have played them.

The oil and moisture always present on your hands is also injurious. To avoid finger marks on the face of records handle them by their edges. Some collectors always use soft gloves or a soft piece of silk when handling their records. There are special velour-covered brushes with soft bristles for dusting records; a delicate circular motion is used.

Like pianos, records should be stored away from heat sources, out of direct sunshine, and at temperatures of 68 to 72 degrees and humidity of 25 to 35 percent. Excessive heat may warp the surface. When the records dry out, the grooves shrink and pinch and much of the tone quality is destroyed. Collectors who have valuable old records insist that records should be played at least once a year to keep them "alive."

Like books, records should be stored vertically and firmly in their wrappers or cases in shelves, ideally partitioned every eight inches. Less dust will be deposited on the wrappers if there is only one half inch between the top of the album and the next shelf, yet there should be space for the free circulation of air. Collectors' items bought before LP's were made are kept in albums.

Take time to index records. You don't have to have a large collection to make an index worthwhile. It is nice to know where a record is when you want it, and as a matter of fact indexing saves wear and tear on records.

Use a simple system, a sticker with a number on the cover of the record or on the album. Under the number in an index book or file list the name of the composer, the artist, and the name of the piece.

30 How to Entertain

Entertaining is an important and pleasant facet of family life. You can't slough off your responsibilities. Analyze the situation in your own household.

When did you entertain last?
Why have you delayed so long in inviting the Smiths over?
Is it because the living room is worn?
Is it because steaks and roasts are too expensive?
Is it because you haven't enough water goblets to go around?
Is it because it is so much trouble?
Is it because your group doesn't seem to entertain much and you would feel queer if you did?

It's fun to entertain once you've broken the ice.

An easy informality has developed in home-entertaining etiquette. Don't hesitate any longer. Collect a group of friends and have a party. Let the children help and reward them with a party of their own.

THE TECHNIQUE

Entertaining isn't easy. It requires planning and advance preparation. We can't all be as casual as Mrs. Wiggs of the Cabbage Patch, who just added more water to the soup if someone appeared at dinnertime. But a little analysis and a little thought will uncover the type of entertaining that you can accomplish easily with what you have.

You may have one or a hundred guests.
You may serve a cup of tea or stuffed snails and champagne.
You may have a breakfast, luncheon, tea, dinner, or supper.
You may serve on the terrace, in the yard, or in the living room, dining room, or even in the kitchen.

You may use china or paper plates, crystal or inexpensive plastic glasses.

You may entertain the Girl Scout troop, your next-door neighbor, a friend from the office, or the new couple down the street. Whom you entertain, where you entertain, and what you serve are not important as long as you discover a formula for home entertaining that works for you.

In one community of small houses where everyone lives simply and incomes and activities are almost identical, entertaining is simple. Several times a week the gang stages a get-together, around ten o'clock at night. They take turns serving coffee to the crowd. When the hour arrives the host goes outdoors and bellows, "Coffee's ready." Four or five couples come over, each bringing their own cups and spoons. With their coffee they have a grand talkfest and they all feel better for the contact.

Another young group in slightly better circumstances entertain twice a month. Instead of serving dinner, they have a dessert bridge. Guests are invited to come immediately after dinner; dessert and coffee are served when they arrive, leaving the rest of the evening free for bridge.

Theater nights bring a young southern group together. To make the occasion into a party an easily prepared buffet supper is served to three or four couples, then they all go to a movie. The menu is usually a casserole dish, a salad, dessert, and coffee.

A teacher in the Middle West has Sunday nights at home. A varied group, young and old, are invited in for an informal evening to discuss current problems. People start coming about six o'clock. Everyone sits on the floor around the fire. About nine o'clock snacks are served, apples, cheese and crackers, popcorn, or doughnuts. It is as simple as that.

Music is the key to one family's recreation. They have collected a wonderful record library as well as a group of friends who enjoy music. The result, of course, is an occasional concert.

In another family the mother and two of the children are talented musicians, and now that the oldest daughter has married a promising young violinist they frequently delight their friends with musical evenings.

A family with a big back yard and a barbecue fireplace have

Saturday-night neighborhood parties to which everyone contributes. Someone brings beans, others potato salad, cake, wienies, rolls. Since everyone contributes one dish, there is no strain on anyone and it's a party of mixed ages, which is good for everyone.

The idea of social exchanges and the home as the center of family activity should begin when children are young. From the time they are little tots, children should be trained to meet guests as well as be guests. Four-year-olds can pass crackers (use a plastic plate to avoid breakage). I've even heard of one two-year-old who knows how to set the table correctly. An eight-year-old helps serve and clear the table.

Children should also have guests their own age. In one Pennsylvania community at least once a week the children stay with a neighbor overnight, usually in a family where there is a child of the same age. As a result they are learning to be guests as well as to entertain. They also are well adjusted if necessity calls their parents away overnight; staying with a neighbor causes no alarm because they are used to it.

In this same neighborhood, two neighbors share Sunday dinners on alternate weeks. The guest family supplies the dessert. With six in one family and four in the other, the table is set for ten or more, and it is quite a sight with children ranging in age from two to twelve.

PARTY POINTERS

Assemble guests thoughtfully. Invite a group who will mix well. If you entertain on a purely chop-for-chop basis, your parties are going to be pretty dull. If most entertaining is within a small group, when it is your turn try to add one couple who may not be known to your set. They will introduce an unknown element and everyone will put on a better performance. It saves the group from becoming too static. The first step then is to invite the right people and to present the picture clearly to guests so that they arrive prepared for the occasion. Will they be the only guests or will there be others? Is it to be informal or are evening clothes indicated? What time are guests due? Is there a guest of honor? Who is it? If it is to be an outdoor party or barbecue make this clear. It may affect the clothes worn.

The food is the next problem. Perhaps you have some specialties.

If so, this is the time to serve one, even if it is corned beef and cabbage. Don't try unusual food on guests; experiment on the family. This is not a new idea. Back in 1860, Ralph Waldo Emerson said that with the unskilled help in the kitchen his family's rule for hospitality was to have the same dinner every day for a year. "Then," he added, "at least the cook could handle it to a nicety and the host learned to carve it and the guests are well served."

As you plan the menu, think in terms of what you can do easily, food you are familiar with, food that will take the least last-minute attention, and food you are equipped to serve. Simple, hearty food calls for a simple, hearty atmosphere and vice versa. Fortunately, today the gay-colored tablecloth and handsome pottery dishes are party equipment just as much as silver and crystal.

Casseroles offer a wonderful solution for guest meals because they look after themselves. The first course—cocktails, tomato or fruit juice, and hors d'ouevres—is served in the living room. Then the casserole can be popped onto the table with some unusual bread and a green salad and there is no running back and forth to the kitchen until time for dessert.

Many hostesses use big electric hot trays for guest meals. With such a tray to keep food warm, the main course may be set out on a serving table in the dining room and each guest can help himself before being seated. This plan calls for good-looking serving dishes.

Even a casserole dish may be a conversation piece. There are interesting ones on the market in a wide range of materials and colors. Every kitchen ought to have several sizes with lids. Casseroles are used for baking, steaming, stewing, boiling, and scalloping and, of course, there will always be one favorite. I have an old French one and my husband declares that anything that is cooked in it is better than average.

Again, if the meal is simple, add special touches. Use pepper grinders on the table instead of pepper shakers. Serve bread or biscuits in a folded napkin in a basket. Use a soup tureen for soup and a handsome bowl for salad. Have a terrific dessert that you or your husband can serve at the table.

Give a party touch by having coffee after dinner in the living room. Set a tray with demitasse cups, coffeepot, creamer, and sugar bowl. If you don't have demitasse spoons use a stick of cinnamon instead, and in addition to cream and sugar include thin lemon slices. After-dinner mints are another nice addition to the coffee tray.

If the dinner is a real party the next elaboration might be a tray of two or three liqueurs or brandies to follow the coffee.

Think through the table service completely. Before guests arrive, lay out on a counter or card table the dishes and silver for each course so that no fishing around is necessary. Have the house sweet and clean. Add fresh leaves or flowers. See that there is an ample supply of fresh ash trays, matches, and cigarettes on hand. Perhaps a dish or two of nuts would be nice. A well-groomed house gives a hostess confidence just as an attracive costume does. Lay a fire in the fireplace and light it the moment the first guest rings the doorbell.

Do most of the work the day before the party so that you aren't worn out. Take a nap and look your best. You will be more relaxed if you aren't tired and your husband will be proud of you.

Greet each guest as he arrives. Go to the door yourself unless it is a big party; then a friend may answer it for you.

When you are a guest you have responsibilities also. You should arrive on time and not stay too late. You should contribute to the conversation but never monopolize it. If you see something you might do to help, such as pass cigarettes or nuts, ask if you may. A helpful guest can do a great deal to make a party a success, but be sure your hostess wants help.

If more than six are invited, dinner may be served buffet style. In such a case guests may be expected to help with the service. Watch for an opportunity to help at an outdoor barbecue party. The host usually officiates at the barbecue, but you may ask if he would like to be relieved or take an intermission. On the other hand, if some particular musical program has been arranged or if some television event is the reason for the party, as a guest it is not your place to change a Beethoven concert for a pop performance or to substitute Shakespeare for a prize fight.

31 How to Keep Holidays

I will admit at once that I am a firm believer in Santa Claus, St. Patrick, the Easter rabbit, witches, the Pilgrim Fathers, anything and everything that creates an excuse for a holiday. To paraphrase Barbara Fritchie's famous words: "Shoot if you must this old gray head but spare our national holidays!"

The responsibility for the celebration of holidays should not be shunted off onto schools, churches, clubs, and community. The gaiety and spirit should start right in the home, and it is the homemaker's responsibility to stage a holiday just as successfully as she whips up a cake. Nothing happens on a holiday unless you make it happen. The fun, the whimsey, the reverence, the renewal of vows, the celebration are the result of conscious planning and a love of tradition. Such family celebrations add to the richness and completeness of life.

It's the holidays that give variety to the calendar and to our days. They enrich our thinking and create a subtle feeling of security, which always comes from a link with the past. Call holidays sentimental if you wish. A certain amount of sentiment is good. It is stabilizing and helps bring the family together. So let's have holidays, even if they do constitute another job for Mother. If she's the woman I think she is, she'll come through.

System is the answer. Holidays need not be all work and no fun. Like all other household activities, advance planning relieves the pressure. Work out a routine for each holiday so that it becomes a family tradition. Change it here, change it there, but keep the same skeleton plan from year to year. Done this way holidays are easy to manage and the children will love the program more for its familiarity. They will feel a part of it and, before many years pass, they will take the whole thing out of your hands.

Establish a holiday closet. As the holidays roll around acquire permanent accessories that can be parked away in labeled boxes to be used each year. For each holiday there may be special mantel ornaments, table decorations, and perhaps hats or costumes for the little children. Papers, ribbons, and odds and ends will be carefully stored also. A special party pantry is also a good idea. It need not be reserved for holidays only. In nothing flat, its resources can turn any dinner into a celebration. Such a pantry should include party snappers, colored straws, marshmallows, gumdrops, and chocolate bits for decoration; gay-colored paper napkins and animal crackers. For more dramatic celebrations, it's worth having a collection of party balloons and colored streamers for the table. With such treasures it would be possible to celebrate a holiday or special occasion without trouble or great expense.

Chart the year. Your household calendar serves as a holiday reminder by having the dates printed in red. Almost every month has one or two. Your holidays might include:

January 1	New Year's Day
January 6	Twelfth Night
February 12	Lincoln's Birthday
February 14	Valentine's Day
February 22	Washington's Birthday
March 17	St. Patrick's Day
March or April (variable)	Easter
April 1	April Fool's Day
May 1	May Day
May (second Sunday)	Mother's Day
May 30	Memorial Day
June 14	Flag Day
June (third Sunday)	Father's Day
July 4	Independence Day
September (first Monday)	Labor Day
October 12	Columbus Day
October 31	Halloween
November 11	Veteran's Day
November (usually last Thursday)	Thanksgiving
December 25	Christmas Day

Also mark family bithdays and anniversaries. Families with roots in foreign countries and with different religious holidays may have special days not mentioned here which they will wish to celebrate. These too should be noted on the calendar.

New Year's—January 1. The festival of the New Year no doubt dates back to the time when the idea of the calendar was first conceived. In some form it is celebrated around the world at one season of the year or another. The mixture of nationalities in this country accounts for the varied spirit of the celebration here.

At homes, in churches, and in clubs Watch Night services are held to see the old year out and the new year in. Older children are permitted to stay up and hear the bells of celebration.

January 1 is the day for making New Year's resolutions and for open house when friends call on friends. In some sections this visiting from house to house has been taken up by groups of children masquerading. Originally these groups did stunts and sang songs; in return they got pennies or food. Eggnog is the traditional drink. Since Christmas trimmings are up, no special decorations are necessary. However, the special symbols of the day include Old Father Time with his scythe, representing the old year; an infant representing the new year; tin horns, confetti, and domino masks for use in the midnight celebration.

Twelfth Night—January 6. Twelfth Night is an old Christian festival It marks the end of the twelve days between Christmas and Epiphany and it is said to determine your luck for the next twelve months. In England Twelfth Day cake was baked with a bean and pea in it. Whoever found the bean was king of the festival, and the pea was the symbol of the queen.

This holiday is not celebrated to any extent in North America but it is a fine one for the housekeeper to adopt because it correctly puts an end to the fuss of Christmas. Traditionally, the end of Twelfth Night was celebrated by "undecking the hall" of Christmas greens. All the evergreens were taken down and burned with a dash of bay, rosemary, and frankincense for good luck. Great care was taken to see that everything was removed. Christmas greens left might be a lurking place for spirits, witches, and elves.

Fireplaces today are not of the magnificent order they were in Old England. Take care, if you burn the greens, not to burn the house down. Feed them in slowly. The sap in evergreens burns with a tremendous roar; flames may lick outside the firebox and may even ignite soot deposits in the chimney.

Lincoln's Birthday—February 12. This is a wonderful opportunity to talk to the children about a great man who had a simple start. At school they will learn the Gettysburg Address, which may be repeated at home. Songs and stories of the Civil War may be reviewed.

Use simple table or mantel decorations. To symbolize the rail splitter, use a handsome small birch log, bury a small hatchet in it, and wreathe it with greens. In honor of the lad in a log cabin, build a miniature cabin, put a horse-and-rider rail fence around it, and a tiny sawbuck and pile of wood in the front yard. Use a big scroll over the fire place with a quotation from the Gettysburg Address printed on it. The children might make this and it could be rolled up and used for years. Add a dashing big red bow and a cluster of greens. It also might be worthwhile to invest in two flags about fifteen inches long, which could be placed above the fireplace on all national holidays.

St. Valentine's Day—February 14. It's the occasion for a party and endless fixings. Over the fireplace put a big red cardboard heart. For a small investment you may find two plaster or paper cupids to hang from the ceiling on each side. Or the cupids may find a place on the mantel.

If there is a mirror over the mantel, let it serve as the center for a valentine. Wreathe it in paper doilies or artificial flowers and with a lipstick write on the mirror, "To My Valentine."

Use a red tablecloth and for place mats white lace-paper doilies. Add white candles and you have a party table whether it's for the family only or for guests.

Let the children use valentines they receive to decorate the family bulletin board. Encourage them to make the valentines they send out. Buying them ready made is dull business and also expensive.

Washington's Birthday—February 22. This is the night for a cherry pie and recalls, of course, the lad who couldn't tell a lie even though he was indiscreet enough to chop down a perfectly good cherry tree. Use a white tablecloth and have the children make big red cherries of cardboard to sprinkle over the tablecloth. If they are really ambitious they could make Washington tricorne hats with red, white, and blue cockades. One youngster I know actually made a small model of Mt. Vernon, Washington's home on the Potomac. It was used as a table centerpiece.

Over the mantel have a picture of Washington with two small flags below. Another amusing possibility is the lithograph of Grant Wood's Parson Weems depicting George cutting down the cherry tree.

St. Patrick's Day—March 17. This is the anniversary of Ireland's patron saint, who freed the country of snakes and converted the heathen to Christianity. The wearing of the green traditionally means the wearing of the three-leafed green shamrock. It is a day of fun and frolic and a night for parties. Characteristic decorations include green stovepipe hats, clay pipes, rubber snakes, white and green color schemes, and shamrocks.

On the dinner table use a green tablecloth. Make a handsome centerpiece of uncooked Irish potatoes set off with leaves and even a few flowers. Make the arrangement in a big copper bowl or perhaps a white soup tureen.

April Fools or All Fools Day—April 1. The origin of this celebration is uncertain but children love it. The first of April is the signal for harmless pranks and the review of endless superstition. Surprises should start at breakfast and go on through the day. Begin by perching a little gumdrop animal on the children's breakfast cereal. As they start off to school, tuck a surprise in their pockets. Leave a note in the kitchen when they get home from school, directing them to look in a bowl on the dining-room table. Place another note there sending them to another spot, and so on. At the end of the hunt there should be a treat.

Easter. This is a big celebration and a wonderful one, at school, at home, and at church. The motifs include colored eggs, eggs in nests, eggs in baskets, rabbits, and chicks. There is the famous egg rolling and Easter egg hunt celebrated on the White House lawn which serves as a pattern for many family celebrations.

One delightful Easter-egg hunt I observed not many years ago was arranged for two brothers, six and eight. The same program had been followed for four years without change. A collection of Easter trophies used in past years, to which fresh hard candy and colored Easter eggs were added, was divided equally and hidden around the living room, half on one side, half on the other. Before breakfast the boy's hunt was staged. Each boy had half the room. By having separate territories, quarrels were avoided and the older boy had no opportunity of running off with all of the loot.

For the centerpiece, use eggs, decorate them with decalcomania, gold and silver stars, and egg stencils. Use them year in and year out. One woman in Pennsylvania has made a hobby of collecting Easter eggs. She has 1,400 which she has acquired in the last twenty years. A really charming mantel arrangement can be composed of antique china and glass eggs of assorted sizes. An alternative is to find undecorated white glass eggs once used by poultry raisers to encourage hens to lay. Decorate them with decalcomania flowers and keep them as permanent props.

Ham is the traditional dish for Easter in many families, and if you want to please the youngsters make a cake with chocolate frosting. Perch on it white marshmallows shaped to look like bunnies.

Pinch one side to form a head and the other to make a tail. Make eyes with cloves or toothpick dipped in chocolate. Cut ears from stiff writing paper and stick in above the eyes. The effect will surprise you.

Don't forget Easter songs. Gather around the piano and sing. Make it a family custom.

May Day—May 1. Teach the children to make May baskets. Surprise them with a big handsome one for the table. If you are ambitious, rig up a Maypole; it isn't too difficult. Traditionally May baskets were filled with flowers and left on the doorstep of a friend. We used to ring the bell, then hide in the shrubbery until the basket was found.

Independence Day—July 4. This is the anniversary of the signing of the Declaration of Independence by the Continental Congress in 1776 separating the American colonies from Great Britain. It means firecrackers, sparklers, and fireworks. It means watermelons and picnics. It means that the summer holiday is really under way. It's the time to bring the flag out. It's the time for patriotic speeches, parades, and red, white, and blue decorations. It's a wonderful day, and there should be something special in the wind for every member of every family.

Why not stage it as an outdoor barbecue for a surprise and bring out a birthday cake to which the children can sing "Happy birthday, dear America, happy birthday to you"?

Labor Day—The first Monday in September. The celebration may resemble the Fourth of July but without the fireworks. It may mean a picnic and it may mean a drive to the country to pick up early apples, peaches for canning, and baskets of tomatoes and late corn. It also may be the day for closing camp and going back to town.

Columbus Day—October 12. Since Halloween is coming, Columbus Day may be passed over lightly unless there appears to be a need to animate history classes.

Halloween, the eve of All Saints' Day—October 31. If you have never swathed yourself in an old sheet with a pillowcase for a head, if you have never carved a grinning face in a pumpkin, if you have never bobbed for apples, or tried to get a bite from an apple on a string, if you have never stumbled down a dark hall with all kinds of miscellany on the floor and had peeled grapes put in your hand with the ghostly advice that they were eyes from a corpse, then you haven't lived. You were a neglected child, and it's time you came to life and discovered how the other half live.

There's fun in Halloween. It's a curious mixture of druid practice and classic mythology. It is a night peopled with ghosts, witches, devils, and pranky little folk. It's the time for fortunetelling and love charms. It's the time to give youngsters an organized party to keep the night from degenerating into a boisterous occasion. Moreover, there is no party of the year easier to give.

Thanksgiving Day—The last Thursday in November. Like Christmas, Thanksgiving is for all the family, young and old, and is the most purely American of all our holidays. It dates back to the Pilgrims in 1621 and is a true celebration of harvest time.

Today it means turkey, cranberry sauce, pumpkin pie, and sweet cider. It means a centerpiece piled with fruits and vegetables. It means place cards made by the youngsters. There are dozens of motifs to select from, such as turkeys, Pilgrims, fruits, and vegetables. It's a day to give thanks for the plenty and goodness that are America. In planning Thanksgiving don't overlook the fireplace. Get a few small pumpkins, some dried corn on the ear, perhaps a squash or two, and make a harvest composition.

Christmas—December 25. Even if Thanksgiving was wonderful, come what will, Christmas must outdo it. Sometimes an adult may not think it's a year to celebrate. But there never has been a Christmas which shouldn't be celebrated.

The spirit oozes from shopping crowds. The great cathedrals and lovely country churches overflow. The air is filled with carols. Christmas is here. Richly celebrated, not in money, but in the pleasure of giving and receiving, it can supply memories for a lifetime.

I'll never forget Christmas shopping in the five-and-ten with my sister when we were very young. The trip was preceded by weeks of planning and maneuvering with our small capital. We were a big family and our allowances weren't large. Often we pooled our dimes to get gifts for our brothers and sisters, but mother and father had to have separate presents.

Father received a succession of homemade gifts from me. Decorated blotters for his desk, tissues made into a pad for cleaning his razor, and felt leaves made into a book for a penwiper. Mother's present usually ran to something for her sewing basket. I realize now that this activity was not all my own doing. Mother guided me, but I thought it was all a profound secret.

I wasn't fooled about my own gift, at least not always. When Mother and Aunt Maud made a magnificent wardrobe for my doll—a pink silk dress and hat, a green velvet cape, a green-striped gingham dress, and lace-trimmed underdrawers and petticoat—I knew it weeks ahead of time. But was I excited when I got the little trunkful of clothes Christmas morning? Just as much as if I hadn't guessed what was in store for me, perhaps more.

The day before Christmas we hung homemade cedar rope in all of the windows and looped it around the entrance door. Christmas Eve we burned a long white candle in every window and in candlelight we busied ourselves with last-minute wrapping. We each had our turn at putting our packages in or around the stockings that hung in front of the fireplace. We were on our honor not to peek at our own stockings.

Tense with excitement we went to bed to wait for our Christmas parade down the steps to the roaring fire in the fireplace in the morning.

The decorations, the dinner table, the food are as much a part of Christmas as any gift, and the preparation must not be a chore. Once Christmas becomes a duty instead of an inspiration and a pleasure, all the joy is gone.

At our house the mincemeat was made before Thanksgiving and even the pies were baked two or three days before Christmas, ready to pop in the oven to heat to a juicy succulence, when the turkey came out. The turkey, too, was dressed the day before to be ready for the oven at eleven o'clock. Only the vegetables remained to be fixed. So with us youngsters to help with the table even Mother could enter into the festivities of Christmas morning.

Christmas means a lot. It is easy to have fun with a big family like ours, but work out a program, a tradition, that is your family Christmas and never let the practice slip. It revitalizes the spirit and brings the whole family together.

Activities such as these outlined here may on first glance seem puny things. But take a larger point of view. Anything that gives a child or a family unit a sense of permanence and togetherness creates a feeling of stability. In a way it is related to what Dr. Bronislaw Malinowski of Yale University, one of the great social anthropologists of our day, was quoted as saying about habits and customs in an article by Eleanor Kittredge in the *New York Times Magazine:*

> Always and everywhere I have found that human life rests on certain very simple fundamentals. To me nationality—framing all the important

differential habits and customs which make the daily round of existence meaningful for those who live—is the substance of life. Once the biological necessities of sleeping, eating and reproducing are met, men—because they are men—must begin to embroider the basic pattern. Civilization, expressed in religion, art, language, the skills of human ingenuity and social institutions man has built, is something we have added to the initial drives of our being.

6 *About the Family*

32 The Children and the House

On a visit to Cleveland some years ago on a rainy afternoon I was chatting comfortably with my hostess over a cup of tea. I glanced out the window and saw a child next door disconsolately standing in the shelter of the house. I commented on it and my friend said, "That child is suffering from homitis. He hasn't got it, but his mother has. This spring she redecorated the house, and it's perfect. It looks just like a picture in a magazine. Even Johnny's room is fixed up. The trouble is, now that the house is attractive, she won't let anyone enjoy it. She spends all her time cleaning and fussing and she has a fit if anything gets out of place. Mr. X. wouldn't let her touch his den and that's the only room left in which even guests can be comfortable."

It's possible to be more comfortable and have more fun in an attractive, clean, well-decorated room than in an unattractive one. I don't hold at all with the idea that you can't have a pleasant, orderly house if there are children. That's ridiculous. But there are some nice points involved. Children haven't acquired the reputation of being house wreckers without reason.

A house must be designed and arranged for the activities of the age groups who use it. There should be one room, or at least a corner, which belongs exclusively to each person in the household. The whole family, old and young, should participate in redecorating programs so that everyone feels a part of it. Furthermore it is important to learn how to let the family enjoy a house once it is a going concern.

THE INFANT

Adjustments in the equipment and organization of a house begin with the arrival of a baby. The infant will fit into the household with less friction if provision is made for his individual wants.

In the kitchen. Set aside one cupboard for the baby's formula and supplies, including bottles, pans, and measuring spoons. Where dupli-

. . . how is the esprit de corps of your household?

cation of standard equipment is necessary, as in measuring cups and spoons, don't hesitate to buy the baby extra equipment. For easy reference post the twenty-four-hour schedule and the formula on the cupboard door. Use thumb tacks, Scotch tape or, if the doors are metal, magnetic holders. It is surprising how this one simple gesture saves hours of time and agonies of frustration by helping to keep the baby's routine running smoothly.

In the bathroom. Assemble all the equipment required for bathing and caring for the infant. Perhaps a wall cupboard or shelves will facilitate handling of the extras. One woman had a hinged shelf fifteen inches wide put on the wall so that it could be let down. It is very solid, as one end rests on the water tank and the other on the rim of the basin. Padded with towels, it is a help in bathing and dressing the baby. Have a diaper hamper at hand in the bathroom, or just outside the door if there isn't enough space inside. Also provide a definite place where the baby's garments or blanket can be kept until you are ready for them. Keep a plastic apron hanging on a hook on the door for your own protection.

If the bathroom and bedroom are on the second floor, many steps may be saved if you have an immersion heater or an electric teakettle in the nursery or bathroom for warming bottles or quickly heating water, especially at night. More steps can be saved if the baby's room is next to the parents' room. This plan may require shifting other members of the family. A certain highhandedness in this case may be justified.

In the bedroom. The same idea of organization before frustration applies to the baby's sleeping quarters. Don't keep the baby's clothes, blankets, and diapers mixed in with general storage. If possible have a separate chest for baby's things exclusively. If a chest isn't possible use painted shelves shielded from dust by a curtain. Such an arrangement is especially necessary if part of your own bedroom must be used for the baby.

THE RUNABOUT

A bassinet and the four sides of a play pen are a baby's first world. By the time a child crawls his world has begun to expand. But the same principle holds as in the first year. The child, until he is grown, should have a part of the house which is his, a chest of drawers, a chair, toys, and a picture that are his property. These things help create a feeling of security, a sense of belonging to the family.

Play space. Ideally there is a room or nursery equipped with the paraphernalia of play where a child may make messes and experiment to his heart's content. In order to be under Mother's eye sometimes this small world is set up in the family room adjoining the kitchen; again a sunroom or an extra bedroom may be used. But even if there is no place but a corner of the dining room or living room, play space must be provided.

One child I know spends hours tinkering with his toys and playing under a card table. The card table has a canvas canopy over it. Doors and windows are painted on the canvas to make it resemble a house. No one else can come in the house with him and he loves its exclusiveness. This contraption isn't particularly decorative and it stands in one corner of an apartment living room because there is no place else to keep it. But it is well worth a sacrifice of space and appearance.

The problem of cramped quarters and inadequate play space in today's small houses and apartments is serious. Child specialists report that lack of play space and few playmates actually account for many childish ills, such as thumb sucking, nail biting, and temper tantrums. It even accounts for slow acceptance of, and participation in, school.

To create extra space in an apartment is difficult and can be done only by arbitrary action. However, by using imagination one can always find some corner to be dedicated to the child and his things. In a house, however, small adjustments can be made, which may not be so drastic. If an entire room in the house cannot be spared for play, there may be a closet, a stair landing, or the end of a hall that can be turned into a child's domain. A paved terrace outside the back door where a child can skate, play, and use his scooter is a possibility. If there is a roof over at least a portion of the terrace a child can and will use it even in rainy weather.

When building a home that will contain young children, include a mud room or, as it is sometimes referred to, "a glory hole" near the back door where rubbers, coats, and all outside garments can be disposed of before the child comes into the house proper. Ideally there should be a space for each child, so arranged that he can hang up and store his own belongings. A lavatory may be included and a planned space which in succession will hold a perambulator, scooter, tricycles, wagons, sleds, bicycles, skis, toboggans, tennis rackets, and golf equipment.

The rest of the house. In a house with a stairway, run a rope halfway between the top rail and the steps, looped through the balusters to keep it tight, to serve as a secondary rail for small, unsteady stair climbers.

Put a long string on the bathroom light so that children can reach it, or, better still, install a low-wattage night light at baseboard level. In a new house if light switches are placed about forty inches above the floor (table height is thirty inches), when the child is old enough to go around the house alone, he can reach them. Have small stair steps in the bathroom to bring children up to wash-basin level. A low rod or a portable rack can hold towels and wash cloths. Closets should be fitted with low hooks, rods, and shoe holders. A sense of cleanliness and order cannot be developed unless the child waits on himself. In the living room have small chairs for the use of the younger members of the family. It will help them feel a part of the group.

At an early age when children first make unguarded steps into the living room review everything in the room carefully. Cover fragile upholstery with slip covers. Remove tippy lamps; they aren't satisfactory anyway. Weed out excess bric-a-brac and irreplaceable objects, but do not strip the room as though you were expecting wild animals to move in.

The next step is to take the child on a tour of inspection. Explain everything in the room. Talk simply and use few words but show how fond you are of lamps, ashtrays, books. Explain how long you have had them. If the object is breakable point that out. It's amazing how much small children understand, especially tone of voice and gestures. Repeat the tour several times. With understanding will come respect and with gentleness will come a feeling for law and order. There are always unruly exceptions, but with the average child this technique works remarkably well.

A superintendent of schools supports the contention that respect for property should be and can be taught. An outbreak of children defacing school property became quite serious in a Pennsylvania school. On investigation the school authorities found that the largest percentage of the children causing the difficulty were living in rented houses, where standards were low and where there was no sense of property. Brief talks were begun on the history, manufacture, care, and use of furniture, books, pictures, china, and silver. Pupils brought china, silver, and glass from home for discussion and exhibition. Without any direct attack on the defacement problem, the vandalism stopped. A property sense developed through understanding.

Children are like wax recorders. Their physical, emotional, and mental habits are the result of what they are exposed to. Excess discipline may lead to outbreaks. Total lack of discipline produces the same reaction, but for a different reason. The child who has had no discipline may not understand the idea or value of control and consideration for others. Too strict discipline enforced arbitrarily is hard for anyone to take, either adult or child.

Even your thoughts and emotions may be received by sensitive children. It is only the well-balanced household that produces truly well-balanced children. Give children courage, discipline, respect for others, and a sense of the joy of living by example, and the child will do the rest.

Children's rooms. As children grow older their rooms should be more like studios and laboratories than bedrooms. Even though couch and bunk beds are not so easy to make as regular beds they are desirable because they save floor space. Linoleum, vinyl, or cork floors are excellent. They are easy to clean, muffle sounds, and offer a smooth surface for important construction efforts.

There should be bookshelves which will hold toys, books, and an endless assortment of things, including hobby collections. There should be a bulletin board and a desk or work table.

A child's curiosity should not be simply tolerated, it should be encouraged. Experiments with flora and fauna may begin on a modest scale. The first step may be a jar of water with a sweet potato or an avocado seed. This may be followed by pots of earth planted with assorted grains. Inevitably, an aquarium will be added, with small turtles, tadpoles, and snails. These efforts may expand to jars of insects in the chrysalis stage. Actual experiments in the growth of penicillin may follow, and in some cases experiments even encompass live frogs, lizards, fish, and snakes. As one mother said of her son's room, "I'm sure they think the family has some Kallikak or Juke blood in it somewhere! To the casual observer Chris's uninhibited room looks like a successful cross between a rabbit's warren and a goat's nest."

Troublesome as live and experimental accessories are, and smelly though they may be, don't throw them out. Set rules for the care of livestock, and insist on owner responsibility. Visit the zoo or a nearby farm and point out what would happen if the zoo keeper or the farmer neglected his charges. Be firm about it.

Then there is the problem of inanimate collections, which may take the form of smooth pebbles, shells, chunks of quartz, or pieces of limestone. Such miscellany may be unintelligible to you but of vital importance to the collector. There may even be a period when insects are impaled on pins. Bird's eggs and bird's nests may appear. These phases will pass. Collecting stamps, match boxes, or even bottle tops has educational value. Be patient with all such interests; even the most violent mania will disappear in due time or endure and become a lifetime hobby.

TEENAGERS

When a child enters his teens is the time that strained relationships develop in a family. It is a period when both too little attention and too much attention may be disastrous. But in any case it is a time when the atmosphere and appearance of the house itself, as well as the appearance of parents, is really important.

If the groundwork of earlier years was well laid, things will proceed smoothly. If a feeling of mutual respect has been established, if home responsibilities are clear, if family councils permit free discussion, friction will be less evident. But only responsible parents can raise responsible children.

Teen rooms. The dolls and toys will gradually disappear along with the collections and the zoo. In girls' rooms a dressing table will encourage hair brushing and manicures. Some girls may welcome a certain frilly atmosphere and turn to flounced beds and ruffled curtains. Others will preserve the studio character. If a room is to be redecorated, let the girl plan the room herself.

To encourage neat closets and clothes care, paint the closet interior a contrasting color. If the room is pink make the closet blue. If the walls are yellow, paint the closet green. A cream-walled room could have coral closets. Then add ruffled shelf edging with matching shoe and clothes bags. Fit dresser drawers with compartment boxes.

Turn over the total responsibility for the care of the room to the child. Boys too should be trained to look after their rooms. Assign daily and weekly chores. Continue to train the child who finds it difficult to be orderly. Tactfully suggest routines and systems. But don't nag.

A boy's room will change more gradually than a girl's. Guns and tennis rackets and footballs may appear with a radio and other miscellany. The room will no doubt be a studio type in manly colors, blue and red, green and orange, or brown and yellow. If it includes a miscellaneous collection of discarded furniture, make it harmonize by painting everything one color. Use a saw on the legs of awkwardly proportioned chairs to lower them. Hack off unnecessary ornaments. Remodel the furniture, fitting it to his present needs. Use woven-plaid washable spreads on the bed so that the gang can lounge on it. Leave his tinkering alone. Privacy is increasingly important in the teens. To be alone is one way of learning to be an adult. He is developing his own world; don't pry into it. Yes, even if he wishes to solve his bedmaking problem by using a sleeping bag, don't interfere. Eventually his wife will reform him.

Boys as well as girls will want a house and garden they can be proud of when they start dating. This may be the time to paint the house, fix up the garden, build a terrace, and do over the interior. They should be encouraged to bring their friends home. If things are too dilapidated teenagers will always go out rather than stay home. More than one child has been completely frank about it. Children are more sensitive and embarrassed than you are over dingy paint, worn rugs, cluttered bathrooms. "But I can't have them here!" they wail.

One youngster of my acquaintance has gone through dreadful pangs over his home, which is really a delightful place. Until recently he loved it. The mistake was made by the parents, who sent him to a prep school for wealthy boys. After he had accepted invitations from two boys with elaborate homes, his parents rightly insisted that his friends be invited to his home.

But Ted's home is simple and his mother does all her own work. His father is a putterer with an electric machine shop in the basement as well as a collection of strange and unusual woods from all over the world. He is a stamp collector and a fine amateur photographer. Such a setup would fascinate any boy and had always pleased Ted. But he suffered agony contemplating his friends' visit.

The guests came for Saturday lunch and had a wonderful time. They adored his mother's home cooking. They were delighted with a parent who had a machine shop and who did all the things they liked to do. Immediately the guests began planning another visit. But even this admiration didn't cheer up Ted. He wanted a mother with perfectly dressed hair and manicured nails, a butler at the door, and a charming house. That's a teenager for you.

Naturally, such whims cannot always be accommodated but the teen-age problem will be eased on both sides if there is joint understanding, even open family discussion of the home and its grounds. Possibly projects can be outlined for the rehabilitation of a house which has become a little dilapidated.

In any case, think and think deeply about your children during this period. The responsibility for juvenile delinquency is more and more laid at the door of parents. The biggest increase in crime comes with the teenagers. Unless personal responsibility and courage to do right can be established at an early age the problem is a serious one. Stern discipline is not so much the answer as guidance and personal example from infancy. The pattern of adult personality is set in childhood. Home direction is more important than that offered by school, church, community, or state. Your children are your personal responsibility. Proper food and clothing are not enough. Training in morals, manners, personal courage, and spiritual rectitude must be established by parents in the home.

A good home may be an apartment, a twelve-room house, a trailer, a farm, in the middle of town or in a suburb, but a child will be happy if—

1. He is loved and wanted—and knows it.
2. He is helped to grow up by not being over- or under-protected.
3. He is allowed a space of his own.
4. He is given a feeling of belonging by being made a part of family fun and group activities.
5. He is exposed to skills—reading, talking, sports and making things—and his work is admired.
6. He is disciplined with understanding and he is corrected without being hurt, shamed, or confused.
7. He has a part in family planning, has duties, and is made to feel needed.
8. He is made to feel that his parents have no favorites among the children.
9. He feels free to talk over any problem he has with his parents without feeling afraid or ashamed.
10. He is given behavior guidelines and standards from infancy, which he must follow or be disciplined, and as he grows older he is given increasing responsibility for his own actions.

11. He is made to feel that his parents are interested without prying into every facet of his life, that they are doing the best they can for him and they know that he is doing the same for them.
12. He has something to believe in and work for because his parents have tried to live up to their ideals.

33 Husbands and the House

Almost every well-regulated family unit is equipped with a husband. They sometimes cause as much trouble as a half-dozen children, but of course all women will agree that men are indispensable, the light and joy of a home, a good interest-bearing investment, and worth the trouble they cause.

Some men make only a cash contribution to the home. There is nothing colder and less inspiring than cash. Interest in any project is aroused only through toil and personal contribution. Mix the sweat of your brow with the soil and timbers of your house for lasting cement. The man who acts like a guest in his own home is not a happy man, nor is it a happy household without some joint contribution.

When joint participation is established, a man deserves certain things that are too often overlooked. There has been a tendency for several decades to overrefine houses, to make them too "cushy." The average man feels completely out of place in a room full of delicate furniture, blond rugs, tippy lamps, mirrors, and tiny fragile ash trays. In a house with a den, a library, or a study, where a man can have rugged leather upholstery, books, guns, and pan-sized ash trays, a fragile living room may be permissible. But if the living room is the only room to sit in outside of the bedroom forgo delicate furnishings and make it a room that can take it.

By all means include a chair that is Father's. Every member of the family should have a chair that suits him, just as in "Goldilocks and the Three Bears." If in your mind's eye you can't see each member of your family settled down in some customary place in your living room, your family life is slipping. You have not been getting together enough and probably the furnishings do not encourage get-togethers.

Bedrooms should be designed with the same consideration for men as the living room. One woman wrote me some years ago, "My bedroom has orchid-colored walls and draperies and apple green woodwork. I have a large flounced dressing table with crystal lamps. I love it, but my husband who is a big he-man with a mustache doesn't. What can I do to make him like it?"

A jointly used room should be planned for the pleasure and satisfaction of both parties. By all means plan complete separation of clothes closets and chests. No man wants his things mixed up with nylon and lace. A separate chest and separate closet are the only solution. Now that there are prefabricated closets there is no excuse for not solving the storage problem. Firmly determine that even if his closet is not as full as yours you will not encroach, you will not even hang the least of your things in his closet. And don't forget that comfort may call for a king-sized bed.

. . . a cave is the ideal home

The bathroom in a one-bathroom house is a personal room which must be used by the whole family and rules are called for. Jampacked medicine cabinets chock a block with curlers, bobby pins, ribbons, and face powder outrage the male. If your husband can be coaxed to use an electric razor it will relieve the bathroom problem somewhat because he can shave just as satisfactorily in the bedroom. Plan a towel rod for each person in the family and desist from hanging hose and girdles to dry in the bathroom. Of course, in a small apartment you may have to make concessions. But to see a cluttered bathroom is annoying not only to men but to everyone.

Male hobbies offer further complications, but they should be as welcome as sunshine and an effort should be made to supply the working area and storage equipment needed. Hooks, racks, and cupboards can be built into the garage for storing fishing and hunting tackle. The basement, garage, or utility room may accommodate a machine shop. An extra bathroom or a pantry off the kitchen can be transformed into a darkroom for photographic adventures. A back yard may be turned into a tennis court or ball park, at least temporarily. In any case, give a man his head in these matters. His hobbies will broaden and enrich the interest and activities of the whole family. Difficulties arise from such activities only when they have not been thought through and provision for time and space arranged.

The kitchen is used by both men and women. Some of the best cooks in the world are men. If your husband isn't already interested, coax him into participating in some one element of meal preparation. Encourage him into mastering and taking over completely making the coffee, mixing the salad, or carving and serving. Encouraging him to acquire these household arts may be more work and trouble in the beginning, but it is worth it. His accomplishments will make him feel as proud as a peacock. Once he has mastered one of these tasks, he will make a fine job of what he does, with perhaps some quirks and turns added that you might not have thought of. It will ease your problem of meal management if you can leave these tasks to him. A really handy man will also set the table and cope with breakfast fruit, wipe the dishes, and help with the food shopping.

Man's real province around the house is in the overall care and repair classification. If you are in possession of an authentic handyman husband, treat him like a dream come true. The comfort that he can bring into a household is beyond words. To have someone at hand who can put up curtain rods, strengthen rickety chairs, put up screens, and do the hundreds of other odd jobs around the house that constantly need attention is to be leagues ahead in the business of keeping house.

Even these upkeep problems should be systematized. Make lists of things that need to be done, such as: clean leaves out of gutters that seemed to be clogged at roof line over terrace; cut vines away from dining-room window; fix drawer in Jean's chest that jams. Such a list of odds and ends could be made almost every week.

In addition to these weekly chores, plan to make a top-to-bottom survey of the house once a year. You should pad right along on this tour so that you understand what's going on too. Use the check list in Chapter 3, "How to Buy or Build a House," as the map for this trip. Overlook no details and make notes of things to be done as the tour progresses. It might be a good idea to carry an oil can in one hand, putting a drop in every door hinge in the house as well as in other moving parts which might be neglected or overlooked.

If your husband is not a fixer, if he just doesn't know how to handle a screwdriver or a plumber's helper, don't risk having him tamper with things. He could make them worse. Locate a handy man and make a deal with him for a semiannual bout of putting things in shape. It will be an economical move.

The children's relations with their father present another situation to analyze. Today sharing equally in the care of children starts from birth. Feeding, changing diapers, mixing formulas, kissing hurt fingers, chanting rhymes, the initiation into the world of wheels via a tricycle or scooter are all the father's as well as the mother's prerogative.

As the children grow older, family sessions that include them should set up codes of behavior, delegate household chores, determine allowance money, and decide whether the young lady of the family is old enough to go to a dance alone without a chaperone.

For success the family and the house must be a closely co-ordinated working unit, as neatly integrated as the motor and the chassis of a car.

Some years ago Alexander Black in his book *American Husbands* pointed out that a good woman needs three husbands:

A business husband to go downtown every day, be important, and earn the cash to run the family.

A handy husband with no office worries who tinkers around the house, looks after the yard, mends the children's toys, paints the house, runs errands, and puts up curtain rods.

A lover husband, a glorified big man with a handsome wardrobe, a feeling for clothes, who says nice things, remembers anniversaries, understands music and art, who always knows a nice little restaurant to go to and who makes you feel like a million dollars.

. . . every woman needs three husbands

How much more delightful to have all these attributes combined into one excellent companion. But even as I describe this satisfying type of fifty-fifty marriage, in which both the everyday problems and the pleasures of homemaking are shared, it must be pointed out that there is another breed of man who is thoroughly dedicated to his work. These men as a rule have neither the time nor the focus for the small joys of the home. As the wife of one of the astronauts said in an interview, "I believe some men are not meant to be tamed and tied down exclusively to hearth and home, pillow and procreation." She added that she was not courageous as much as she was conditioned, that she could have enjoyed a simple life, but her man chose another way, and that she is fully committed to his world and the demands it makes. She brushed off the idea that she was making a great sacrifice and explained that a woman who lives on these terms gives her man a gift—the freedom to do what he would with his life in the service of mankind.

34 You and the House

A house is only as good as the life in it. Creating that life is not all cooking, cleaning, and washing. More important than anything else is the *esprit de corps* of the household. But you can't go out and buy the stuff like so much Joy or Chanel No. 5. It is extremely volatile and comes entirely from within.

Creating a happy household requires physical energy as well as headwork and is a full-time job even if it follows an eight-hour day at the office. It requires rare understanding and study to achieve it. It is a creative job and an exciting one. There are no prepared mixes or mechanical aids to speed it up or make it easier. It is a job for women but it calls for masculine cooperation.

If a woman is bored the whole household is bored and the rush to escape to the club, to the golf course, or to the movies begins, and before long the home is nothing but a rooming house.

If a woman is not handy around the house she will be driven to distraction. She will complain and exaggerate the problems and the whole household will be equally unhappy.

If a woman does not respect the job she is doing she will not do it well and she will be no blessing to herself or anyone else.

If a woman will not assume adult responsibilities, if she is a whining, sniveling thing, either the household will go to pieces or her husband will have to carry the load.

If a woman imagines herself the center of the universe and tries to escape realities via the movies and beauty parlors there will never be a home under her roof.

On the other hand if a woman loves her husband and her children, if she respects her job and herself, there won't be enough hours in the day to do all the interesting, exciting things there are to do. Work, the law of activity, is the solution of endless imaginary ills. There is a poem by an unknown author called "Work" that begins:

If you are poor, work,
If you are rich continue to work,
If you are happy keep right on working,
Idleness gives room for doubts and fears,
If disappointments come, work . . .

Perhaps you think women are doing a good job. Any number of books on the subject make this debatable. They may take too black a view of women, but they do provoke thought. In an informal poll on male reactions about their homes, here are a few comments:

"For years I've wanted my wife to fix up the living room, but somehow she doesn't get around to it."

"We usually entertain at the club, as my wife is always too tired to entertain at home."

"All I want is a good reading lamp in the living room, but I'll be dead before I get it."

"I'm fed up with stockings and stuff hanging around the bathroom."

"There's no place left where a fellow can relax with his coat and shoes off."

When such reactions come spilling out, sub rosa, there's something incomplete about the job women are doing. Complaints don't end there. In another checkup in one suburban block, it was found that in twelve households only four husbands had a complete breakfast at home before leaving for work and two made it themselves. One of the two served his wife breakfast in bed on a tray —but they had been married less than one year. Three more men in the block grabbed up a cup of coffee on the run and the others "sometimes" get breakfast in town.

Permitting such a condition at breakfast time is not the way to make a happy home. A woman who hasn't the stuff in her to get up and see that her family starts off with a good breakfast doesn't deserve a home and may not keep one.

Now let's take a look at the children's side of it. The *New York Times* ran a news item under the heading "Children's Essays Deflate Parents," pointing out that while there was considerable misspelling there was surprising unanimity among the young writers as they checked through a list of "good" and "bad" parental qualities. "Honesty" was given the highest rating. Justice, courtesy, and a "quiet voice" were other characteristics which rated high on the list of "good" qualifications.

On the other side of the picture, nagging stood out in sharp focus as the most objectionable parental quality. Ninety-three percent put it at the top of their negative list. Forgetting promises, fussiness, and a complaining nature were tied for second place on the "bad side."

All of these complaints cannot be laid entirely to mothers but they do seem to point in that direction. The list of complaints is a disarming one. The good qualities are those desirable in any long-term relationship and the bad qualities would damage even the best of friendships. Perhaps a new book of etiquette for the home is indicated.

Needless to say, women if consulted would have a long list of complaints to make too, about their husbands and their children. These complaints are so well known and so often reviewed that there is no need to list them here. However, it isn't a bright woman who lets minor annoyances eat into her good nature. The trick, as generations of women know, is to work out a method of counteracting the irritant before it becomes a rankling sore.

Many annoying situations call for nothing more than tact or finesse. If seeing your husband read the paper in the evening or at breakfast bothers you, order two papers and read when he does. It will be good for you. It will keep you up with things and keep you from being sorry for yourself. Before you know it you may be sufficiently familiar with current events to have a good time discussing them and reading the paper will involve pleasant interchange of ideas.

If your husband has a way of coming in late for meals, hold the meal only as long as you can without feeling sorry for yourself. As soon as the martyr spirit leers at you, serve dinner and put a plate aside for your husband. At all costs avoid a martyr complex. It is one of the most insidious things a woman has to deal with.

If your husband won't hang up his clothes or prefers a chair back, check and see if his closet is well equipped and easy to use. It might even be worthwhile to get a silent valet, a stand topped with coat hanger and trouser and tie rack. They are neat, made for the purpose, and will keep the furniture clear.

In any case don't try to force a man to acquire new habits. Success comes only with indirect and gentle persuasion. If this method is tried seriously it can be remarkably successful. The control and discipline it imposes becomes a valuable asset. Since it requires concentration on the problem of pleasant relations in the household,

. . . order two papers and read when he does

the life of the family becomes richer and finer. Like vintage wines and good tweeds, a happy household if carefully nurtured will improve with age.

Still another problem women seem to have has nothing to do with anyone else. It is purely a personal thing. Believe it or not, many women seem to have difficulty coping with the hours they have to spend with themselves. After the bustle of school, business, or teaching, a house is pretty empty. When the children are little they are company, but in a few years school absorbs them and the problem of being alone comes up again. Time hangs heavier still when the children marry and leave home.

Girls should be trained to cope with these hours alone. An attitude of mind is needed. Time is one of the most beautiful and precious things we have and the idea of wasting it or being disturbed by time alone is unfortunate. When children are growing up they should be exposed to activities and should be encouraged to develop hobbies. It may be photography, music, sketching, reading, gardening, sewing, or sports. Acquired in youth such activities can supply lifelong pleasure and help fill those empty hours. The most absorbing type of hobbies are those which require head or hand work. These are hobbies as a rule requiring no companion.

The time women must be alone totals thousands of hours in a lifetime. These hours can be most rewarding if they are used to enrich and rebuild oneself.

It sometimes appears that everything would work out right if women would only relax. Relax regardless of what happens. Relax if a cake burns, or the milk is spoiled. Relax if Johnny throws a stone and breaks a neighbor's window. Relax in the middle of a quarrel. Relax when completely alone. The results of relaxing are amazing. By shedding physical tension and mental disturbance you can reduce any problem to its proper size and often the solution may be apparent.

C. Northcote Parkinson, the British economist who is well known for his Parkinson's "laws," maintains that work done with a feeling of pressure produces excess heat which expands and fills the mind. When everything goes wrong—the toaster jams, the milk boils over, Reggie breaks a piece of your fine china, and frustrations build up—the professor suggests that you stop what you are doing, sit down, collect your thoughts, and tell yourself it isn't so; it's just a hallucination. If that doesn't work, even if it is only ten o'clock in the morning, run a tub of cold water, submerge to the neck three times and much of the heat and pressure will drain out with the water.

An alternative, but definitely not as successful, is to call up a friend for a chat and ask her over for a quick cup of coffee.

The professor also suggests that you should never look at incoming mail until you have time to read it and you should never answer the phone if you are in the middle of something you shouldn't interrupt.

Analyze and rationalize every problem that comes up in the house; don't let it worry you into a tizzy. Make yours a happily used house with everyone sharing the responsiblity and fun. Such a state of affairs does not come about without effort. Like cleaning the house, it takes work to get results. Only by thinking together, planning together, reading together, and doing things together can a solid team be built.

Now ask yourself, would you like to have *you* as a wife or mother? Put yourself in your husband's and your children's shoes, and take the quiz below.

1. Are you always available when anyone in the family needs advice, information, or assistance?
2. Does the family feel your genuine personal interest in their affairs?
3. Are you generous with praise when it's deserved, and do you lend a guiding hand when it's needed?
4. Do you make the whole family feel wanted and a part of the operation of the household? Do you encourage a sense of participation?
5. Are you flexible and considerate about the familiar dates, appointments, and outside responsibilities?
6. Are you predictable, or do you blow hot and cold? Do you lose your temper? Do you scream and become abusive?
7. When you make a promise do you keep it?
8. Do you plan and serve meals that are attractive and varied?
9. Do you always or almost always look trim and neat around the house, hair combed, frock clean?
10. Do you remember anniversaries, birthdays, and holidays, and plan special surprises?
11. Do you plan family events that are fun—picnics, song fests and barbecues in the back yard?
12. Do you keep an eye on your budget, occasionally robbing Peter to pay Paul, but on the whole keeping money matters under control?
13. Is the house orderly enough so that it is a restful, pleasant place to come home to?
14. Do you keep the whole family informed about the doings of

grandparents and other relatives so that the children have a sense of background?

15. Does the family feel free to invite friends home?
16. Do you keep up with what's going on in the world to broaden your outlook for your own satisfaction and growth and to have intelligent discussions with your husband?
17. Do you occasionally take time to do nothing, just dream a little?
18. Do you always manage to have clean shirts and darned socks available for the men of the family?
19. Are you gently insistent about everyone in the family picking up his own personal belongings even though it would be easier for you to do it yourself?

Well, how about it? What is your score as a housewife and mother?

35 How to Enjoy a House

There is a real trick to living in a house. Some people know how to get fun out of it, but others never seem to get the knack of it. There are several reasons for failing to enjoy a house. Those who let the house obsess them will never succeed. Give a house its head and it will demand this, that, and the other. In this sort of dictation a house can be worse than a woman and much more devastating on the bank account.

If you want to be happy in a house, you have to budget its demands and put your foot down on too much dressing up. If you get rugs that are too delicate, sofas too elegant, and too many precious things, it's impossible to enjoy the place any more. You must retreat to the basement, attic, or garage if you want to do anything really entertaining.

Second, if you let a house turn you into a housemaid and to keep the thing satisfied you spend all your time manicuring, massaging, and shampooing it, enjoyment has gone out the window. You have permitted the house to be boss. If this type of thing goes too far, the house can actually make your husband and family feel as though they are unimportant in comparison. When this happens only a radical awakening will correct the situation.

Finally, just to show what a delicate balance there is between enjoying and not enjoying a house, if you don't really honestly in your heart love your house it will get cold and sulky. Even strangers visiting the house for the first time will sense that something is wrong.

It is only the house that is loved but not slaved over, it is only the house which is not demanding and not furnished for show, that will make a real home that you can live in and enjoy in every part. When all is said the house is worthless without the right spirit.

Alexander Calder's wife, who is a great-niece of Henry James, seems to have created an aura of well-being in their home. She is said to carry off any situation with aplomb. The house is not tidy in a prudish sense. There is nothing fixed or constructive about the kind of order she produces but there is always a feeling of serenity. The rooms seem to say, "One's own house is a place to be at ease."

One of my neighbors has a quaint wood plaque hanging beside her entrance door and printed on it are these words: "Come in, sit down, relax, converse; our house doesn't always look like this; sometimes it's even worse."

With a happy housekeeper and a cooperative family almost any house, regardless of how simple and limited, can be a joyous place. When there are children a home is far more than a retreat or a cold piece of real estate. It is a miniature world where children are first exposed to the potentials of living. Books establish a library; pictures create a consciousness of art; tools—a hammer, screwdriver, and a saw—spell repair shop; well-stocked closets suggest the home store. A piano or other musical instruments turn a home into a concert hall; a garden or indoor plants introduce the world of growing things; a pet which must be tended and fed is a lesson in responsibility. An allowance introduces economics, and to be a part of family councils and discussions is exposure to diplomacy, arbitration, and committee procedures.

All in all a home is a staging ground for the family's contact with the world. It is a fortress against intrusions as well as a wonderful entrée to what the world has to offer.

In 1874 Benjamin Disraeli summed it up in these words: "The best security for civilization is the dwelling, and upon proper and becoming dwellings depends more than anything else the improvements of mankind."

I recall a case in the Middle West. A college chum had married and had five children. I hadn't seen her for years but on visiting her town I called her on the telephone and went out to call.

When I first saw the house I thought how wise she was to move her family into a big old Victorian house where the children would have room to spread out. When I got close enough to see the yard I had misgivings. It was as trampled down and dilapidated as a barnyard. The front door was marred and beaten up, and when I stepped into the living room I really was aghast.

The floor finish was completely gone, the woodwork was marred, the upholstery was blackened, and the whole place a shambles. The youngsters swarmed around like little animals. It was shocking.

Eventually I learned that their mother was up in her room. I retreated up the stairs and found X. calmly sitting in her room, reading, paying no mind to the hubbub downstairs. What was she reading? A book on philosophy by William James. "Oh," she said, "I let the children look after themselves. Grace [the oldest] does the cooking and the younger girls look after the house."

It was easy to understand why for years her husband had preferred engineering jobs that took him to the far corners of the globe. I really don't believe a sane man could live in that house.

The sequel: The two older girls are married and two better housekeepers you couldn't find.

Family rooms, hobby rooms, tool shops, studios, and closets are the real solution to keeping an orderly house. Such areas confine messes while they encourage creative pursuits.

There is a couple in Kansas who have gained the cooperation of their house by a little forethought. Before they built they made a list of the things they wanted their new home to do for them. The list was long and the house was small. Organized in the usual way, a twelve-hundred-square-foot house just couldn't offer all of the things they expected.

Mrs. B. liked to cook, weave on a loom, model ceramics, paint, and sew. Mr. B. was a fine amateur photographer, a good carpenter, and also enjoyed doing metal and leather work. These activities were not suitable for a living room. Still the house had no basement or attic.

The answer was to reduce the living room to parlor size and have a large room adjoining the kitchen. Vinyl-asbestos tile floors, room for solid work tables, looms, and other equipment, plus good lighting and easy-to-shift chairs, make this room a perfect workshop. The result is that the parlor is used rarely and the B.'s regret that they gave any space to it.

Obviously the business of living in a house requires more thought than it usually is given. It requires a state of mind and an understanding of the problem as well as a house that is designed and furnished in a suitable manner. A house should not be taken for granted. If this is truly understood, it should lead to honest study of all subjects related to houses, and houses designed for status' sake would disappear.

The more one knows about a subject the more interesting it becomes, and the subject of houses opens up fascinating fields.

Subjects which might be studied are:

- antiques
- architectural styles
- art
- child care
- china and glassware
- city planning
- color
- decorating
- fabrics
- flower arrangement
- gardening
- growth and habits of families
- household management
- house construction
- kitchen design
- landscape design
- lighting
- modern design
- neighborhood development
- rugs and carpets
- safety practices

The list of subjects relating to the practice of keeping house is almost endless, long enough to offer a lifetime of study. Inevitably as one wanders in and out through columns of subjects as varied and interesting as the foregoing list, certain fields will loom up as more vital and appealing than others.

I know one woman who quite unexpectedly became an expert gardener because she was faced with an unkempt yard. Another woman started collecting antiques as a hobby and ended by writing a book and lecturing on small antiques. A third took a course in modern ceramics because she wanted to get away from the house for an evening every week. Then she started collecting fine pieces and now she has a shop specializing in modern accessories.

As we women keep house and do the multiplicity of things that must be done, we will fare better if we are not completely absorbed in the job right under our noses. If we remember that the world out there is full of fascinating things, we can explore much of it from our own firesides if we have the will to do it.

As we vote, so go elections.

As we are concerned with schools and community affairs, city reforms are launched.

As we buy clothes and food, we are a factor in the economics of the country. We are actively affecting Wall Street.

As we accept or reject new products, we are an influence in our national economy.

As we keep up our house and grounds, we are influencing property values and the growth of the city.

As we train our children, we are affecting the standards of future generations.

As we decide on English, American, or Italian pottery for the table, we have our finger in world markets.

As we decide to shampoo our own heads or go to a beauty parlor, we are a factor in a business that involves millions of dollars a year.

No action we take is free of important implications. No woman running a house and a family is operating from an isolated position. She is a part of the great pattern of society and the age in which we live.

Index

ABOUT THE AUTHOR

Mary Davis Gillies was born in Kansas but grew up and went to college in the state of Washington. She taught household arts at the University of Oregon for two years and then served for a time in the United States Department of Agriculture's Bureau of Home Economics. After a stint with a New York advertising agency, she went to *McCall's* magazine as Decorating and Architectural Editor.

In 1965 and 1966, Mrs. Gillies conducted eight conferences on better living in cities from the East Coast to the West. They were held in Boston, Cleveland, Pittsburgh, Louisville, Denver, Seattle, Cape Coral, Florida, and Phoenix. Many ideas expressed by women at these conferences have been included in *The New How to Keep House.*

Mrs. Gillies is a press member of the American Institute of Interior Designers, the Fashion Group, and various other professional organizations. In her work at *McCall's* she decorated and photographed houses all over the country. There, too, she was also exposed to the latest developments and ideas related to the home.

She and her husband divide their time between a New York City apartment and a thirteen-acre place in New Jersey which was built by Thomas A. Edison. Among her hobbies and interests are travel, gardening, birds, painting, cooking, and an important one—wild flowers. She has 213 varieties growing. Yellow is her preferred decorating color—the precise shade of marsh marigolds.

p. 69
p. 79 - Before bed, once-over.
81 - Daily Brushups
82 } Weekly - Order of Cleaning
to 84 } + Occasional + Seasonal Cleaning.
85 Bedroom
87 Bathroom
125 House smells.

Format by Paula Wiener
Set in Linotype Times Roman
Composed and bound by The Haddon Craftsmen, Inc.
Printed by The Murray Printing Company
HARPER & ROW, PUBLISHERS, INCORPORATED

70 71 72 73 10 9 8 7 6 5 4 3